Inflection Journal
Volume 08 - Presence
December 2021

Inflection Journal is published annually by the Melbourne School of Design at the University of Melbourne and Melbourne Books.

Editors: Michaela Prunotto, Kate Donaldson and Manning McBride

Deputy Editors: Isabella Chow, Jack Le Riche and Bridget McNab

Collaborators: Qiyu Chen, Saibal Dutta, Thandi Lane, Michael Minghi Park, Alessandra Prunotto, Alex Rayne, Angelica Roache-Wilson, Amelia Wells and Janice Williem

Editorial Advisors: Louis O'Connor and Arinah Rizal

Academic Advisor: Dr. AnnMarie Brennan

Academic Advisory Board: Dr. AnnMarie Brennan and Prof. Alan Pert

The editors would like to thank all those involved in the production of this journal for their generous assistance and support.

Special thanks are due to AnnMarie Brennan, whose continual support, guidance and encouragement has been invaluable.

For editorial enquiries contact:
editorial@inflectionjournal.com

For sales enquiries contact:
info@melbournebooks.com.au

inflectionjournal.com
facebook.com/inflectionjournal
instagram.com/inflectionjournal

ISSN 2199-8094

ISBN 9781925556759

Melbourne Books
Level 9, 100 Collins Street,
Melbourne, VIC 3000,
Australia
www.melbournebooks.com.au
info@melbournebooks.com.au

CONGRATULATIONS
INFLECTION JOURNAL
VOLUME 07 - BOUNDARIES

WINNER OF THE 2021
BATES SMART AWARD FOR
ARCHITECTURE IN MEDIA
(STATE AWARD)

Cover image:
Lake Conjola, bushfires © Matthew Abbott/The New York Times/Headpress.

Inside cover:
Aerial Bushfire 6214 © John Gollings AM.

msd
Melbourne School of Design

M
MELBOURNE BOOKS

A catalogue record for this book is available from the National Library of Australia

CONTRIBUTORS

Alexis Kalagas
Kalagas is Head of Public Programs at Molonglo and leads an advanced studies unit at MADA exploring the impacts of 'smartphone urbanism.' Previously a foreign policy advisor with the Department of the Prime Minister & Cabinet, he worked on projects internationally with the Zürich-based practice Urban-Think Tank. He has researched the complex economic, social, and technological forces reshaping our experience of urban space and the home as a Harvard GSD Richard Rogers Fellow and a Future Architecture Fellow.

Alexandra Pereira-Edwards
Pereira-Edwards is a designer, writer and recent Master of Architecture graduate from Carleton University's Azrieli School of Architecture in Canada. Situated in Tiohtià:ke (Montréal), she was one of three fellowship recipients at the Canadian Centre for Architecture in 2020, where she collaborated on an open-access syllabus project intent on addressing architecture's role in settler colonial processes. Her work centres on the politics of space, infrastructure and the affective bonds that unite us.

Amanda Achmadi
Achmadi is a Senior Lecturer in Architectural Design (Asian Architecture and Urbanism) at the University of Melbourne, Faculty of Architecture, Building and Planning. She holds a Bachelor degree in architecture and a PhD in architecture and Asian studies. Her research works explore the interrelated history of architecture, urban forms and identity politics in colonial and postcolonial Indonesia, as well as Southeast Asia. Her writing has been published in leading academic journals such as *Fabrications* and *ABE Journal*.

Bernard Khoury
Khoury is an architect situated in Beirut, Lebanon. He studied architecture at the Rhode Island School of Design and obtained a Master of Architecture from Harvard University. Khoury's office has developed an international reputation and a significant portfolio of diverse projects both locally and internationally. He has taught, lectured and exhibited his work in prestigious academic institutions in over 35 countries.

Boyd Hellier Knox
Knox is an Australian architect at Reiulf Ramstad Arkitekter, Oslo. He previously worked at Wood Marsh Architecture, Melbourne. Graduating from the Melbourne School of Design in 2020, Boyd received The Ernest Fooks Memorial Award, nominations for the RIBA Silver Medal and INDE's Graduate Award. He has also studied at University College Dublin, Stockholm's Royal Institute of Technology and the Australian National University. Knox is the current curator of the Alistair Knox Foundation.

Bruce Pascoe
Pascoe is a Yuin, Bunurong and Tasmanian man born in the Melbourne suburb of Richmond. He has worked as a teacher, farmer, fisherman, barman, fencing contracter, lecturer, Aboriginal language researcher, archaeological site worker and editor. He has written over thirty books, among them *Dark Emu* (Magabala books), which won Book of the Year and the Indigenous Writer's Prize at the NSW Premier's Literary Awards in 2016.

Bureau Architectures Sans Titre
BAST is an architectural practice founded in Toulouse in 2013. They adopt an anonymous approach and a proactive research posture to experiment with the diverse potentialities of each project. At each step of their design process, solutions are found and contiguously questioned in an iterative way. As a result, their projects do not follow a formal method, but instead develop in an evolutionary way, which in turn works to define the identity of the office.

Cameron McEwan
McEwan is an architectural theorist and educator at the University of Central Lancashire Institute of Architecture and director of the AE Foundation, an independent research institute for architecture and education. He is an editor of *Accounts* (Pelinu, 2019) and *Architecture and Collective Life* (Routledge, 2021). His research focuses on the relationship between architecture, representation and subjectivity to engage the city as a critical project. McEwan is writing a book entitled *Analogical City*.

Ciro Miguel
Miguel is an architect, photographer and doctoral fellow of the Institute for History and Theory of Architecture at ETH Zürich, where his research focuses on the intersections between architecture, photography, and mass media. His work has been exhibited at biennales in Venice and São Paulo, and in museums internationally, such as Architekturmuseum der TUM in the Pinakothek der Moderne and SAM Basel. He was co-curator of *Todo dia/ Everyday*, the 12th International Architecture Biennale of São Paulo (2019).

Colby Vexler
Vexler is an architectural researcher and practitioner. He has co-led Melbourne School of Design research unit and design studio *Housing Home and Contents: A Soft Focus on Domestic Things* with Pricilla Heung since 2016. In late 2020, Vexler and Heung founded Office Heuler, an architecture practice committed to contemporary residential architecture, to extend the lines of inquiry established by Studio 26 into an industry context. Vexler is also the editor of online contemporary architectural publication, *cc:Journal*.

Daniela Mitterberger
Mitterberger is an architect and researcher with an interest in new media and the Human/Body relationship within digital fabrication and emerging technologies. She is co-founder and director of «MAEID [Büro für Architektur und transmediale Kunst]», a multidisciplinary architecture practice based in Vienna. Currently, Mitterberger is a PhD researcher and A&T PhD Fellow at ETH Zürich, the Chair of Architecture and Digital Fabrication (Gramazio Kohler Research).

Domenic Trimboli
Trimboli is a registered architect, freelance writer and recipient of the Nell Norris Fellowship for a PhD in Architecture at The University of Melbourne. His research asks us to reconsider our relationship with existing cemeteries in Australia's cities and to think about how we might create new ones over the course of the 21st century. Trimboli is also a tutor of architecture and urban planning. His writing has been published across several design journals nationally and internationally.

Feifei Zhou
Zhou is a Chinese-born artist and architect. She holds a Master of Architecture from the Royal College of Art in London and was a guest researcher at Aarhus University Research on the Anthropocene (AURA). Her work explores spatial, cultural and ecological impacts of the industrialised built environment. She co-edited the digital publication *Feral Atlas: The More-than-Human Anthropocene* with Anna Tsing, Jennifer Deger and Alder Keleman Saxena, which was published in October 2020. She currently lives and works between London and China.

Frida Escobedo
Escobedo is an architect and designer based in Mexico City. Her work focuses largely on the reactivation of urban spaces that are considered to be residual or forgotten. In addition to her practice, Escobedo has taught at the Columbia University Graduate School of Architecture, Planning and Preservation, Harvard Graduate School of Design, and Rice University. In 2018, she was selected to design the 18th Serpentine Summer Pavilion in London.

Helen Rix Runting
Runting is an architectural theorist (PhD), planner and partner in the Stockholm-based architecture office Secretary. She has edited books and newspapers, published essays and exhibited installations internationally. Presently, Runting is a Research Fellow in Architectural Theories and Critical Design Practices at the University of Melbourne. Her work is motivated by a feminist ethos and a commitment to an affirmative biopolitics of the designed living environment.

Igor Sladoljev
Sladoljev is an Amsterdam-based architect and urbanist working in both practice and research. He acquired his Master of Architecture and Urban Planning at the University of Zagreb. In 2019 he took part in 'The New Normal' think-tank and research program at Strelka Institute of Media, Architecture and Design. His work has been showcased at museums and large scale exhibitions internationally. At present, Sladoljev works as a research lead at de Architekten Cie.

Katja Wagner
Wagner is an architectural graduate currently practicing in Melbourne. She completed her Master of Architecture in November 2020 and continues to muse upon the confluence of place, space and museums. Her independent thesis project, *Cook Cloak*, has its roots in a proposition formed for The Ian Potter Museum of Art Miegunyah Student Project Award 2018 and was recognised with the Bates Smart Award at its conclusion in 2020.

Liam Young
Young is a speculative architect and director who operates in the spaces between design, fiction and futures. He is co-founder of Tomorrows Thoughts Today, an urban futures think tank, and Unknown Fields, a nomadic research studio. His worldbuilding for the film industry has been acclaimed in both mainstream and architectural media. He currently runs the Master of Fiction and Entertainment at SCI-Arc in Los Angeles.

Lucia Amies
Lucia Amies graduated with a Master of Architecture from the University of Melbourne in 2019, during which she was twice awarded the Nell Norris Scholarship for academic merit. She is a tutor, guest critic and previous research assistant at the Melbourne School of Design, as well as co-editor of *Inflection* Volume 5. Currently, Lucia is an Associate at Olaver Architecture. Her interests lie at the intersection of architecture and landscape, with a particular affinity for small-scale interventions.

Marc Boumeester
Boumeester is the Director of AKI Academy of Art and Design, University of the Arts ArtEZ. Previously, Boumeester was a researcher at the Delft University of Technology (Faculty of Architecture) and Head of the Department of Interactive Media Design at the Royal Academy of Art in The Hague. His research focuses on the interplay between non-anthropocentric desire, architectural conditions and unstable media. He holds a PhD from Leiden University and he publishes in the fields of media-philosophy and art-theory.

March Studio
March Studio is a collective of architects, designers and creators located in Melbourne, Australia. They are focused on realising projects with ingenuity and respect for location, materials, processes and people. They have an unconventional knowledge of materials and fabrication processes and are constantly testing, prototyping and refining them for deployment in current and future projects.

Mitul Desai
Desai joined Studio Mumbai for an internship after graduating from Washington University, St. Louis (Master of Architecture, 2008). This engagement continues as a collaboration on publications and exhibitions in India as well as abroad. Desai has his own architectural practice and continues to engage with various design institutions in his hometown, Surat, India. Urban fringes, industrial landscapes, demolition, materiality and informal architecture are a few of his many photography and research interests.

Pınar Balat
Balat is an Amsterdam-based architect and urbanist. Before acquiring her Master of Architecture from TU Delft, she completed her Bachelor studies in METU, Ankara and her Master of Collective Housing in UPM, Madrid. In 2015, she founded her own office, Studio Pınar Balat. Balat is a member of the Advisory Committee of Architectuurcentrum Amsterdam. As a researcher, she focuses on contributing to socially integrated, equitable and sustainable urban environments.

Sarah Akigbogun
Akigbogun is an architect, filmmaker, writer and educator. She is founding director at Studio Aki, one of Wallpaper's Emerging practices of 2021, and of theatre collective Appropri8. She is an elected member of RIBA Council, Vice-Chair of Women In Architecture and founder of The XXAOC Project. Sarah is currently an Associate Lecturer at Canterbury School of Architecture and tutor at the Architectural Association. Her current film explores the stories of female architects of colour.

Timothy Hill
Hill is the founder of architectural practice Partners Hill. His work has been awarded at the national and international levels and is deliberately unspecialised; projects have ranged through furniture commissions, city centre masterplans, landscapes, campus buildings, office towers and in a continuous stream, houses. He investigates alternate models of housing that provide flexibility throughout the lifespan of their inhabitants as alternatives to nuclear family housing.

Vicky Shukuroglou
Shukuroglou is an artist and researcher who endeavours to deepen our understanding and care of our precious world and each other. She seeks to ignite joy and fulfilment through careful exploration of our environment and intimate connection with its complexity. Scientists, musicians, Indigenous communities and young people are among Vicky's collaborators. In consultation with diverse Indigenous communities, Vicky recently co-authored *Loving Country: A Guide to Sacred Australia.*

CONTENTS

BUILDINGS ARE BURNING

EDITORIAL

Michaela Prunotto, Kate Donaldson and Manning McBride

Inflection *acknowledges the Traditional Custodians of the land on which we work and are published, the Wurundjeri People of the Kulin Nation. We pay our respects to their Elders past, present and emerging, and acknowledge First Nations people as our first storytellers and architects.*

Beds Are Burning is a song by the Australian rock band Midnight Oil that was released in the months leading up to Australia's bicentenary in 1988—the 200th anniversary of the First Fleet's arrival at Botany Bay. This iconic song protested for action on Aboriginal and Torres Strait Islander land rights through the provocative question: "How can we sleep while our beds are burning?" Through their politically-charged metaphor, Midnight Oil conflated the presence of a violent, disruptive catalyst ("burning" fire) with the domestic interior ("our beds"). Counterintuitively, protest rock lyrics brazenly infiltrated the hermetically sealed interior world of the colonial Anglo-Australian, albeit through a voice that was white and male. Like *Beds Are Burning, Inflection* Vol. 08 positions 'presence' as a subversion of that which is established or dominant—whether it be a building, urban system, infrastructure or individual—and as the making of space for a multiplicity of voices in the fields of architecture and design. For the purposes of this editorial, one might understand 'fire' as mimetic to 'presence': both are forces that paradoxically wield both an immense constructive and destructive power over architecture, landscape and humanity.

Fire as Villain

The cover image of this journal was taken by photojournalist Matt Abbott at Lake Conjola, NSW, during the Black Summer (2019-2020) bushfires. Black Summer was an exceptionally severe bushfire season; its fires burned through some 12.6 million hectares of land, destroyed 3000 homes and took 30 human lives.[1] While the country burned, its Prime Minister holidayed in Hawaii. The Australian bushfire has been illuminated as a violent, destructive and uncontrollable presence on the local and global media stage. Fire in Australia has become synonymous with trauma, for its immediately perceivable harmful effects on animals, humans and the built environment. The cover image of this volume is best read by flipping from the front to back cover. Doing so reveals the full story of Matt Abbott's image, which is captioned: "A man hoses a property to defend it from a fire in a neighbouring house."[2] Indeed the act of "defend[ing]" by negation constructs fire as a virulent force of attack.

This image of a guerrilla firefighter's brave yet seemingly futile defense of a burning suburban house invokes the architectural profession's attempt to address not only catastrophes such as Black Summer, but also its close companion, climate change. The image sits in humble but fierce contradistinction to *Inflection* Vol. 08's initial Call for Papers, which featured the image of a burning Notre-Dame Cathedral in Paris. When an accidental blaze razed the roof and spire of Notre-Dame in 2019, igniting the renowned edifice into a searing global spotlight, gothic evocations of fire as a frightening destroyer of architecture ran rife. The cathedral's gruesome, charred remains have imparted an indelible spectre of nostalgia and sorrow to many, not least the rich and famous, some of whom have donated millions of dollars to rebuild the cathedral—or perhaps, to reconstruct the image. Admittedly, the exo-identity of a Western 'cultural epicentre,' Paris, had lapsed from its sanitised image of bourgeois tradition and immaculately preserved historical monumentality, to one of smoke, disorder, volatility and above all, ruin. During this crisis, no lives were lost, although many art and religious relics suffered from smoke or flame damage.

Fire as Hero

Black Summer has also spurred important discussions on the rich and ancient history of fire as an ecological tool, wielded as a promoter of biological diversity and flourishing ecosystems. For 1.7 million years, humans have been using fire; we are "fire organisms."[3] Wiradjuri man and Assistant Dean in the Faculty of Science at the University of Melbourne, Associate Professor Michael-Shawn Fletcher works to fill the absence of empirical data that demonstrates fire as a tool with which Aboriginal people have profoundly shaped and managed the landscape. 'Cultural burning' is the First Australian utilisation of low-intensity fires which remove the accumulation of fine fuels such as leaves, twigs, or dry grass, to promote new growth.[4] Fletcher describes this kind of fire management as "intimate and reflexive to local settings," performed for a range of reasons: spiritual and ritual, pragmatic and economic.[5] He argues that the net effect of cultural burning is that of increased biodiversity, reduced landscape fuel loads, protection of fire-sensitive ecosystems, as well as connection to Country and improved Indigenous lives and livelihoods.[6] Catastrophe can illuminate the ironies and contradictions of an anthropocentric existence and provoke us to challenge our approach to erasure, memory and place-making.

In the midst of Black Summer, Swedish climate activist Greta Thunberg shared one of Matt Abbott's photographs of the Australian bushfires to her 12 million Instagram followers. In her caption for the post, she wrote:

> The fires have spewed 2/3 of the nation's national annual CO2 emissions, according to the Sydney Morning Herald. The smoke has covered glaciers in distant New Zealand (!) making them warm and melt faster because of the albedo effect. And yet. All of this still has not resulted in any political action. Because we still fail to make the connection between the climate crisis and increased extreme weather events and nature disasters like the #AustraliaFires.[7]

Greta's words reverberate in light of the International Panel on Climate Change's Assessment report, released August 9, 2021, which unequivocally puts the blame on climate change as human-made. Keeping in mind that the construction and operation of buildings accounts for 25% of greenhouse gas emissions in Australia,[8] *Inflection* Vol. 08's cover image of a house on fire is rendered paradoxical, as at once human-designed, human-made, human-destroyed and human-protected. Conversely, Fletcher's research paves the way for an Indigenous Futurism, in which solutions to vast ecological and climatic problems reside in the proliferation of Indigenous land knowledge and maintenance systems. Fire is thus illuminated as a powerfully constructive force. When wielded with the right hands, fire has the potential to foster and promote Indigenous Australian knowledge networks and place-making practices, which in turn could mitigate ecological decline, as well as the rate and effects of climate change.

A hopeful reminder on the paradox of 'presence'

Although all buildings must eventually die, whether it be due to fire, time or a wrecking ball, a seed of something new can emerge during or after this process. For indeed, a natural component of demolition and its close companion of 'absence,' is reconstruction, rebirth or 'presence.' Just as the architecture of a banksia plant relies on the heat of a bushfire to prise open its pods and release seeds to germinate, so too do architectural terrains grow and evolve under the pressure of extreme external conditions. Architecture often deals with the physicality of form and space, but following catastrophe, it is the presence of what remains—as physical residue, cerebral memory, tangible or ideological regrowth—that is most powerful.

Victorian bushfires, Cann River.
Aerial bushfire © John Gollings AM, 2020.

01 Matthew Abbot, "Australia's Bushfire Crisis," *World Press Photo*, 2020 Photo Contest (2020).
02 Ibid.
03 Michael-Shawn Fletcher, interview by Rae Johnston, "Indigenous Fire Practices Have Prevented Bushfires for Thousands of Years," *Science Gallery*, November 8, 2020.
04 Tim Lee, "Scientist investigating Australia's past says Indigenous cultural burning key to controlling bushfires," *ABC News*, June 26, 2021.
05 Fletcher, interview by Johnston, "Indigenous Fire."
06 Ibid.
07 Greta Thunberg, "Australia is on Fire," *Instagram*, January 5, 2020. Accessed September 9, 2021.
08 Igor Martek and M. Reza Hosseini, "Buildings produce 25% of Australia's emissions. What will it take to make them 'green' - and who'll pay?" *The Conversation*, January 15, 2019.

COUNTER-INFRASTRUCTURES

PLACEMAKING AS RESISTANCE

Alexandra Pereira-Edwards

"We recognize that a renewed relationship [with Indigenous Peoples] cannot be built using colonial structures."[1] These words were tweeted by Canadian Prime Minister Justin Trudeau less than a year before his government purchased the rights to the Trans Mountain Pipeline, an infrastructural project set to carve up unceded Secwepemc territory, in the North-West of Canada. The $4.5 billion purchase, made in 2018, exists as part of an ongoing lineage of settler colonial violence within the territory presently known as Canada. Although the pipeline has a dangerous capacity to cause environmental, cultural and emotional damage, Trudeau's tweet speaks to the settler government's tendency to diminish its harms. As both a symbolically and materially colonial structure, the project has been vehemently opposed by Indigenous land defenders and allies alike.

Settler colonialism in Canada has long been reified by the building of new infrastructures that work to normalise practices of dispossession, often under the guise of progress or economic prosperity. There is certainly an urgency to uncover the ways that this colonial agenda unfolds—for it is also a practice in revealing the roots of hegemony—but it remains equally as important to recognise established and emergent forms of resistance. To situate one such oppositional force, we can look to the women-led Tiny House Warriors, a group of Secwepemc land and water defenders prohibiting the Trans Mountain Pipeline from pushing through their unceded territory by building ten mobile tiny houses along its path. Through practices of community-building, the Tiny House Warriors continue to assert Secwepemc jurisdiction over their lands and waters, actualising a mode of resistance that merges placemaking with protest, and which can be conceptualised as a *counter-infrastructure*.[2] Infrastructures materialise power formations, so by applying an infrastructural lens to both the destruction and protection of land, we can begin to examine the multi-directional and multi-scalar flows of power that govern the present day.

Settler Colonial Structures

Canada has been fundamentally formed by its infrastructures, both concrete and immaterial, which ascribe distinct socio-spatial relationships between bodies, spaces and objects. Infrastructure is understood as the physical networks of roads, railways and ferries that transport materials and bodies across the landscape; the hidden networks that carry clean water or sewer waste; ubiquitous cell towers and power lines that serve to connect some and disconnect others; and the associated laws and policies that function within hegemonic systems to ultimately render racism and colonial violence invisible. However, looking with a critical eye toward both the technical and affective dimensions of infrastructure—seen in the way that the Trans Mountain Pipeline serves as a macro-structural conduit for oil as much as for coloniality—allows us to assess the tangible and intangible systems that regulate power.

In "The Commons: Infrastructures for Troubling Times," Lauren Berlant asserts that infrastructure is "not identical to system or structure, as we currently see them, because infrastructure is defined by the movement or patterning of social forms."[3] By shifting the focus from material manifestations and stagnant networks toward patterns and movement, Berlant poses an expansive framework for recognising infrastructure's inherently relational nature. These relations forge distinct hierarchies within Canada, where power is often asserted to impose and sustain settler jurisdiction, thereby exposing the inequality that underpins material networks of colonialism.

Top: A tiny house situated at the village site near Blue River. Image courtesy of Tiny House Warriors, 2021.

Bottom: The Trans Mountain Pipeline's Westridge Terminal in Vancouver, British Columbia. Image courtesy of Trans Mountain Pipeline Company.

Crucially, contemporary infrastructural analysis brings up the 'who' associated with infrastructure: who is impacted, who is disadvantaged and who benefits?[4] Which human and non-human actors are assimilated into capitalist and colonial modes of extraction and production and which are supported to exist otherwise?[5] Infrastructures can be understood not just as latent objects within the built environment, but rather as active constituents of sociality and the political formation of space.

The Myth of Progress

If transportation networks were the original 'how' of Canada's settler colonial project—exemplified in the way that the Canadian Pacific Railway, an early nation-building tool, was constructed through racialised labour and colonial dispossession—this colonising enabler has shifted prominently to energy systems.[6] Winona LaDuke and Deborah Cowen write, "the transformation of ecologies of the many into systems of circulation and accumulation to serve the few is the project of settler colonial infrastructure."[7] Indeed, settler colonialism remains deeply intertwined with land ownership, profits and extraction, seen no more clearly today than through the construction of oil pipelines through Indigenous territories.

Pipelines serve as material archives of the settler colonial process: a violent history literally embedded in the land. Expansions to these systems of extractive capitalism are advertised by the Canadian government as prominent job creators and economy stimulators. Despite the prevalence of such claims, they are consistently being proven otherwise by Indigenous communities and independent researchers. Unless the country plans to significantly increase oil sands production at levels that exceed the established limits of climate pollution, there remains no good reason to expand pipeline projects.[8] Moving forward with pipeline expansion pushes the country toward a future of fossil fuel production that the earth cannot handle.[9]

Of the more prominent and contentious infrastructural projects within current media discourse is the expansion of the Trans Mountain Pipeline that was initially proposed by Kinder Morgan Canada in 2012. In 2018, the project was sold to the Canadian government, despite never having received consent from the Secwepemc Nation. The existing 1,150-kilometre pipeline, put into operation in 1953, transports oil from Alberta tar sands to the coast of British Columbia through 518 kilometres of unceded Secwepemc territory. The expansion would serve as a 'twin' to the current line, increasing the amount of oil able to be distributed overseas. Despite numerous stops and starts over the course of development, construction of the pipeline continues to lurch ahead.

These elements of technical functioning remain mono-dimensional facets of the pipeline's existence. Beyond financial or logistical details lie lands, lives and relationships that will ultimately be impacted by the project's construction and operation, both immediately and well into the future. When it was initially built, the Trans Mountain Pipeline was not approved by the Secwepemc people precisely because the Indian Act—a colonial legal structure—prohibited them from asserting their land rights between 1926-1951.[10] Now the project is strongly and vocally opposed by many Secwepemc land and water defenders, who have not provided their free, prior and informed consent to the Canadian government. Nevertheless, as the presence of the pipeline and its workers threaten both communities and river systems across the unceded territory, many community members have faced arrest and subsequent legal charges for asserting their sovereignty.

Counter-Infrastructures

We look ahead to the next 10,000 years. If our ancestors have been here for 10,000 years and we are still able to drink from the glacier-fed streams today, what do we have to do to ensure 10,000 more years of clean water for future generations?

—Kanahus Manuel[11]

Kanahus Manuel, Indigenous activist and founder of the Tiny House Warriors, has warned of the environmental devastation that the pipeline, its disruptive construction processes and its toxic bitumen supply could cause to the ecosystem, food chain and glacial waters that exist within Secwepemc Territory.[12] Regardless of these risks and the oil industry's path toward obsolescence, plans to sell the project to Indigenous groups are underway.[13] These negotiations simultaneously serve as a way to relieve the government of accusations of insufficient consultation with First Nations, and to place the burden of a failing infrastructure and dying industry onto Indigenous communities. True to the settler colonial logic, the relationship between humans and the land is reduced to that of owner and property.

In seeking to re-establish village sites on their traditional lands and thereby disrupt this colonial imposition, the Tiny House Warriors have constructed solar-powered tiny houses on wheels along the planned pathway of the Trans Mountain Pipeline expansion. These wood-framed structures provide shelter to Secwepemc families, simultaneously creating presence and protection. Such placemaking serves as a counter-infrastructure, in that it both counteracts the settler pipeline project and constitutes an infrastructural system in and of itself; the tiny houses provide warmth and shelter, while the affective infrastructure of care creates critically-binding networks of resistance.

The tiny houses were first activated as counter-infrastructure in 2018, when three of the structures were moved to occupy North Thompson River Provincial Park. After facing arrest and being forcibly removed from this occupation by the Royal Canadian Mounted Police, the Tiny House Warriors relocated to their current village site near Blue River, across from a planned man-camp for pipeline workers. This strategic blockade within Secwepemc Territory, comprised of a growing number of tiny houses, works as counter-infrastructure to defy the presence of the colonial pipeline and its builders.[14] Although the encampment exists to house a community, it is not without conflict. It has been the site of multiple arrests and of tangible violence, most notably during a nighttime attack by three white men and one white woman who tore down a memorial for missing and murdered Indigenous women and girls, assaulted an Indigenous man and rammed a stolen truck into an inhabited tiny house.[15] These civilian and institutional violences cause further financial damage to an already economically disadvantaged group. Tracing capital flows that govern infrastructure versus counter-infrastructure offers deeper insight into this economic disparity. While the pipeline is funded with taxpayer dollars on a massive scale, the Tiny House Warriors rely largely on crowdfunding to support not only the construction of the houses themselves, but also the payment of legal fees.

Above: Indigenous leaders march in Burnaby, B.C., to oppose the Trans Mountain Pipeline expansion. Image courtesy of Darryl Dyck, Canadian Press, 2018.

Next page: Construction of the original Trans Mountain Pipeline, completed in 1953. Image courtesy of Trans Mountain Pipeline Company.

Although the houses are presently stationed at the Blue River site, their mobility also serves a more expansive purpose. Building each house atop a wheeled trailer base allows the land defenders to create strategic, mobile barriers along the pipeline's path while reclaiming a traditional nomadic lifestyle.[16] Each house is equipped with a wood-burning stove and composting toilet, again positioning the counter-infrastructure and its self-sufficient operation as a tangible counterpoint to the pipeline's extractive and environmentally devastating methods.

Reflection

Despite the covert proliferation of colonial violence, we must not lose sight of the fact that power is multidirectional; it can be exercised in the form of white supremacy and the imposition of settler jurisdiction, but also through unifying and resistant practices. In the case of the Tiny House Warriors, place-making becomes a practice of political advocacy, as processes of colonisation are met with anti-colonial acts of protest. In this context, building and occupation become tools to counteract settler colonialism. While those who push the monumental pipeline forward seek to claim space, property and resources, the Tiny House Warriors assert the right to protect their contested land through visibility and a sustained, mobile, human-scale presence. Looking toward these counter-infrastructures serves as a way to understand the expansive power of community, but also how the built environment has the capacity to satisfy or disrupt the colonial consciousness.

Within this context, counter-infrastructures serve as a way to claim space and assert a collective responsibility.[17] This understanding leads us further toward the critical task of reassessing how we understand infrastructures, for while they can cause significant harm, they also have constructive capacities. The task is not only to parse apart infrastructural relations in order to address the connections and inequalities that lie just below the surface, but also to reflect on what this conceptualisation might offer to building the world otherwise.

Counter-infrastructure within anti-colonial frameworks can serve as a form of sustenance and as a basis for resistance.[18] By maintaining their presence as both a physical barrier and a symbol of defiance, the Tiny House Warriors continue to defend their land and fight for a collective future. As asserted by Kanahus Manuel, "Our land is home. We're putting tiny houses out there to scream that message to the world: pushing a pipeline through is tearing through our home."[19]

01 Justin Trudeau (@JustinTrudeau), "We recognize that a renewed relationship can't be built using colonial structures," Twitter, August 28, 2017, https://twitter.com/JustinTrudeau/status/902234336250007553W.

02 The term 'counter-infrastructure' has been used by Muna Dajani and Michael Mason in discussions of water infrastructures constructed by Syrian farmers to resist settler colonial transgressions. While the cultural and geographic contexts differ, Dajani and Mason aptly describe the power of resistance through anti-colonial presence, the likes of which run parallel to discussions of the Tiny House Warriors. See: Muna Dajani and Michael Mason, "Counter-Infrastructure as Resistance in the Hydrosocial Territory of the Occupied Golan Heights," in *Water, Technology, and the Nation-State* (London: Routledge, 2018), 147-162.

03 Lauren Berlant, "The Commons: Infrastructures for Troubling Times," *Environment and Planning D: Society and Space* 34, no.3 (2016): 393.

04 Ara Wilson, "The Infrastructure of Intimacy," *Signs: Journal of Women in Culture and Society* 41, no.2 (January, 2016): 247.

05 Bettina Stoetzer, "Infrastructure-Peripheral Visions and Bodies that Matter: A Commentary," *Engagement*, August 23, 2016, https://aesengagement.wordpress.com/2016/08/23/infrastructure-peripheral-visions-and-bodies-that-matter-a-commentary/.

06 Deborah Cowen, "#SHUTCANADADOWN: Anti-Colonial Counterlogics for Indigenous Sovereignty," *The Funambulist* 28 (March-April 2020), https://thefunambulist.net/articles/shutcanadadown-anti-%E2%80%A8colonial-counterlogistics-for-indigenous-sovereignty-by-deborahcowen.

07 Winona LaDuke and Deborah Cowen, "Beyond Wiindigo Infrastructure," *The South Atlantic Quarterly* 119, no. 2 (2020): 245.

08 Oil Change International, "Reconsidering the Need for New Oil Pipeline Capacity in Canada," October 2016, http://priceofoil.org/content/uploads/2016/10/cappmath-biefing-final-v3.pdf.

09 International Energy Agency, *World Energy Outlook, 2011* (Paris: OECD/IEA, 2011), 229, https://www.iea.org/reports/world-energy-outlook-2011.

10 Arthur Manuel, "An Open Letter to Prime Minister Trudeau Regarding the Kinder Morgan Trans Mountain Pipeline Expansion through Secwepemc Territory," November 28, 2016, https://intercontinentalcry.org/open-letter-prime-minister-trudeau/.

11 Kanahus Manuel, interview with Alicia Kroemer, in *Minority and Indigenous Trends 2019: Focus on Climate Justice*, ed. Peter Grant (Minority Rights Group International), 97.

12 Ibid., 96.

13 Kyle Bakx, "Plans to Sell Trans Mountain Pipeline to Indigenous Groups Take Another Step Forward," *CBC*, February 19,2021, https://www.cbc.ca/ news/business/bakx-tmx-pipeline-negotiations-1.5918712.

14 Tiny House Warriors, "...The TMX Pipeline Will Never Be Built," June 18, 2019, http://www.tinyhousewarriors.com/2020/05/the-tmx-pipeline-will-never-be-built/.

15 Jerome Turner, "Land Defenders Describe a Violent Night Attack on Their Camp," May 4, 2020, https://thetyee.ca/News/2020/05/04/Land-Defenders-Describe-A-Violent-Night-On-Their-Camp/.

16 Janice Cantieri, "Indigenous Women Built These Tiny Houses to Block a Pipeline-and Reclaim Nomadic Traditions," May 6, 2018, https://www.yesmagazine.org/democracy/2018/05/16/indigenous-women-built-these-tiny-houses-to-block-a-pipeline-and-reclaim-nomadic-traditions.

17 "About," *Tiny House Warriors*, http://www.tinyhousewarriors.com.

18 LaDuke and Cowen, "Beyond Wiindigo Infrastructure," 252.

19 Ashifa Kassam, "'Our Land is Our Home': Canadians Build Tiny Homes in Bid to Thwart Pipeline," *The Guardian*, May 8, 2018.

ENTANGLING FIRE, BONE + FRAGMENTS

IN CONVERSATION WITH FRIDA ESCOBEDO

Interview by Michaela Prunotto

With special thanks to Sol Camacho and Diogo Horvath from Instituto Bardi, São Paulo, Brazil.

Above: Frida Escobedo.
Image courtesy of FE Architects,
photo by Manuel Zúñiga.

Below: Lina Bo Bardi.
Image © Instituto Bardi/Casa de Vidro,
photo by Pietro Maria Bardi, 1947.

Characterised by both its artistry and playfulness, Frida Escobedo's architectural oeuvre explores the spontaneity of social relations, gritty realities of various social contexts, and the visceral experience of a raw, neutral space. Credit to her experimental and sincere approach, in 2018, Escobedo became one of two sole women practitioners ever commissioned to design a built Serpentine Pavilion, the other being Zaha Hadid. Based in Mexico City, Frida Escobedo Architects work with a wide range of typologies, which they categorise either as 'permanent' (cafe, library, hotel, shop, gallery, house) or 'temporary' (pavilion, exhibition content or design, research). At the time of this interview, one of Escobedo's most recent projects was her design for the Lina Bo Bardi: Habitat *exhibition at Museo Jumex (2020). Lina Bo Bardi was an Italian émigré who established herself as one of Brazil's most important and prolific modernist architects, working there from 1946–92. Taught as a student by Italian rationalists, Bo Bardi was not only architecturally energetic but also socially, politically and intellectually engaged, with many of her buildings anti-pretentious, playfully poetic and open to the public. Bo Bardi also created, edited and illustrated for numerous publications, including her and Pietro Maria Bardi's* Habitat *art magazine, and* Domus*. In talking to Escobedo, a noteworthy number of similarities emerged between the praxis of the two architects. Where Olivia De Oliviera's 1991 interview with Lina Bo Bardi begins in her hometown—"I'd like to start in Italy"—my first question for Frida Escobedo, posed March 26, 2021 via the virtual interface of Zoom, follows suit. Escobedo's dialogue subsequently imparts to us stories of luminous archives, vital ruins, and the power of voids as public architecture.*

In an interview with Chilean poet Alejandro Zambra (2018) you briefly describe your hometown of Mexico City as "like fire."

Like fire, the city is intense, and there is a feeling that everything is happening in public space. Life is flourishing on every corner; we have food, exchange, protests, gatherings. Every layer is overlapping and in a constant state of transformation. There is a vibrancy to it.

Any places in particular?

Paseo de la Reforma is one of the main avenues, and it is full of activity. Festivals and parades, like the Pride Parade and the Women's March, go through here. Before the pandemic, we would have weekends where they would close up the streets for people to come out with bikes and skates. There are also little tents where you can have Zumba lessons, or aerobic lessons. It is really like an ongoing party out there! And of course, Reforma is connected with some of the main plazas, like Monumento a la Revolución, and it also leads to Zócalo. So it is part of a procession, especially for protests.

How does one begin to build in this kind of context?

If you walk towards Zócalo, there are many neighbourhoods where everything spills out into the streets. Here, there are so-called informal markets, which I believe to be quite organised: they have a very precise structure. These markets begin to take over the whole street. Some of the streets have even been paved in a different way—with hardwood floors—because this setup has become permanent. The built environment then only works as storage space, with stores 'folding in' during the evening, and then 'pouring out' onto the street when it is daytime. This rhythm expresses a breathing effect of the city, where life pours into the public space and then it goes back to sleep for a few hours.

In equally evocative language, Lina Bo Bardi has described her hometown, the harsh business district of São Paulo, as a "pile of bones." This quote gives rise to Bo Bardi's rough, exposed concrete surfaces, which seem skeletal. In actuality, there is a lot of life, vibrancy and colour going on within.

This is especially visible within the São Paulo Museum of Art, where Lina created this very strict structure. It is quite heavy, it is geometric, it has a presence.

Ultimately, one comes to understand that the importance of this building is not the built fabric that is cantilevered between these two massive red columns, but rather the space underneath it. It is the void that is most important, because this is where many of the social activities happen, where people gather, play, dance, protest. So, the question is how do you create spaces, whereby doing one thing, you actually achieve many. I think that is crucial in a context like Latin America or Mexico.

A socially engaged take on the old dictum, 'less is more...'

Yes, we always have to do more with very little. Resources are often limited and so there is a need to find ways to optimise. Luckily, in Mexico there is nice weather, which means we can build with less layers, and with raw, exposed materials. And that works. But at the same time, this rawness has to do with an economy that prolongs itself. It's not just a moment of construction, but also about maintenance and ageing. There is also the question of how to create simple spaces that can be appropriated in different ways. It is not just about fulfilling one single program, but also about expanding to become neutral. Neutral architecture can be appropriated by the public and by people who inhabit that space.

In 2020, you designed the exhibition *Lina Bo Bardi: Habitat* at Museo Jumex. Do you feel an affinity with Bo Bardi?

Of course. She has been a great influence, I think, for many of us. And the exhibition design was a really interesting project, because we were able to access a huge number of archives and materials. Looking at her drawings, some of them were technical and very precise, but many of them were depicting life. One can see how a major integration of vegetation, people and objects was really important to her. And, how this priority worked to evolve her body of work from being about big gestures to something that was more about the richness of space or the experience.

Recreating some of Bo Bardi's furniture for the exhibition was also a way to understand the fabrication process, logic, and inspiration behind it. Designing this exhibition became like a research experiment to me, which was a pleasure. Talking with the curator, Julieta González, was really great. So was having the opportunity to talk to Sol Camacho, who is in charge of the Lina Bo Bardi Foundation in Brazil. She really is an expert.

I wonder if you begin to form a picture of her persona by piecing together all these archives...

That's true. It is weird, in a way, that for this exhibition there was access to some of the professional work, but also to her personal archive—for example, to some of the postcards Lina was sending when she arrived in Brazil, which depict photographs of some very personal moments. In addition to the architect, you see the human being. And this is a reminder that we architects have more vulnerable and familiar facets than the ones that we project as professionalism.

What do you believe are some of Bo Bardi's most important buildings?

The iconic MASP, mentioned earlier. Also, SESC Pompeia, where she decided to stack things that usually would have been distributed, like the volleyball and basketball courts. This stacking frees up space to allow for social areas to be at the most accessible [ground] level of the building, which has become like a large living room for everyone in the community. Here, there are spaces for reading, for spending an afternoon close to the water, playing cards, having a meal. She put in the foreground—on the ground level—what was most important to the community.

Which of her archives speak to you?

There are these very tiny, very early drawings that are like jewels, just because they are so different and so special: miniature studies of volume, light and colour. Also, there is a collection of objects that Lina gathered throughout her life, in particular a special piece that Julieta González, the curator, showed me. This piece was a tiny lamp made out of tin, with a bare light bulb (but just the glass piece). It is as though the electrical system was taken out and then filled with just a cord. So, it could be used as an oil lamp, which was quite a contradiction, and expressed the need to adapt in the face of scarcity. To me this is a very special piece.

Your design for La Tallera—a public art gallery that was the former studio and home of painter David Alfaro Siqueiros (1896–1974)—is an exercise in adaptive reuse, reactivation, and community-centred architecture. These rich and conscientious characteristics are all familiar to Bo Bardi, but what would you say is unique to La Tallera?

I am not trying to compare myself with Lina Bo Bardi in any way, but I think there was a need here for open space. Rather than to have more building, it was about having less building, and to create possibilities by doing tiny things that would dilute the museum's property line. For example, repositioning Siqueiros' massive mural structures, by rotating them to face outwards, opened up his private courtyard to enable more expansive public program. And this was a risk because people would say, 'No, I'm losing my ground inside the complex,' but then they ultimately understood that it was gaining the plaza.

One of the things people often talk about in regard to this building are the *celosia*, or breezeblocks. Why did you select *celosia* as a material?

The museum is located very close to Mexico City in a place that has very nice weather, called the city of eternal springtime (Cuernavaca). *Celosia* create an effect of porosity, filtering fresh light and air through to workshop spaces, the reading room, courtyards and communal areas. The *celosia* envelope also imbues the museum with an institutional feel, or public presence. This was originally a building that had been constructed in little fragments; initially it was just a workshop, and then there was one addition, and another, and so on.

Top: SESC Pompeia towers, Lina Bo Bardi. Bottom right: The lightbulb of Nordeste. Images © Instituto Bardi/Casa de Vidro. Bottom left: La Tallera, Frida Escobedo. Image courtesy of FE Architects + Rafael Gamo.

With all these fragments it was almost like a coral reef. So there was an opportunity to create an envelope by adding to, rather than erasing, this layering effect. When you look through the *celosia*, you can actually read some of the fragments if you pay close enough attention. And in the evening, by peeking through, you can see into the exhibition space without necessarily going into the museum.

It seems that yourself and Bo Bardi approach materiality in a similar way: rough, low-cost, timeworn.

Inevitably, this is related to how we have learned to do more with less, very early on. Since my very first few projects, this has been a condition. For example, one might realise the opportunities of raw cinderblock (which is used at the periphery by many people who build their homes without architects) as a material that is not only cheap, but also has its own beauty and expression. Why keep adding layers of things that need to be maintained?

Your recent Niddo Cafe is clad in vibrant green tiles, and appears different to some of your other buildings which adopt neutral or raw tones. Why so?

We usually steer away from colour at the studio, but we felt that green was not a colour on that corner because of the context. It is actually a very deep green, almost emerald. So the surroundings are reflected, and the material surface becomes quite neutral; there are beautiful trees all around, and it feels like you are bringing the trees outside-in, while also reflecting the movement of people and light. The tiles also create a textural effect in the evening, so that when the lights are lower, the shopfront is atmospherically reflective and glittering. And of course tiles work well in a coffee shop, as you need something that can be easily cleaned and maintained.

What kind of tile was it?

It is a glazed terracotta tile, which were very common in Mexico, but now are slowly being displaced by ceramic tiles, which come in bigger formats, and are cheaper to install and produce. And often those materials have a pattern that is trying to be something else. You can find ceramic tiles that pretend to be marble or some of them even pretend to be wood, which is insane. I don't know why, they are always trying to create some sort of effect, or illusion, and some developers love it. It's like, "Don't use wood, just use this fake wood tile!" But the wood is about sound, temperature, and feel. It's not just about the photograph that you're going to present on your web page. So, I think we are misreading the potentials of what that ceramic tile could be. Because it could be a beautiful thing if we really understand its characteristics. Since terracotta is glazed, I think that has a specific form of expression as a crafted material. It is not completely industrialised. You can see the small variations and the tones, the reaction of the enamel happening on the surface of the terracotta, as opposed to having something stamped on a tile.

In an RIBA lecture (2019), when discussing your research on an anonymous Mexican modernist building that is "intact yet changing, eroding yet accumulating," you mention a personal fascination with ruins. Why are ruins interesting to you?

They are a fixation, but I think that is just part of growing up in Mexico City. You find ruins everywhere, they are a big part of the city's landscape. There are ruins that have been preserved, namely, the monuments. But there is also another type of ruin, a kind of unfinished thing, that could be in the process of being built or in the process of decay. And sometimes you find buildings that do both: there are houses that have not finished being built, but are falling into disrepair. So, you realise that a building is something that is not static but rather completely changing. Once I went to my Master of Architecture degree and took this fantastic class by Erika Naginski, it all made sense. I realised that through these transient fragments we can actually read different kinds of stories and project ourselves in a different way. When something is completely finished, it is hard to find facets which talk to you. But when something is fragmented, it's easier to project yourself into that narrative.

Left: *Celosia* at La Tallera.
Image courtesy of FE Architects + Rafael Gamo.
Right: Terracotta tiles at Niddo Cafe.
Image courtesy of FE Architects + Fabián Martínez.

Lina Bo Bardi's São Paulo Museum of Art (MASP), during construction. © Instituto Bardi/Casa de Vidro + Flieg.

In 2010, you designed a pavilion that people could 'take home' with them, block by block, and in doing so gradually erase the pavilion (Pavilion Eco). What inspired this? Was it these notions of decay and constant flux?

At that time, it was not framed in that way, but nevertheless is related to this idea. The pavilion becomes like a shoreline where people are constantly shifting and moving pieces, and to me this is how life happens. There are two layers, the one that is programmed or prescribed, but then when people start shifting its fundamental fabric, they counteract the strict pattern through agentic movement. So, for me, that was one of the reasons why this modular object worked so well, because you could actually read decay in the composition. Because decay is also a composition, no? And yes, eventually the pavilion also disappeared at the end of the exhibition without leaving any marks. So that was important.

Before it disappeared totally, what happened? Were there any surprises when the public began to interact with Pavilion Eco?

It was really fun. Some of the pictures that I share in lectures show these two girls moving pieces around. And usually when I show that in other countries, they say, "What do you mean? Kids are moving pieces. That's a liability problem." But not in Mexico, there were no accidents. Seeing people constructing their space was a special moment, and so was seeing artists or people who are older just becoming children again, and moving these pieces around. And sometimes they were asking, "Am I able to really move this thing?" or "Can I touch it?" And then usually, once you say yes, they really move them. So it's interesting, this idea that you can participate in the process of the creation of a piece, and by participating you're blurring the authorship into a collective.

Was there a sign at the front, something to let visitors know they could move the blocks?

I think at the beginning, they might have had someone who would tell people they were free to move the pieces. But then when people saw others doing it, they copied. And then, once there were little mounds of pieces that were disarranged, people understood very quickly that this was a moving landscape. There were some more controlled interventions, there were artists who were creating patterns, or things like that. And of course, people would play, just because they're having a good time!

Left: Pavilion Eco, 2010.
Image courtesy of FE Architects + Rafael Gamo.

Lisbon Civic Stage, 2013. Image courtesy of FE Architects + Catalina Botelho.

Would you say the performative aspect of Pavilion Eco is translated to your Civic Stage, at Lisbon (2013)? The Civic Stage has been described by FE Architects as a circular see-saw platform, which pivots so that the more the audience grows, the higher the performer rises, amplifying the civic gesture.

Both the Eco Pavilion and the Civic Stage are somehow trying to make something invisible visible. But they are different kinds of dynamics. One is mouldable, it reacts to that invisibility, and then it's materialised. And the other one has to do more with a movement, but the piece remains static, it does not change. Perhaps it is the neutrality of both pavilions which allows these forces to be seen in a more evident way. The Civic Stage was influenced by a very beautiful piece of art by a friend of mine, Rodolfo Díaz Cervantes. He had created a checkerboard, with a little bowl underneath, and the idea was that when you were placing the chess pieces, the balance would shift (but these were not the typical chess pieces, they were for example a little onyx elephant, or a plastic figurine of Mickey Mouse, and then a little car, these random objects). This piece was talking about human relationships, participation, and hierarchy.

With both of these pavilions, you seem to be playing with things that are dynamic, or constantly shifting and changing. Does this tie into the allegory of 'building with fire'?

Not really. Everyone who has worked or is working on the creative field, they have to portray their reality. So maybe this is my way of portraying what I see and experience in the city. I am not intentionally saying, "let's represent this particular thing." Instead, it is about asking questions and making little experiments to see how things react, and then drawing stories and narrative from those experiments. It is more like an open question, rather than trying to depict a specific situation.

SESC Pompeia, Bo Bardi's sketch for a snack bar at the sports block. © Instituto Bardi/Casa de Vidro + Henrique Luz.

Mohsen Mostafavi commended your Serpentine Pavilion commission (2018) as a performative, constructed environment, as opposed to yet another feat in representation. What entails meaningful architecture to you?

As architects, sometimes we feel the need to design objects that are very recognisable, and have a specific, memorable shape. Instead, I am interested in how people move through and perceive a space. The Serpentine Pavilion erased the idea of an object. It was more about shifting the experience of those who were visiting. If you look online, there is no typical 'moniker' for the pavilion. When you see pictures, it's really bad, just a box made out of roof tiles, or a wall, there is nothing recognisable or special. But that's because user experience was a priority; when you walked through the diagonal space of the walls, they would become more opaque or transparent; the alignment of the roof allowed you to see the movement of the sun; gaps in the tiles filtered in sounds and a breeze; a pool of water reflected the skyscape and a ceiling mirror reflected the earthscape. It came to be about experiencing things that were outside the pavilion, both metaphorically and literally. You could locate yourself in a larger geography, a larger cosmography of space, and understand how it is constructed in a very abstract way.

I've heard you speak about a memory of a place potentially being separate to the experience of it. Can you elaborate on this idea?

Sometimes, we 'remember' images more so through media information than our personal experience. For example, I remember being in Paris, and I remember the Eiffel Tower, but mainly out of photographs and not my actual experience in that place, because it is so recognisable, and so over-mediatised.

Opposite (top): Frida Escobedo's Serpentine Pavilion.
Image courtesy FE Architects + Rafael Gamo.

Opposite (bottom): Lina Bo Bardi's SESC Pompeia interior, social ground-level area.
Fishing in the San Francisco River, 1982.
© Instituto Bardi/Casa de Vidro + Antônio Saggese.

Right: Lina Bo Bardi's SESC Pompeia interior, social area furniture.
© Instituto Bardi/Casa de Vidro.

But when you are in the Serpentine Pavilion, that is a diffuse thing, you have to be paying close attention. There are specific devices that inform snippets or fragments of your own presence and experience, like seeing a face in a reflective ceiling, feeling the sun heating the floor, inhaling the particular breeze that was happening that day, was it fresher? Or warmer? Were there kids playing around? Was there a specific echo? So, I think a vivid memory can be informed by a whole-body experience of a place, rather than remembering an image through one's eyes only.

We began this interview speaking of Mexico City and São Paulo… how would you describe the habitat of your Serpentine Pavilion, London?

That is a tough question. Even though I spent some time there, it does not feel like I have the same sensibility towards London as I do towards my hometown Mexico City, or the familiarity that we share with São Paulo (because they have so many things in common, it's easier for me to have a read on what is happening). What I would say about London is that it is a collage of cultures. At the same time, many of the spaces arise as constructions to preserve capital. It is a fascinating city because it's trying to hold onto this production and preservation of a specific economy, but at the same time many things are happening underneath. It is very vibrant. There are many people from many countries contributing to what being a Londoner is. So, I would not say it has a single image. It is more like a multiplicity of cities within one. It is not as easy to read as some other grid-like cities, this is more of a fragmented city.

In a well-known quote from her correspondence—which has been popularised in part due to Isaac Julien's recent film installation *A Marvellous Entanglement* (2020)—Lina Bo Bardi writes: "*Linear time is a Western invention. Time is not linear, it is a marvellous tangle, where, at any moment, points can be selected and solutions invented, without beginning or end.*"

That is a beautiful quote, one that I had kind of forgotten, but really it is marvellous. Because you realise how often we are focused on the process, and not the experience of the process. This is especially the case for architects, who are constantly trying to finish something, to accomplish something as if it were completable, when really, we are just a temporary moment in the production of that kind of space. Architects are only a tiny piece in this never ending puzzle of transformation. The space was already there, the material was already there, it is just being displaced from somewhere else. These components are constructed into an object, which is then modified by the way people use it, not just over the years, but almost every second. Space is changing every second, and it is never going to be the same; the light that is coming through the window right now is never going to be the same. So, we have to be very aware of these slight shifts and how to connect with them. This approach has to do with what I would say is a more 'feminine eye,' where it is not just about the milestone that we need to achieve, but also the connections that we make in the process. I think this is very valuable from Lina. It's a big lesson.

TRACING THE ANTHROPOCENE

Feifei Zhou

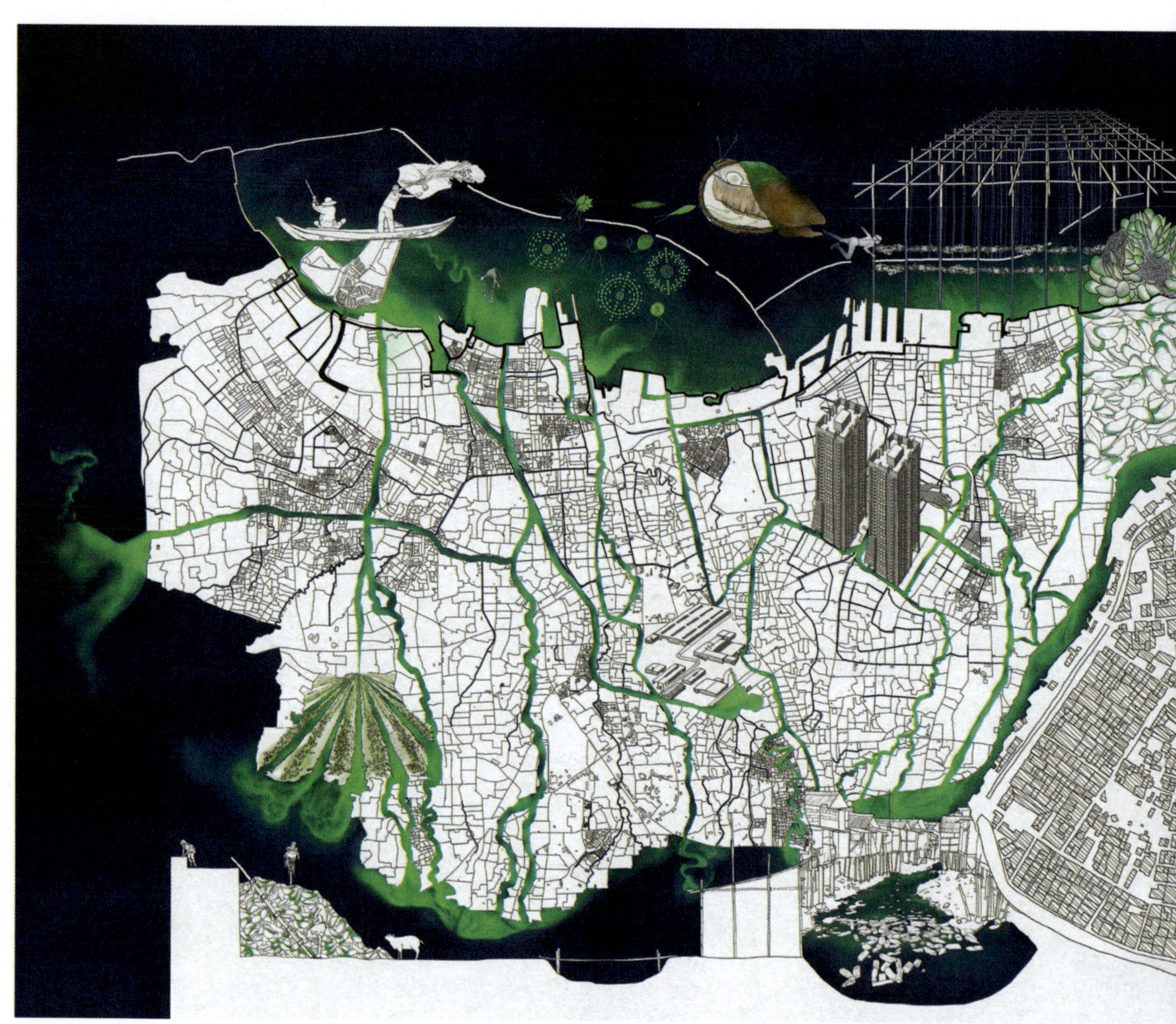

Imagine you are building a shed in your backyard. You bought some timber from the local workshop, perhaps some wood chips for the path, and some lovely flowers from the flower market.

If you live in an urban area like me, there is a good chance that your commercial timber, plants or even soil, have gone through long-distance transfers to arrive in your yard. The transportation of commodities throughout global trade routes often amasses silent, intrepid nomads; living or non-living organisms that touch down and lay claim to new ecosystems, resulting in unintended ecological collisions and potentially feral consequences. Pathogens, antibiotics and agrochemicals are the stowaways of commercial shipments that might just have crept into your shed and home. A simple shed contains the imported by-products of its timber, plants and soil: the ubiquitous yet buried stories of a global system. This system of globalisation makes almost everything around us part of one or multiple supply chains. Simply through the act of building a shed, you become a participant in this system, most likely without even realising.

In a recently published research project *Feral Atlas: The More-than-Human Anthropocene*, we assembled 79 first-hand field reports that tell stories of these 'feral' effects emerging around us.[1] Often unnoticed, these effects emerge and spread with the aid of man-made infrastructure projects but beyond humanity's control. They are a condition that characterises this geological epoch we call 'the Anthropocene.'

Left: 'Flow Toxins,' by Feifei Zhou and Kirsten Keller. Image originally commissioned by Forum do Futuro, Porto, and published in *Vita Nova*, eds. Guilherme Blanc, Shumon Basar, Filipa Ramos, Jenna Sutela (Galeria Municipal do Porto/Bom Dia Boa Tarde Boa Noite, 2020).

The Anthropocene is uneven. It is formed by non-human responses to landscape programmes, which are distributed unevenly across the earth.[2] We cannot simply determine the environmental consequences of anthropogenic activities with generality, because these consequences are trans-spatial and temporal, and underpinned by mechanisms of power and justice. Our daily practices, though seemingly negligible on an individual scale, are very possibly contributing to ecological catastrophes. Feral dynamics are ubiquitous, and simultaneously affecting humans and non-humans, though unevenly.

Buildings play a crucial role in this feral dynamic, yet such connections remain unseen or even dismissed by architects. As a result, our increasingly intensified built environment has become a battleground for the Anthropocene. Intricate entanglements between the built environment and ecologies are making it impossible to design something that could stand as absolutely 'regional.' Admittedly, spatial impacts of arguably any architectural designs are cross-regional and multi-scalar. In something as seemingly insignificant as a shed, particular attention is required in understanding the oft-unnoticed feral dynamics: what has disappeared, what may disappear, and what may proliferate—which sometimes might be far too significant to ignore. To design something small, we must first think big.

Opposite: 'Relic manufacturing sites, Jewelry District neighborhood, Providence, Rhode Island.' Map by Thomas Marlow, post-doctoral researcher at New York University, Abu Dhabi. Image published in *Feral Atlas: The More-Than-Human Anthropocene*.

Imagine a shed at Maura Angke, a fishing port and settlement in Jakarta Bay, Indonesia. Semi-permanent structures in the informal settlement are built by Jakarta's fishermen, a marginalised community threatened by speculative urbanism and industrialisation. Anthropologist Kirsten Keller's field research in Jakarta Bay investigates intricate coastal interactions, exploring social and ecological histories, as well as contemporary relations. Often evicted to marginal, swampy areas to make way for urban development, the urban poor have used vernacular and other salvaged materials like bamboo and scrap wood to construct temporary homes, via a combination of traditional architectural techniques, such as *rumah panggung* (stilted homes). Bamboo is also used to build structures for cultivation of Asian green mussels, an increasingly important livelihood practice as heavy water pollution and large-scale coastal infrastructure instigates the decline of small-scale fishing.

Alarmingly, the interaction between waste and infrastructure is causing Jakarta to sink. Sewage, industrial effluents and agricultural runoff are discharged into the city's canals and rivers, and flow to the sea as a cocktail of nutrients and heavy metal. Inadequate public water treatment and provision of infrastructure encourages upper class and industrial users to rely on intensive, unregulated private groundwater extraction. Depletion of the aquifer causes land subsidence (sinking). In response, massive seawall infrastructure is being constructed in an effort to prevent Jakarta's coast from sinking into the sea. This threatens to displace fishermen who live in informal settlements where land rights are ambiguous, and to ruin the marine ecosystem.

Many fishermen rely on the aforementioned cultivation of Asian green mussels, creatures which not only survive, but can thrive in polluted water. As filter feeders, green mussels consume nutrients, algae and heavy metals, helping to clean the water, but also rendering the mussels themselves toxic to human and non-human consumption in the process. The mussel cultivation activities also result in the accumulation of tons and tons of shells, which rather than being simply discarded, provide material for habitation. Mussels shells, along with the waste and concrete debris left by the construction of seawalls, become the material for spontaneous land reclamations, creating new informal lands to dwell upon in the face of displacement and subsidence.

A shed in Maura Angke is not only a shed. Alongside piles of mussel shells and a monumental seawall, it is material evidence of the city's entangled complexity, which is underpinned by social and environmental injustices.

Imagine a shed that sits alone on an abandoned lot in downtown Providence, Rhode Island, USA. Right underneath that shed, the urban soil has long preserved Providence's once prosperous manufacturing industry with toxic residues from oil spills and chemical leakage. Despite the area's above ground transformations, pipes, sewers, tanks and other industrial projects with all their associated wastes are left buried in the earth, whether they are abandoned or still functioning.

Once in a while, what was buried comes back to haunt us. Sociologist Scott Frickel told us—in his field report for *Feral Atlas*—about his 'ghostly' encounter during a morning run in the rain around the urban side of Providence. While he was running, a heavy rainstorm liberated the buried toxins from below the ground; they engulfed the city's fresh air with sharp, irritating odors of volatilizing chemicals.[3]

The conclusion of Frickel's encounter was that we, city-builders, cover up the underground chemical residues excreted by old mills and factories with new homes, new schools, and those inconspicuous sheds, only to forget that out-of-sight toxins have spread through our soil, water and air, causing complications for both the present and the future.[4]

A shed on a brownfield is not only a shed. It is a futile attempt to patch over the city's buried yet virulent industrial history, and a reminder for us to unmask the urban past in order to reinvent the future of the built environment.

In *Feral Atlas*, we argued that infrastructure is responsible for the feral effects of the Anthropocene. The term 'infrastructure' here represents public land/water/air-scape modification projects, which are integral to the case studies unpacked in this essay. Instead of focusing on the kind of work infrastructure intentionally aims to do, *Feral Atlas* seeks out the undesigned, unnoticed and uncontrollable consequences arising from our activities.

These infrastructure projects not only alter the shape of our terrains, but also block access to natural resources from indigenous communities. Such projects also upset and disrupt formerly balanced ecological rhythms and cycles; our garbage in the communal bins ends up in landfill sites or swirling in the ocean with other wastes, becoming hazards for marine ecosystems. This feral effect is visibly scattered around us, but there are more: commercial shipping on large scales transfer pathogen-laced products across the globe, spreading fatal disease; excessive ground energy extraction becomes responsible for anthropogenic disasters such as earthquakes and extinctions; toxic waste is gathered and distributed, overloading our bodies and homes without us even realising.

The simple construction of a shed in our backyard could trigger a chain of ecological disturbances, often unnoticed. With its ability of territorial forming and landscape shaping, architecture in the Anthropocene should avoid itself becoming the by-product of our skewed power structures and environmental inequalities. For this to happen, we ought to start noticing the unnoticed.

Now, imagine building a shed.

01 Feral Atlas is a collective project of more than one hundred scientists, humanists and artists.

02 Anna L. Tsing, Jennifer Deger, Alder Keleman Saxena, and Feifei Zhou. *Feral Atlas: The More-Than-Human Anthropocene*, (Redwood City: Stanford University Press 2021).

03 Scott Frickel, "Cities are subterranean disasters," in *Feral Atlas: The More-Than-Human Anthropocene*, (Redwood City: Stanford University Press 2021).

04 Max Liboiron, Manuel Tironi, and Nerea Calvillo, "Toxic politics: Acting in a permanently polluted world," *Social Studies of Science* 48, no.3, (2018): 331-349.

WHOSE ARCHITECTURE

Vicky Shukuroglou and Bruce Pascoe

An echidna presses up against a woman's calf. With her skin mostly exposed, its textures straighten her back, just a little. Its skin is flaky and pink, hair thinned, many quills broken. She knew the creature was unwell, and wondered if its senses were now affected. Echidna continued to show no sign of caution when the woman lightly stomped, attempting to keep it still, close.

A tree is cut at the base. The procedure is methodical, considered, and more than 200,000 times faster than the time it took the tree to reach its growing height and girth. Suddenly, shade disappears. Life transforms. Roots that kept it still and strong and also made it vulnerable, now receive different messages.

That echidna knew the woman. She had become part of its place; familiar, like the tree.

The woman knew the echidna and kept a lookout for it and signs of its rummaging. Seeing its instinctive defence of burrowing when a stranger appeared, helped the woman realise how well the echidna sensed her. She loves the echidna, and so her understanding shifts.

For those who know the tree, the absence of shade expands the details of their understanding.

Some who notice the increased sun, yet previously barely saw the rooted tree, allow their mind to contemplate it, and what they might have loved. In the time of the tree's presence, some had noticed the calls of birds, the rustle of leaves pushed by wings in flight, cracked nuts dispersed below. Seasonally, those nuts gathered in such number they were easily heard while walking through them.

None who walk know there is a particularly fine piece of stone nestled among the tree's more fibrous roots. At the time the stone was sought out and held skyward for the sun to better reveal its structure, the tree had not even sprouted. Its grandparent was just a sapling growing near the drip-line of its parent.

The stone had been traded from afar because it was ideal for what a maker was seeking – fine grain, no 'impurities', and of good size. The piece now entangled in the fibrous roots had been reduced to its precise form by angled strikes from other tools, controlled by human hands. When deftly worked, this material reveals sharp and shapely edges so effectively, that across the earth we see evidence of matching craft and use by people over many tens of thousands of years. Other stones also extracted from where that finely crafted one originated, ended up nearby but with a century's distance, in the process of making the city's footpaths. Such are the chances with the mingling layers of human habitation.

The woman who knew the echidna peered at various stones around her lightly treading feet. In her contemplations was the lineage of echidnas of that particular place. She wondered about living spaces, and how perceptions form and give shape, allow for presence or absence.

She thought of the ground hugging echidna, the soil particles dotting its eyes, encrusting its moist nostrils, and distinctly scenting its body. Echidna's perspective is of another world to hers—its horizons varied—its architecture imbued with subtlety *of* that place. And the architecture of an echidna living in the snowy mountains is surely different to one in a tropical rainforest, or arid region of Australia.

The woman further contemplated this as she slipped into her bed that night, between sheets, behind solid walls which stand in opposition to any echidna's architecture. She had always preferred sleeping on the other side of these walls and, staring at them, wondered what inclusions and exclusions were made in the building of structures across the world. The people who settled here, in Australia, perhaps a hundred thousand years ago, observed and responded to this land. Like all who settle, they held a certain consciousness for their own survival.

Photography by Vicky Shukuroglou.

Housing is important. If you find a good house, keep it.

It's pretty clear he was in residence but like many people, he was only house minding. The previous residents were dead, murdered. It happened quite often in this place.

It was an interesting house. Cathedral ceilings, panoramic view of the valley, energy efficient, the walls thick and designed to release heat slowly in winter. The winters are cold, giant boulders are cloven in two. The detonation from those frost incidents must have resounded through the valley like a cannonade.

Cleft tors strew the valley as a reminder how frequently those cannons must have boomed.

We saw him under circumstances which would have been difficult for him. We had ascended the mountain in order to more closely inspect his house which we had come across the day before, in falling light. One wall in particular intrigued us and we needed to examine its construction in daylight. Anyway, he met us first. He must have heard us labouring up the slopes, and because he had a question to ask he decided to watch our approach.

There was a nice stone terrace behind his house and that's where we glimpsed him, but he was a shy sort of creature, almost hermitic. At the last minute he became wary and dashed off, but must have remembered his question and so he waited for us.

We arrived, he watched our approach and then held up his paw to show us his problem. He was a dingo with an injury. He seemed to want us to notice. Perhaps he needed advice or help. He approached us with tentative steps but at the last moment he was startled by something and bounded away despite his injury.

It seemed indecent to inspect his house in his absence but we needed to know how it had been constructed. We knelt before the wall facing the valley and just as we suspected it had been made by human hands using available stone to fill in an aperture in the tors; a feature designed with cold winters in mind.

Those old hands had done a fine job in construction. We had seen their handiwork in creating other structures in the valley. They seemed to be for the purpose of animal control but it is just speculation for the moment. Because the builders are gone. Killed in the war.

You can still see their tools strewn around the valley corners and their art is still preserved in the galleries of stone but they, the builders, gamekeepers and artists of this place, are gone.

Their descendants stand with us, trying to understand the remnants of the town, an anguish of loss palpable on their faces; all of our faces. This has been a terrible history.

And now the dingo is the caretaker and he too is injured. From his mountain eyrie he must listen to the frosty night cannonades too. We yearn to watch his face on those occasions, deep in the warmth of his environmentally friendly home. But that privilege of contiguity is too much to expect of such a wild beast.

He let us see his home and that will have to be enough. Prolonged dinner conversation with uprights is not his thing.

Photography by Vicky Shukuroglou.

HOUSE ON A HOUSE

Mitul Desai

During our travels in India, we come across conditions where spatial qualities arise out of the need to function in restricted environments. It is a spontaneous act to resolve all basic requirements where available space and resources are limited. These spaces are considerate to human interaction. They are modest and free.

—Bijoy Jain, Studio Mumbai

This photo essay captures moments of permanence and ephemerality across Gujarat, Rajasthan and Uttar Pradesh states in North and West India. Moving through this landscape with a sense of curiosity and wonderment, at times we stumble upon seemingly anachronistic spaces and places that are phenomenal, atmospheric and ingenious. It is my concern, through fieldwork undertaken in association with Studio Mumbai, to look closely at these urban and rural anomalies. Such encounters become visceral memories that sustain and nourish the instinct. An ensuing repository of body-memory imparts spontaneity, and reminds us to build with graceful humility. The final set of images in this study shares a designed response to this fieldwork by my practice, Studio ii. This design is named 'House on a House,' and it aspires to the sophisticated creations that precede it.

Demolition, Surat

If construction is an act of defying gravity, demolition embraces it. In that sense, demolition is axially opposite to construction where gravity becomes the primary actor and humans, the catalyst. Demolition is not destruction. It is a careful, intentional, and systematic extraction of material and habitation from architecture. Demolition sites are nothing less than fleeting archaeological specimens where the 'cut' is through culture and time as much as it is through the building. These sites are constantly in flux and complete at any given moment. In the act of demolition, many unprecedented spatial configurations occur that cannot be approached through rational construction of spaces but only emerge in the act of deconstruction. They offer a sensory and visual depository: an archive of pure spatial possibilities.

Sand dredging, Surat
Dredgers leave for the river mouth, outside of regulatory zones, early in the morning to dredge sand in the cooler hours. Heavy sand-loaded boats return to the banks, borne by the force of the morning tide. Dredging is aligned to the rhythm of tides because none of the boats have motors. Every morning, boat owners, dredgers and truckers self-organise this real estate-underbelly of a fast growing city. Underground labour, construction resource-extraction and togetherness coalesce.

Bushy Curtainwalls, Phalodi
On a highway stretching across semi-arid landscape, the only places of pause are roadside inns, locally called *dhabas*. Here, truckers and travelers stop for shade, rest, water and food, before continuing the scorching journey. Built with frugal means, *dhabas* have facades gracefully constructed with bamboo, and bushes sourced from the nearby vicinity. These curtainwalls filter out harsh sun, storm dust and hostility of the desert, while still allowing gentle breezes to pass through, rendering the interiors humane and restful.

Wood Plank Houses, Surat
Wood planks from industrial crates and pallets are upcycled as a cheap house material. Thick coats of oil paint protect this low-grade and temporary material from weather, promoting longevity. In the same region, there are houses constructed using the same approach, but with local teak timber, that are more than a generation old. This uncanny mirroring of structures connected by time, place and ethnicity assures that tacit knowledge remains ingrained in culture and materials alike.

Saree Building, Surat
A residential building is appropriated by the informal textile industry. Migrant workers live and work relentlessly in these spaces, applying finishing touches to sarees, the traditional dressing for Indian women. These sarees are left out to dry after their final wash, veiling the building before they are packed and transported to various parts of the country. Although the textile process capitalises on the height and form of the building for pragmatic reasons, as a result the building assumes a colourful identity.

Brick Monoliths, Sarnath
Buddhist relics were long ago buried under these brick mammoths to protect them from any and all eventualities. Timelessness is embedded into the construction of these ancient stupas, which continue to outlive their ancient life. Built with humble brick, the stupas transcend limitations of material and process. The safe-guarding mechanism of these monoliths is unsuspecting; although they may seem to be protected by their sheer scale, in actuality it is the careful and strategic layering of brick which resists penetration. When foreign invaders destroyed every possible architectural landmark of this time to the ground, they could hardly scratch the surface of these monoliths. These structures by design could only be re-claimed and built upon, but never destroyed.

Monkey Grills, Mathura
Monkeys during the day and thieves at night meander the city, scouring for openings to enter homes, searching for food or valuables. Through the use of grills, the city closes itself to the menace, yet remains open to other elements. Courtyards, balconies, verandas, terraces and openings are layered with these filters, which allow homes to be impartial to any intruders and remain congenial to the street. The rain, the sun, the breeze and the night are as welcome as ever in the household. The monkeys and the thieves coexist.

All photography pages 34-43 by Mitul Desai.

House on a House, Surat

By Studio ii

A couple build their first house atop their parents' house, with continuation of structure, access and form. Although demolition sometimes precedes expansion, this dwelling instead builds on what was already there to promote growth. Resources, memory, and togetherness are preserved and protected, without encroaching on further land area. This infill approach is not only economically feasible, but also at a larger scale, inhibits urban sprawl.

Approached either from the in-house staircase or through direct elevator (which facilitates mobility for elderly parents), the house finds its own expression of space and tectonics, paradoxically independent of—but also in response to—the house below. Its central courtyard is like a spine, extending out to all the spaces and connecting the house from the earth to the sky.

At the upper level, a porous grilled and blinded box wraps the courtyard on two sides, allowing the house to constantly breathe in this semi-arid climate, and for the external atmosphere to permeate the interior. Across and below, large openings with louvered doors offer variable levels of porosity.

At the ground floor, both living and dining rooms can either open to a North facing outdoor terrace, or more intimately to a central courtyard. When all of these walls are opened, almost the entire ground floor becomes one large gathering space.

Taking cues from local teakwood 'wood plank' houses of the old city, and inspired from traditional spatial-materiality, the house's interior detailing is rooted deeply in the craft of building and space-making. Custom designed light fittings and brass hardware subtly ornament the otherwise simple spaces.

Restraint in materials, connection with the sky, as well as spatial articulation and thoughtful detailing, evokes the house as a seamless entity in its parts or as a whole. Be it an anchored concrete floor on the ground level or lightweight teak flooring on the first level; sandstone in the bathrooms with open-roof showers or the roofless central courtyard staircase; visceral sensorial experiences govern the user experience within. The house allows stillness to settle into its spaces, even as seasonal and daily rhythms of both the family and the weather wash over and through it.

PLANET CITY

IN CONVERSATION WITH LIAM YOUNG

Liam Young is a speculative architect and director who operates in the spaces between design, fiction and futures. He is co-founder of Tomorrows Thoughts Today, an urban futures think tank exploring the local and global implications of new technologies and Unknown Fields, a nomadic research studio that travels on expeditions to chronicle these emerging conditions as they occur on the ground. Young's narrative approach sits between documentary and fiction as he focuses on projects that aim to reveal the invisible connections and systems that make the modern world work. He currently manages his time between exploring distant landscapes and visualising the future worlds he extrapolates from them.

Young's most recent project, Planet City, *is a film and book that explores the productive potential of extreme densification, where 10 billion people surrender the rest of the planet to a global wilderness and the return of stolen lands. The* Planet City *book is published and available by Uro Pubications.*

With our curiosity piqued by the recent exhibition of Planet City *at the National Gallery of Victoria Triennial,* Inflection *Vol. 08 editors initiated a dialogue with Liam on architectural education, the expansive role of the architect and how fictional futures bring the present realities into focus.*

Indoor Mega Farm, Planet City, 2020. Visualisation.
Image by Liam Young.

How does your work as a speculative architect differ from your work as an educator? If you were to speculate on the future of architectural education, what might an alternate pedagogy entail?

As a speculative architect, I do not design buildings as endpoints or outputs. But I would still argue that what I do is architectural, or at least, it is architecture in some form. Instead of creating buildings themselves, I tell stories about the global, urban and architectural implications of emerging technologies. The dominant forces of the past that shaped our cities, buildings and public spaces are now being displaced by technologies, systems, networks, and stacks. Thus, the architect needs to change their model of practice in order to remain relevant. The architect now needs to intervene in these systems beyond shaping physical buildings, and that is really about telling stories of how they operate. Speculative architects mostly create narratives about how new technologies and networks influence space, culture and community. They try to imagine where new forms of agency exist within cities changed by these new processes.

For me, architecture is really a practice of telling stories with and through space. Most architects, whether they call themselves that or not, have been speculative architects for much of their careers. For example, most competition entries remain unbuilt and the client never pays for them. These are speculative projects that have never been legitimised within the profession or education. So I think the claim in speculative architecture is actually not to say that it's a new discipline but to legitimise and formalise it in a way that it has not been before. Many of the graduates from architecture school do not go on to work traditionally as 'building-making' architects. Yet, rarely does an architectural program acknowledge and support alternative career paths. Typically, we see them as alternative routes but today, I would argue that non-building architects are actually far more the mainstream. I set up a new Master of Fiction and Entertainment program on speculative architecture at Sci-Arc to try to establish it as a clear genre of architecture and a clear career path, not being something that you fall into because no one will pay you to build anything but something that is really meaningful and critical.

How does a project like *Planet City* evolve as a collaborative work? How could non-fictional works benefit from such a process?

Although wildly speculative, the project is a grounded and possible proposal developed from real calculations, cutting edge research and the support of a distributed council of acclaimed environmental scientists, technologists, economists and authors from all over the world. We look at what possible urban forms might emerge if we fully embraced these technologies and implemented them at their most extreme scale. This is a necessary form of prototyping and speculation that is not an attempt to impose a singular vision but rather the development of counter narratives that could be discussed, debated and scaffold larger scale cultural engagement in their possible implications. The front line of the climate change fight is no longer technological, it is now an economic, political and cultural battle.

A lot of these technologies that we talk about when we are thinking about smart cities or our future cities are what I define as 'before-culture technologies.' Since ideology rarely evolves at the same pace as technology, speculative practices and processes are really a form of prototyping cultural responses to consequences of technologies that are not quite here yet. These projects are based in fiction but I think they suggest methodologies that are critical in applied and non-fictional works as well. That is why speculation and futures are really important. It is a way of engaging an audience and empowering them to make decisions about the futures that they want to live in because inevitably, the future is a verb, not a noun. The future is not something that just washes over us like water. It is something that we actively shape and define.

Opposite: 'Solar Fields,' *Planet City*, 2020. Visualisation. Image by Liam Young.

If we imagine *Planet City* as a site to prototype narratives, what might the role of the architect entail? How would they work and who would they work with?

Planet City presents the idea that we need to radically embrace the uncomfortable place we now occupy in a world where we can no longer be at its centre. At present, we chart territory for the extraction of wealth and the fulfillment of our own desires. But *Planet City* imagines that the rest of the globe outside of its walls are defined specifically in order for us to leave it empty. Suggestive of a national park boundary, we might draw this line on the earth not to own, develop, or occupy but to keep us out and scaffold its recovery. In *Planet City*, technology is deployed to intensify human activity and make more room for an intentional landscape, a carbon sink wilderness and a voluntary exclusion zone. The beginnings of *Planet City* is the necessary end of human-centered design and the foregrounding of action for non-human species and the development of positions such as 'wetlands-centered design,' 'atmosphere-centered design' or 'whooping crane-centered design.'

Unfortunately, nation states, governments and large corporations that have really failed us when it comes to climate change. Traditional forms of architecture and the architect are both enabled by and complicit with these entities. We perpetuate the problems they create and the systems of power and finance through which they operate. What we are seeing is how completely ineffective these forms have been in addressing problems of this scale and time frame. Without change at this level, no architectural invention or proposal has any hope. If we understand that climate change is now a cultural problem not a technological one, then the issue is that too often architects fail to operate as cultural or political agents and instead fetishise or attempt to impose simplified technological solutions to extraordinarily layered and complex social problems. If the battleground of climate change is in cultural and ideological discourse, then we need to make projects that have resonance in that space, not repeat outmoded master planning projects with the hubris and megalomaniacal tendencies of previous generations. The type of imagination needed as designers and architects is based around rethinking our relationship to these structural forces and developing new models of practice and projects that can engage audiences in these underlying problems.

Above Left: 'Beekeeper,' *Planet City*, 2020. Photograph.

Above Middle: 'Code Walker,' *Planet City*, 2020. Photograph.

Above Right: 'Algae Diver,' *Planet City*, 2020. Photograph.

Opposite: 'Indoor Mega Farm,' *Planet City*, 2020. Visualisation.

All images by Liam Young.

An emerging interest in regional expansion has been made all the more prescient by the pandemic. The susceptibility of urban centres and proliferation of online work and study has afforded flexibility in places of residence. How do you reconcile this trend with your speculative future in *Planet City*?

We are all already residents of a planetary city. Following centuries of colonisation, globalisation and never-ending economic extraction we have remade the world from the scale of the cell to the tectonic plate. Urban development has forever changed the composition of the atmosphere, the oceans and the earth. The notion of centre and periphery has fundamentally changed to the point where it really no longer has relevance. There is no city and country anymore, no nature and technology. Instead, we have now engineered a continuous urban construct that stretches across the entirety of the earth, an unevenly distributed megastructure hiding in plain sight. It was not masterplanned by a single imperial power, or a cyberpunk megacorporation. It was slowly stitched together from stolen lands by planetary logistics where landscapes have become resource fields, countries have become factory floors, the countryside has become industrialised agriculture and the oceans have become conveyor belts.

Planet City is not a plan for direct implementation but rather, serves as a grounded provocation that prototypes the necessary systemic and lifestyle changes that may be required in order for our world to continue to support human life. It affords us this critical distance from which to re-evaluate ourselves and helps us to see that normal is the actual problem. What comes into focus are not the extremes of this fictional city but the catastrophic models of everyday urbanism. The live-action dystopian film we all occupy in the present moment is just as fantastic, implausible and incalculable as any science fiction imagining. In a world that is post-truth, post-logic and post-geography, *Planet City* is both already here and entirely imaginary. Projects like this one hope to contribute to a necessary collective conversation about the futures we all want to be a part of. It is a call to arms, a hope that we will keep making stories and building worlds that become vessels for critical ideas—Trojan Horses hidden within the mediums of popular culture.

DEFAMILIARISING ARCHITECTURE

SPATIAL AGENCY IN CITIES OF THE SOUTHERN LATITUDES

Amanda Achmadi

Cities of the Southern Latitudes, such as those in Asia-Pacific, Latin America and Africa have emerged as the epicentres of urbanisation in the 21st century. Yet, the empirical complexities of inhabitations emerging in these vast regions, as well as the configurations and transfigurations of their architectural and urban formations, have not quite captured the imagination of design studio curriculums and design pedagogy in most parts of the world, including those within the regions themselves. Instead, Euro-American traditions and buildings, as well as the professional design culture of the developed world, continue to remain the canon and benchmark in all major domains of architectural teaching—history and theory, construction technology and design.

Architectural education in the 21st century has not substantially engaged with the socio-spatial dynamics of the unprecedented scale of urbanisation of its own time. What, then, is the role of architecture and design thinking in the vast landscape of spatial contingency, multiplicity and temporality of lived urban experiences unravelling in the Global South?

Contrasting urban conditions of Bandung in West Java, a formal colonial settlement with a population of 2.5 million. Image by the author.

In this essay, a series of urban conditions in two major Indonesian cities—Jakarta and Bandung—will be considered as examples of lived urban experiences in the Global South. These conditions challenge the way we see and analyse urban forms, including their architectural components. This is an exercise of *defamiliarising architecture*. It is an attempt to shift from a preoccupation with architecture as highly controlled built form or final design outcome into a consideration of the multiple urban processes and contingencies in which architecture is part of and dependent on.[1] The urban conditions of Jakarta and Bandung are sites of myriad urban processes and socio-spatial practices that constantly destabilise any illusion of spatial order, coherence or finality of a built system.

The complex landscapes of resilience and transformation that characterise cities in the Global South have been critically interpreted, theorised and lucidly narrated elsewhere through interdisciplinary methods by contemporary scholars such as AbdouMaliq Simone, Jeff Hou, Ananya Roy, Ross King, Kim Dovey and Abidin Kusno.[2] In *City Life from Jakarta to Dakar: Movements at the Crossroads*, Simone theorises that urban conditions of the Southern Latitudes have exposed the limit of the formal language, vocabulary and conceptual apparatus of both the scholarly and professional fields of architecture and urban planning.[3] He warns us that cities in the Southern Latitudes are socio-spatial environments in a continual state of flux and contestation. These are cities that cannot be contained or sufficiently described and analysed by the seemingly finite, predictable and contained taxonomy of urban morphology or architectural typology associated with cities of the Global North. Such complex urban landscapes, Simone argues, have instead called for a new mode of urban inhabitation, processes and built forms.

When architects and planners attempt to transplant their pre-existing disciplinary apparatus and vocabularies to the shaping and forming of cities such as Jakarta and Bandung, they impose a system of spatial order and morphological coherence onto complex fields of urban processes that do not conform to the same formal taxonomy. Such architectural endeavours generate built forms that appear foreign, fictional, artificial, or staged—architectural and urban spectacles of highly curated and controlled built perfection. They appear to be hyperreal, out of place, frozen in time. It is not surprising, then, that such spectacles are soon overwhelmed by the vast, unravelling flux of urban processes, mobilities and agencies that do not have the capacity or opportunity to stop and appreciate formally designed architecture. In many instances, these top-down planned urban neighbourhoods—shopping malls, office towers, elite apartment complexes, housing estates and satellite towns—are literally separated and even 'defended' from their urban contexts through a construction of elevated podiums, solid brick walls and layers of security checks; they are rendered a series of urban fortresses.

Easily marketable urban and architectural spectacles are utilised to brand the city as progressive, smart, sustainable and 'global.' At the same time, they become powerful tools to marginalise, and in many cases delegitimise, the indigenous urban forms and the urban population's own capacity to envision and manage their built environments. Postcolonial architectural scholars and critical urbanists, such as Lawrence Vale, Abidin Kusno, Anoma Pieris, Kim Dovey and Ananya Roy, have argued in their separate studies that architecture and urban planning's preoccupation with the ordering of space and more recently the branding of cities, have made the disciplines and the associated professions susceptible to the ruling ideologies of colonial and postcolonial states of the Southern Latitudes.[4] Through architecture, urban design and planning, state authorities impose power structures and social hierarchies onto the space of everyday life. Typically, indigenous and vernacular built forms—urban shanties, the *kampung* and other types of urban habitat imagined and built by the majority population who are not in the position to engage professional services of architects or urban planners—are relegated as the underdeveloped, backward, or the pre-urban. Here, architecture and planning become parts of the ruling elite's spatial and visual rhetoric.

Through flagship master plans and architectural projects, ruling postcolonial authorities construct and visualise what being urban, modern and successful should look like, regardless of the vernacular urban forms and the diversity of social and economic life of a place. Instead, cities and large-scale neighbourhoods have been planned and constructed primarily for the professional urban middle classes, thereby displacing and pushing aside diverse socio-spatial practices of those who have already resided there for generations. Formally planned cities and their architecturally designed buildings become rhetorical urban forms through which postcolonial states shape, govern and control their territory and social subjects, under the guise of projecting a progressive national or urban identity to the world. Architecture is indeed a powerful tool in realising an imagined identity, including that of a nation.[5]

Meanwhile, the 21st century's image economy continues to ascribe primacy to the visual effect of architecture. Architectural experiences and qualities are now instantly flattened and disseminated beyond their unique social contexts through online platforms. They are edited and then reproduced throughout the world primarily as architectural objects—projected through photoshopped photography or realistic digital rendering—often with a shadow cast over post-occupation conditions. Anecdotal stories abound where life and all their messy traces have to be packed away or cropped out of architectural objects so that they can be heroically featured in professional design media and Instagram platforms. Digital visualisation of architectural ideas typically features exterior views framed from certain dramatic angles not attainable from human-eye (future user) perspectives. Architecture is imagined and represented as a field of formal abstractions and aesthetics, conceived outside and regardless of, the dynamic socio-spatial realities of our time. In the era of advanced graphic editing softwares, it has become even easier to omit, blur, or darken the messiness of everyday inhabitations and urban contexts, as though architecture could overcome contingent occupations of space. As Jeremy Till's book, *Architecture Depends* reminds us:

> An associated effect of the computer's confusion of representation and reality is that it reinforces architecture's autonomy. In severing time from the architectural scene, while giving the illusion that it is there, architects are provided the luxury of preoccupying themselves with form alone, undisturbed by the social and physical flux of contemporary life.[6]

The fashion industry has been widely criticised for its narrow definition of beauty ideals and obsession with the 'flawless' appearance through image manipulation by removing any traces of wrinkles, bumps and less-than-ideal proportions. A parallel of this preoccupation resides in the quest for a heroic representation of architecture, that occurs through the deceptive graphic marketing of unrealistic scenes, which are frequently devoid of lived-in traces of people and time.

These stratifying and deceptive tendencies in the field of architecture and planning are problematic for two core reasons. Firstly, the demographic composition of cities in Southern Latitudes entails social environments where the middle class—the main clientele of the design professionals in the Global North—are a minority if not a distant aspiration.

In cities such as Jakarta, Kuala Lumpur, Mumbai, Colombo, Lagos, Santiago and Mexico City, architects and their pursuit of spatial order and gravitas continue to be dependent on a small pool of private clients, primarily those of the affluent upper and upper-middle class, or the design-as-brand minded developers and ambitious authorities. In reality, or once realised, the scale and impact of designed places are consistently dwarfed and overwhelmed by the multiplicity of social identities and temporalities that operate in cities of the Southern Latitudes. Architectural imagination becomes an isolated exercise, a speculative imagining of built forms that appear more and more as a field of spectacles, as exceptionally curated built places that are detached from the lived experience beyond. The production of spectacular architecture in Southern Latitudes are ostensibly part of the operation that Guy Debord chillingly predicted:

Walkability and play space within Kampung Siliwangi, Bandung. Image by James Connor.

> The whole life of those societies in which modern conditions of production prevail presents itself as an immense accumulation of spectacles. All that once was directly lived has become mere representation.[7]

Secondly, the cities of the Global North have access to resources, technology and infrastructure that are less available in the Global South. To associate cutting-edge design with advanced technology and computational methods, is to associate architecture with a certain level of infrastructural capability and affluence. Such technologies are neither readily available nor essential for the majority of the urban population in the region—the working classes and the urban poor—who are yet to address the basic challenges of survival and inhabitation after years of being neglected and seen as invisible subjects in their own cities. Instead, these groups rely on social capital arising from tight informal networks. One such network of shared responsibilities, shared amenities, and collective opportunities, is to be found at the Kampung Lebak Siliwangi in Bandung, formerly a major colonial settlement and today the capital city of West Java province, Indonesia (see image on p.53). In this urban neighbourhood, rural migrants, low income workers, and university students from regional Indonesia have found their home, in the form of diverse and affordable housing options ranging from rented rooms to boarding houses, all embedded within the bustling settlement. Here, transient groups are supported by the holistic social infrastructure of the *kampung* neighbourhood in a way that defies the colonial, European vision of a top-down planned urban formation elsewhere in the city.

Often, the resilience of Southern Latitudinal populations relies on the adaptability and opportunistic durability of their informal labour networks, within 'informal' urban forms, such as the *kampung*.[8] This is because the formal urban infrastructure that has been set up to support future cities in the Global South frequently works to exclude the urban poor, rural migrants and working classes, despite the fact that these groups constitute the majority urban population.[9] Ironically, the ever opportunistic spatial tactics of informal urbanism crucially support the functioning of the rigidly designed formal cities. As Saskia Sassen notes in her seminal book *The Global City*, even the functioning of iconic cities such as New York, Tokyo and London rely on a very mixed labour market, from those working in the financial sectors down to the cleaners and garbage collectors.[10] All these urban labourers operate and live in these cities; such a diverse market, in turn, necessitates a diverse urban environment.

Urban habitats built by people outside the 'official' planning and design process—such as the *kampung*—are providers of affordable urban co-habitation and diverse services (see image at left). They are elastic buffer zones of walkability and mixed-use inhabitation. Importantly, however, these informal urban habitats are also responsive to the needs of the adjacent 'official' cities, which tend to be unequipped to support the entire spectrum of urban production alone. The informal neighbourhoods of cities in South-East Asia, the Middle East, Africa and Latin America provide a crucial 'urban backstage' to facilitate the region's quests in creating the next urban spectacle. This 'urban backstage' offers affordable accommodation, as well as cheap and lively street food culture, allowing junior office workers, university students, blue-collar workers and other urban labourers to prop up the operations of towering offices, glittery shopping malls and executive apartment complexes. These informal networks of intense urbanity are never finished and are constantly being repurposed, precisely to support the functioning of the megacities of the Global South.

This essay began by questioning the role and purpose of architecture in the vast landscape of spatial contingency, multiplicity and temporality of cities in the Global South. Perhaps before we can provide any kind of tentative answer to this question, we need to first learn to see and read the mechanisms that allow cities in the Southern Latitudes to function in the midst of unprecedented, rapid urbanisation. One step to do so is to situate the complex built environments of the Southern Latitudes at the centre of 21st-century architectural education. We need to form a new capacity among our future architects, planners and urban designers to see, analyse and reimagine those socio-spatial practices that destabilise and defamiliarise the existing canon of the discipline and the profession.

Opposite: Community-based co-housing prototype in Kampung Tongkol, Jakarta. Image by the author.

01 See Jeremy Till, *Architecture Depends* (Cambridge: MIT Press, 2009) for his thought-provoking argument on the limits of architecture.

02 See Abidin Kusno, *Behind the Postcolonial: Architecture, Urban Space and Political Cultures in Indonesia* (London: Routledge, 2000); Ananya Roy and Nezar AlSayyad eds. *Urban Informality: Transnational Perspectives from the Middle East, Latin America, and South Asia* (Berkeley: Lanham Centre for Middle Eastern Studies, 2004); Jeffrey Hou, *Messy Urbanism: Understanding the "Other" Cities of Asia* (Hong Kong: University of Hong Kong Press, 2016); AbdouMaliq Simone, *For the City Yet to Come: Urban Life in Four African Cities* (Durham, N.C. and London: Duke University Press, 2004); Ross King, *Reading Bangkok* (Singapore: NUS Press, 2011); and Kim Dovey and Ross King, "Forms of Informality: Morphology and Visibility of Informal Settlements," *Built Environment* 37, no. 1 (2011): 11-29.

03 AbdouMaliq Simone, *City Life from Jakarta to Dakar: Movements at the Crossroads* (New York, London: Routledge, 2009), Chapter 1.

04 See Lawrence Vale, "Designing National Identity: Post-Colonial Capitols as Intercultural Dilemmas," in *Forms of Dominance: On the Architecture and Urbanism of the Colonial Enterprise*, ed. by Nezar AlSayyad (Aldershot: Avebury, 1992), pp. 315-338; Abidin Kusno, *Behind the Postcolonial* (London: Routledge, 2000); Anoma Pieris, *Hidden Hands and Divided Landscapes: A Penal History of Singapore's Plural Society* (Honolulu: University of Hawai'i Press, 2009); also *Architecture and Nationalism in Sri Lanka: The Trouser Under the Cloth*, (London: Routledge, 2009); Kim Dovey, *Framing Places: Mediating Power in Built Form*, (London: Routledge, 1999); Ananya Roy and Aihwa Ong eds. *Worlding Cities: Asian Experiments and the Art of Being Global* (Hoboken: Wiley, 2011).

05 Benedict Anderson, *Language and Power: Exploring Political Cultures in Indonesia* (Ithaca: Cornell University Press, 1990).

06 Jeremy Till, *Architecture Depends*, 87.

07 Guy Debord, *The Society of the Spectacle*, translated by Donald Nicholson-Smith (New York: Zone Books, 1994 [1967]) 91.

08 Kim Dovey, "Informal Settlement and Complex Adaptive Assemblage," in *International Development Planning Review* 34, no.3 (2012): 371-90.

09 Kim Dovey, Brian Cook and Amanda Achmadi, "Contested riverscapes in Jakarta: flooding, forced eviction and urban image," *Space and Polity* 23, no.3 (2019): 265-282.

10 Saskia Sassen, *The Global City* (New York, London, Tokyo: Princeton University Press, 2001 [1991]).

PLACE AS IMAGE, IMAGE AS PLACE

Marc Boumeester

The historical parallel unfolding of two types of human organisation, the civil and the nomadic, has been named a tale of 'dark twins,' indicating the false juxtaposition of a history of linear progression and human prosperity (the Citizen), with a parallel narration of underdevelopment, poverty and primitivism (the Barbarian). The paramount fallacy in conceiving this apparent juxtaposition between the Citizen and the Barbarian is to centre its organisational *effects*, rather than its social causes. Both perspectives centre the 'urban identity' and the socio-economic and cultural consequences of civil development. The nomadic is placed outside civilisation, but it originates from within. Therefore, it is unwise to distinguish between organisation of life within the urban as opposed to those in the rural, and rather inspect origins such as rootedness, agency, affect and mental imagery as deciding elements in any classification of civilisation or barbarism. In this context, civilisation is an organisational form that discards, and nomadism is the residue that includes all other discarded elements, inside or outside the urban constitution. The juxtaposition is thus a fabricated dichotomy that obscures a far more subtle ecology of social agencies, significations and affective economies.

The concept of *image* plays a crucial role in this ecology, as it is the embodiment of subjective perception, cloaked as an objective entity. In other words: no image is ever the same as no spectator is ever the same as no experience is ever the same. Therefore, the image acts as a place for occupation by thought, and places consist only out of images formed by those who experience them. These places are thus both literal and metaphorical, as visions of selection and aspiration.

Drawing on Affect Theory this essay will voice elements, biological and non-biological, human and non-human that act, shape, modulate, resist, counter and question the optimistic and supreme chronology of progress and growth to make way for a critical and rooted realism of *presence* as a result of agency and not of identity.[1] The two case studies will show two extreme nodes in the fabric of a large socio-economic ecology, rather than a ranking of the two on a binary scale, although both are products of urban development. Firstly, we examine a place that can never escape being more than its own image and secondly a place that unwillingly re-identifies itself constantly because of its tenacious rootedness.

View of Times Square New York. Digital photography by the author 2018.

Times Square, or the place that can never be itself
Times Square in New York is a place that evokes recollection in many people's minds, if not from first-hand memory, then from the image that has been conveyed through media exposure. And yet—unlike many other landmarks—the image of Times Square is far from stable and it is not the architecture that forms (the appearance of) its properties either. The image of Times Square is predominantly formed by images of advertisements that cover large areas of the built environment, and since these expressions have a commercially-driven momentum of expiration, they are replaced regularly. The image of the place is thus formed by a continuously changing set of images, and though the place itself remains undeniably largely unchanged, its visual properties are highly unstable. In that sense the place is a medium itself, in the same way a newspaper is no more than a distinct format of paper that daily changes its content, yet still we can speak of a stable entity. On a more abstract level, we could say that the collective recollection of this place (either based on live-experience or on the image of it that has been created) can only exist of this meta-image of its properties. Yet even this is not stable. As every spectator attaches different connotations, interpretations, significations and affects to the image of the place, even a simultaneous exposure of the same place to two observers will never produce an identical experience. Experiences are highly individual as they are not primarily rooted in stimuli, but in the reaction or perception of the individuals to them. Architect-philosopher Andrej Radman explains: "Perception cannot be considered independently of the environment since it is defined as an evolved adaptive and constructive relation between the organism and the environment."[2] Therefore, we cannot speak of perception 'of' something, instead perception 'is' something. The capacity to affect relates to the capacity to be affected in a two-way manner: affect is capacity, affection is actualisation. In this view, one could also claim that Times Square is made by the perception of its visitors, rather literally because the advertisements are there to be perceived for commercial purposes, and metaphorically as no single image of this place could ever be the same. This place is an image, its image is the place.

Mediascape: interconnecting flows that create realities without necessarily actualising them
This place/image conflation is part of what Arjun Appadurai would name the 'Mediascape,' that in turn is part of his interconnecting system of global flows, including Technoscapes, Ethnoscapes, Financescapes and Ideoscapes, that connect and influence citizens of the world.[3] Elsewhere, I have

altered 'ethnoscapes' into 'ethoscapes,' as the latter ostensibly reaches a deeper level of human processing and action. By changing ethnoscape into ethoscape, a crucial modification can be achieved without losing some of ethnoscape's stronger capacities, such as interrelations and fluidity, while attaching many more. Ethnos defines itself along specific social, cultural and racial lines, whereas ethos opens a gateway to a more complex set of definitions. Individuals are at least in part formed by their ethnos, but we cannot reduce the individual to these definitions. Ethos is self-referential, ethnos is not, ethnos is always multiple, ethos is always singular.[4]

Citizenship comes with the participation in the interconnecting system of global flows; the city is its most efficient form of organisation and Times Square is perhaps a supreme embodiment of this system. The interconnecting system of global flows enables and ensures the operation of a system of technological and industrial progression and growth. Yet the logic and justification of this so-called linear 'development' can be only expressed in terms of its relative success. Alternative modes of development that do not build on industrial progression have been historically underappreciated. Indeed, the average quality of human life has risen over the centuries, yet certainly not for everyone and at great expense to the world at large, with damage that might be irrepairable. It is the justification of linear development that has prioritised the history of citizenship over that of the Barbarian, which in this context can be described as the rooted, local and empowered in terms other than its *own* development.[5] The Barbaric can thus be defined as any form of progression that is not commodifiable or detached from its rooted intentions; a Barbarian has its own ethos that does not respond to the interconnecting flows of global development.

The term 'Barbarian' is loaded with negative connotations, as that was the whole purpose of the invention of the term: in the ancient Greek civilisation anyone who did not match the Greek cultural coding of language, culture and customs was classified and excluded from the civilisation as *Barbaros*. But even long before that, many civilisations had special terms for those outside of their own cultivation, all favouring their societal form over other social forms of existence. It served many purposes to attribute all sorts of 'negative' qualifications to this group, as this contributed to the idealisation of the civil. And thus started a long, historical tradition of juxtaposing 'the good and the bad;' the winners versus the losers, the successful versus the unsuccessful, the rich versus the poor etcetera, in terms of being inside or outside civilisation. Earlier critique of the bourgeois capitalist system often included a third leg to the inside/outside juxtaposition of civilisation. Writers in the Marxist tradition such as Rosa Luxemburg and Karl Kautsky presented the triangle: "Capitalist civilisation cannot continue; we must either move forward into socialism or fall back into Barbarism."[6] Again, Barbarism is portrayed as the daunting alternative to ideology, set against a failing yet civil society. The implicit threat of regression into a state less refined as civilisation sadly does not come with the opportunity to rethink and reconceptualise the civil state itself.

Exo-identity: how the image makes the place

The organisation of state—either based on a linear progression of capitalist development or ideological equality—has overtaken the alternatives that centre individual experience as the main parameters for growth, success and wealth. Alternative societies that prioritise *a presence in the now, rather than a future of growth* do not produce wealth in a commodifiable way. In the aforementioned two- or three-legged juxtapositions a crucial movement has been denied access to visibility, yet it has unfolded steadily and strongly. Similar to a genetic code that has one dominant gene, this movement has been dominated by the anthropocentric viewpoint that submits rooted perception (as an act) in favour of imposed perception (as a commodity). Rooted perception demands an individuated action to perceive a singular exceptional moment, including a selection of what is defined as exceptional, whereas imposed perception is flattened and isolated to be transferable in a non-ambivalent way: spotting a Kookaburra in the wild versus seeing a cat video on YouTube, so to speak. Both have always been there, in the same place, yet only the latter is counted as being inside the civil, whereas the first is discarded as not-civil (Barbaric) and especially as it is not commodifiable, it does not fall into the system of global flows as described by Appadurai.

An *exo-identity* is a mental image of place, culture, behaviour or social status that only exists on a meta-level, just like Times Square only exists in the image that we have of it. It does not contain a presence in the here and now, but it creates a set of values that can be filled with transferred experiences. *Exo-identities* are created over time and consist of expectations that need to be met, but will never actually truly fit the promise. Paris, for example, has a strong exo-identity—as have many other cities—and although we have a clear image of what this city offers, we will not find there any bereted citizens carrying a baguette under their arm anytime soon. Neither is the City of Love filled with joyful couples flirting alongside the banks of the Seine, unless these couples are ourselves. The image of the city is formed 'over it' and we are most eager to actualise it by our own interventions, steered by the image that we impose upon the place. It is a similar phenomenon to 'our' experience of Times Square, which may be predicated on the image we have of it. This does not mean that these images are not real, they are of great influence and possess significant agency. The question, however, is 'what image is it that we (want to) see and what causes it to be seen?' A long romantic weekend in Paris will most likely be experienced in that way, because if the expectancy is set, we cognitively bias our perception to register our experiences to fall within that expectancy. The image of a place creates a biased perception that largely goes undetected because of the expectancy that is created by its *exo-identity*.

Civilisation has been developed to act as a logical state of organisation, using *exo-identities* as blueprint for an organisational structure. In this view, the rural serves as the extended city, meaning that the planning and modification of the landscapes, seascapes and airscapes can best be seen and valued in terms of its function in the greater romance of urban endeavour. This view can be addressed historically by tracing the accumulation of human capital, the opportunities created for commodification, and the disconnection of value from costs and profit. In this constellation, the landscape serves as a tool for urban development and accumulation of capital, whereas—as the subsequent sections of this essay posit—its true potential lies on a far more complex, crucial and interesting level. Nevertheless, we have witnessed the geographic dislodging of a global industry of finance, services and entertainment that has spread a ubiquitous network of non-local identities over many cities, which in turn are increasingly transforming into petrified images of their own historical importance. These 'living presences' are commodified to serve as beacons for the aforementioned industry of *exo-identity*, with tourism, trade and financial laws as its paramount instruments.[7]

Presence: how agency does not need an embodiment to act

Simultaneously, there is a narrative to be told that draws on the unembellished and therefore unavoidable necessity of rural rootedness, a literal ecological perspective that acts in a different way to formalise its importance, its effects on humanity as well as its strength on other futures that have been created. This is not a tale of biology and 'natural' ecology alone, its discourse centres empowerment and involvement, congregating aesthetics, rootedness and locality in search for a non-petrified *presence* that is not supreme nor excluding, yet nevertheless undetachable and endowing.[8] And therefore, not commodifiable or transferable: it is a *presence* that only exists in action and relation to others. This 'non-local local' *presence* does not focus on specific distinctiveness, but on the degree of participation and investment of both sender/creator and receiver/audience that shape non-transferable rooted experiences. New materialism opposes abstract and humanist traditions in cultural theory that are grounded on dualist structures; instead, it offers an enticing alternative by opening up theoretical formulations in which matter is a very strong actor.[9] Thus, the prerogative on agency shifts from the anthropocentric signification to a shared domain of non-signification (matter, medium, mind, body). Feminist philosopher Karen Barad summarises: "Agency is not held, it is not a property of persons or things; rather, agency is an enactment, a matter of possibilities for reconfiguring entanglements."[10] This makes way for an unbiased and inclusive perspective on a world within the now, rather than on an illusory future ahead.

Kaiser-Wilhelm-Gedähtniskirche:
Civil symbolism turning into barbaric presence

The Kaiser-Wilhelm-Gedächtniskirche serves as an exemplification of this thought, and was deliberately chosen as it is a known landmark in an unmistakably urban setting, in the midst of a highly commercial area of former West Berlin. As the original church was dedicated to the memorial of Emperor Wilhelm I, the place was historically symbolic from its inception. After its destruction in World War II, a replacement church in high-modernist style was designed by Egon Eiermann, initially planned to utterly erase and supersede the ruins, but after local interference the remains of the church were integrated in the site's new planning. Its ruins signify the monstrosity of war, whereas the 'newbuilt' parts already carry the reminiscence of an era driven by an extreme belief in the makeable society. A certain similarity to the history of the Genbaku Dome in Hiroshima springs to mind, which started as an exhibition space for industrial progression, but was 'involuntarily' transformed into the atomic bomb memorial site after long deliberations about the desirability of such intense reminder of monstrosity.[11]

What makes the Kaiser-Wilhelm-Gedächtniskirche particularly interesting to this discussion is the transformation of its symbolic yet rooted value as the predominant constant element of its existence. The content of its symbolism has changed several times over, but the mere presence of its structure and its tenacity to stay rooted lifts this place from one era to another to another.[12] It is not a nice or warm place; its setting has a distinct hardness and the exteriors of both old church and 'new' church do not convey much inviting or comforting affects. Standing in an area dominated by shiny flagship stores of global brands, uninvitingly accessible by the intercutting of several roads and trenched in an atmosphere of neglect, the churches seem to be in constant battle not to be pushed out of their place, both literal and metaphorical.

Although the more recent Eiermann building functions as a church, it is most often occupied as a temporary refuge for homeless people. This place has a highly attractive quality to it, once one opens up to it in a non-signifying somaesthetic way. The unmediated *agency* of both ruins and modernist symbolism conveys a breakability that comes with its own hardship. The nowness of the Church's existence, throughout its own history, is unfiltered and present. Just like the city of Berlin, this place is reinventing itself repeatedly. However, its story is continuously evolving without overwriting the older parts of it. Continuous decay of both older and newer structures emphasises the erosion of both physical and symbolic state in the passing of time, not only by the palpable digressing state of its properties, but also by the multiple recontextualisations of its significance and presence. This in contrast to the image of Times Square that is constantly refreshed to depict an exo-identity of the near future, showing products that are to be bought, just one click away. Both Times Square and the Kaiser-Wilhelm-Gedächtniskirche are real places, it is not helpful to dichotomise the two, yet the ground in which this reality holds foot is very different for every place. Whereas Times Square flashforwards a near consumer-preoccupied future, the Kaiser-Wilhelm Church holds ground in the present: a presence formed by its history, carried by its decaying material structure and harsh exposure of human failing, yet lived in the now. The rootedness of the place is evoked by the presence of both creation and destruction, tangible in all aspects of the architecture as well as its setting, both in literal and metaphorical ways. This is a chronicle of that which does not fall within the civil, it is a story of rootedness and locality that does not hide or discard its scars or vulnerability. It is a saga of loss, not of progression, which can be seen as a submissive story amidst stories of dominance; it is a tale that gives true hope exactly because it has lost hope itself, many times. This can only be sensed if one is open to the experience of contributing to the making of this history, without any prerogative or ranking in the establishment of the symbolic orders, like religion or signification. The place has become a memorial of itself, inviting others to become part of it. Its image cannot be made apart from its agency, nor apart of those experiencing its presence by participating in it.

Conclusion

The parallel history of the Civil and the Barbaric is frequently reduced to a narrative of that which is 'inside' versus that which is 'outside' a system of linear progression. This narrative entails a collocation of value judgement that dismisses the weaker in favour of the stronger. Yet on closer inspection we can see that the strong might not exist outside of its own image—an image based on an *exo-identity*—while the narrative of the weak is unfolding in parallel and shows great durability, recreating a rooted identity over and over again. Experience as an *act* (as opposed to experience *of*) can unveil that the true value of presence is non-negotiable, nor commodifiable. The Barbaric is not a state of regression, it is a state of inclusion, inclusion of stories told and affect felt. When we extrapolate the duet of the two places presented in this essay, we can find many more stories untold that have always been embedded in civil history, but not been part of it. The civil has been an instrument of exclusion that favoured one particular view on humanity. By unfolding this insight there are many 'older futures' that have been developing indigenously, nomadically, non-normatively and out-centred to be perceived. Within the urban, civil fabric we have showcased two exceptional nodes of presence. Whereas Times Square can never be truly experienced, as it consists only of the image that we made of it, the entire history of the Kaiser-Wilhelm-Gedächtniskirche serves as a precondition to shelter one homeless person today. Rooted, actualised, inclusive and unfiltered, in other words: Barbaric.

Top Left: View on the original Kaiser-Wilhelm-Gedächtniskirche, Berlin.
Postcard collection of the author, dated 1909.

Bottom Left: View on replacement of Kaiser-Wilhelm-Gedächtniskirche, Berlin, by Egon Eiermann, 1957. Instant photography by the author 2021. Instant or diapositive photography offers the closest to unmediated imaging, which indicates the closeness to the subject matter in the experience.

Right: View on Kaiser-Wilhelm-Gedächtniskirche Berlin. Instant photography by the author 2021.

01 For an introduction in this field see: *The Affect Theory Reader*, Melissa Gregg and Gregory J. Seigworth (Durham: Duke University Press, 2010).

02 Andrej Radman, *Gibsonism* (Delft: Delft University, 2012), 51.

03 Arjun Appadurai, *Modernity At Large: Cultural Dimensions of Globalization* (Minneapolis: University of Minnesota Press, 1996), 32.

04 Marc Boumeester, *The Desire of the Medium* (Arhem: ArtEZ University Press, 2017), 40.

05 "State and nonstate peoples, agriculturists and foragers, 'barbarians' and 'civilized' are twins, both in reality and semiotically. Each member of the pair conjures up its partner. And despite abundant historical evidence to the contrary, the peoples who have historically identified themselves as belonging to the ostensibly more 'evolved' member of each pair - state people, agriculturalists, the 'civilized' - have taken their identity as essential, permanent, and superior." James C. Scott, *A Deep History of the Earliest States* (New Haven and London: Yale University Press, 2017), 148-149.

06 Karl Kautsky, *Erfurt Program* (New York: Franklin Classics ([1877] 2018), 21.

07 Enrico Conti of the Istituto Regionale Programmazione economica della Toscana names the massive invasion of travelers towards the historic city 'hit and run' tourism, as most visitors are only focused on collecting images of the iconic landmarks, whilst a significant part of the revenue of their visit 'leaks' away to out of state ownership of commodities.

08 There is no such thing as an 'environment as such,' let alone the environment. Speculative realist Levy R. Bryant points out that 'environments cannot be treated as something that is simply given or there such that the organism subsequently fills a niche that already existed in the environment.' He argues that organisms perform actively in the construction of their own environment. Levi R. Bryant, 'The Democracy of Objects' (2011) http://openhumanitiespress.org/democracy-of-objects.html [accessed 25 July 2016].

09 Jane Bennett, *Vibrant Matter: A Political Ecology of Things* (Durham: Duke University Press, 2012).

10 Karen Barad, "Meeting the Universe Halfway", in *Feminism, Science and the Philosophy of Science*, eds. L.H. Nelson and J. Nelson. (Dordrecht: Kluwer Academic Publishers, 1991) 214.

11 See also: William Logan, *Places of Pain and Shame: Dealing with 'Difficult Heritage'*(London: Routledge, 2008).

12 Another interesting case study is the 'Völkerschlachtdenkmal' in Leipzig, Germany, which originated as a memorial site for the biggest battle in the wars of Napoleon Bonaparte, but was 'rebranded' as a monument for the glorification of respectively the Weimar Republic, National Socialism and the Deutsche Demokratische Republic (DDR).

NATURE'S UNDERWORLD

A MICROSCOPIC (OVER)VIEW INTO SUBNATURAL MANIFESTATIONS WITHIN OUR ENVIRONMENTS

Lucia Amies

Toilet seat	186 bacteria per square centimetre
Kitchen bench	269 bacteria per square centimetre
Self-checkout screen	698 bacteria per square centimetre
Door handle	1,340 bacteria per square centimetre[1]

Our concept of 'nature' in today's society is conditioned to promote an idealism found exclusively in the prehuman elements of sun, air and greenery. In reality, the nature of our environments is not inherently clean or green. In an approach that has been refined over millennia, these selective natures have been championed with the aim to create 'healthy' environments for people to dwell in. Meanwhile, other natures deemed inferior—known collectively as 'subnatures'—have been neglected, discouraged and increasingly omitted through our designs. Our attitudes toward environmental cleanliness have remained steadfast amidst the global pandemic and our current trajectory is geared toward increasing the sterilisation of our homes and cities; yet at what cost? Under perpetual cleaning regimes, the ecological health and resilience of our environments suffer; so too (ironically) does our immunity, which depends on a rich and diverse microflora.[2] The ongoing trend toward the sanitisation of nature in architecture also begs us to reconsider the underlying social and economic agenda. In charting a brief history of perspectives on this topic, a better understanding of subnature's endemic presence within our environments may be garnered, ultimately breeding productive forms of cooperation between subnatures and humans in our designs, particularly at the scale of the micro.

Current notions of 'nature' within our environments are underpinned by a historical conditioning on the subject. In fact, the nature-architecture dialectic can be traced from antiquity until well into the 20th century. In the first century BC, Roman scholar Vitruvius wrote on the relationship between selective natures and 'healthfulness,' insisting that this be the architect's chief focus.[3] Like the Greeks before him, Vitruvius believed in a 'humoral' theory of medicine that pertained to bodily fluids (bile, blood and phlegm) and prescribed the careful siting of any project so to avoid these "noxious humours."[4] Throughout his treatise *De Architectura (Ten Books on Architecture)*, Vitruvius promotes an architecture in which the sun, wind and plants are central protagonists.[5] Unsurprisingly, with the rediscovery of ancient texts such as Vitruvius' in the mid-15th century, Renaissance architects looked to further emphasise the role of prehuman nature in architecture, albeit with a more anatomical focus.[6] In fact, humourism—alongside an analogous Hippocratic theory known as miasma (the belief that 'bad air' was the cause of disease)—remained a popular conviction and impetus for design well into the 18th and 19th centuries, when city streets were surfaced in an uninterrupted blanket of stone pavement to superficially seal miasmatic vapours beneath.[7]

The widespread acceptance of miasma as the dominant hypothesis until the mid-19th century overshadowed the emerging 'germ theory,' which eventually took its place in 1876 with evidence that bacteria caused disease. The theory developed in response to an 1854 outbreak of cholera in Soho, London, that led physician John Snow to discover a single contaminated water pump as the source.[8] Snow's investigative mappings correlated incidences of the disease with potential geographic sources in order to reveal the clustering of cases. As author Carolyn Steel notes:

> The incident showed for the first time that infectious diseases were carried not by some form of bad air, or 'miasma', but by the spread of germs in a physical medium – in this case, water. The discovery of so-called 'germ theory' was both a crucial step in the history of microbiology, and the start of a psychological shift in people's attitudes towards their fellow humans. All of a sudden, rubbing up against one's neighbours didn't seem quite so appealing.[9]

Opposite: Teresa van Dongen, *Mud Well*, 2017, installation. Image by Alex Hamstra, courtesy of the artist.

REVISTA NACIONAL DE ARQUITECTURA
Año XII
Núm. 126
Junio 1952
In the present state of the environmental art, no mechanical device can make the rain go back to Spain; the standard-of-living package is apt to need some sort of an umbrella for emergencies, and it could well be a plastic dome inflated by conditioned air blown out by the package itself.

In response, sanitary reforms sought to minimise interactions with germs through the redesign of cities, infrastructure, architecture and interiors.[10] Corridors were introduced within houses to create distinct routes through space and thus reduce human contact.[11] Within household interiors, ornamentation such as architectural mouldings, ornately carved furniture and velvet-textured flock wallpapers were banished so as to discourage the accumulation and spread of dust into inhabitants' lungs.[12] Meanwhile, the installation of plumbing within domestic settings corresponded to the privatisation of waste and hygiene industries, whose maintenance burden fell upon residents. Consequently, the upkeep of personal hygiene and a clean abode became inseparable from inhabitants being perceived as 'healthy.'[13]

With the advent of Modernism in the early 20th century, architecture's function and aesthetic went further in advocating 'health' through cleanliness. Architectural historian and author of *X-Ray Architecture*, Beatriz Colomina, asserts that "modern architecture was shaped by the dominant medical obsession of its time—tuberculosis." She observes that "the widespread success of modern architecture depended on its association with health, its internationalism the consequence of the global spread of the disease it was meant to resist."[14] Much like tuberculosis, architecture itself was placed under the microscope. Realising the unseen threat of bacteria within our environments, modern architects adopted the role of bacteriologists, and generated architectural and urban design principles as both a literal and metaphorical reaction to the presence of microbes.[15] In aesthetic terms, the resultant International Style championed whiteness and transparency. From a functional standpoint, buildings themselves transformed into medical instruments for treating inhabitants, solar devices for capturing light and cleaning contraptions for filtering air (Fig. 1).[16] The modern approach espoused by architects such as Le Corbusier, Alvar Aalto and Richard Neutra, among many others, highlighted an increasingly sanitised and idealised deployment of nature in architecture through the campaign for sunlight, open space and greenery. By the mid-late century, atmospheric manipulation of these elements had become the focus. The then-burgeoning sci-fi approach speculated on hermetically sealed spaces in the form of pneumatic bubble structures, as evidenced in the work of Buckminster Fuller, Archigram, Cedric Price and Coop Himmelb(l)au. One such project was proposed by Reyner Banham and François Dallegret in *The Environment-Bubble*, the ultimate conditioned environment designed so that "dirty old Nature could be kept under the proper degree of control"[17] (Fig. 2).

This history of the evolving relationship between architecture and nature is fundamental to an understanding of how we have come to see a microbiology of 'germs' as antagonists in our environments. As such, it is no surprise that prehuman nature continues to be seen as desirable in the design of 'healthy' spaces.[18] Yet, often under the guise of 'greening,' the perpetual cleaning of our domestic and urban environments with these select natures manifests a classist and capitalist agenda often overlooked, wherein these idealised forms of nature are exploited to cleanse our homes and cities.[19] Seen as a productive instrument, this kind of nature is accorded a monetary value; an act which threatens to commodify nature and make it exclusive to only those who can afford it.[20] Through our own invention, we are led to believe that only lush, light and airy environments are 'clean' and that all other environments are, by extrapolation, dirty and inferior, as are their inhabitants.[21] Within this conception of nature based on 'cleanliness,' the suggestion of social cleansing is deeply troubling.[22] In protest, academics and practitioners across several disciplines have turned their attention to alternative realisations of nature in architecture.

Architectural theorist Hélène Frichot's pivotal book, *Dirty Theory*, argues that our perception of what constitutes 'nature' is distorted by a hierarchical conception. Expanding upon the definition put forward by anthropologist Mary Douglas—that "dirt is matter out of place"[23]—Frichot notes that it is "matter located where it is judged not to belong. Judged as such by someone, or rather, judged by some societal context organised around societal norms and structures."[24] This philosophy can be understood with regard to other peripheral and denigrated natures too. 'Weeds' are plants sprouting in unwanted places and 'germs' describe the microbes that make us sick. These examples are a select few that fit into the concept of 'subnature' theorised by author David Gissen. In his book of the same name, Gissen explains that "forms of nature become subnatural when they are envisioned as threatening to inhabitants or to the material formations and ideas that constitute architecture."[25] They emerge within our buildings and cities in the form of dust, dirt, debris, mould, smog, smoke, puddles and pigeons.[26] By this definition, Gissen's subset could be easily expanded to recognise 'germs' and microbes more generally as an invisible yet widespread subnature.

Whether we choose to accept it, subnatures persist within our designed environments, often evading human attempts at containment or concealment. The accumulation of dust on a windowsill or weeds which spill from cracks in pavement and roof gutters denote our indifference towards the persistence of some subnatures, while, in some cases, human efforts to actively discourage or curtail subnatures has led to further architectural response. Even so, these attempts have often been in vain, given their entropic tendency. Working to destigmatise their presence, many contemporary practitioners highlight the omnipresence of subnatures and demonstrate creative ways in which to harness their power. Artist and architectural preservationist Jorge Otero-Pailos creates casts of architectural facades, elements and spaces with his ongoing series titled *The Ethics of Dust*. In doing so, he preserves the dust collected upon their surfaces while at the same time cleaning them of pollutants (Fig. 3). Likewise, the work of artist Hannah Bertram explores the interdependency of subnature and architecture as she crafts dust collected in streets, studios and vacuum cleaners into complex and intricate patterns, resembling traditional household decoration (Fig. 4 and Fig. 5). Through making apparent the minute manifestation of dust in space, Bertram's work tackles the transformation of this particular subnature from a worthless abject into a valuable agent.

Visibility becomes a particular challenge in the destigmatisation of subnature at the scale of the micro. To many, the unseen magnitude of microscopic organisms is unnerving and precisely that which poses a threat. The global spread of the COVID-19 coronavirus disease has prompted us to revert to increased sterilisation of our environments. Hands-free devices, automation systems and the frequent use of disinfectant products have become customary. Such mechanisms for cleaning are an extension of the modernist dogma that may, without careful consideration, lead to hyper-sterilised environments and mindsets. This trend is observed by architect Hilary Sample, who purports that "in the age of self-cleaning buildings, there remains a desire for whiteness and pureness."[27] Likewise, with the aim to reduce our physical contact, the erasure of tactile fixtures in contemporary buildings has simultaneously deprived us of a phenomenological engagement with the environments we occupy.

While the current pandemic has awakened the global consciousness of the spread of germs in our homes and in our cities, we need not fear the microbiome altogether. This invisible form of subnature is in fact beneficial to human health. Scientific research is leading the discussion in this sphere along the lines of the 'hygiene hypothesis,' which contends that exposure to diverse microflora protects against allergenic diseases and strengthens immunity.[28] Another benefit of a rich microbiome is increased resistance to invasive and potentially harmful bacteria.[29] In fact, it has been shown that common household cleaning products cause household bacteria to mutate and become resistant to antibiotics.[30] Hyper-hygienic environments are thus non-conducive to overall human or ecological health.

Alerting us to the possibilities of a more diverse subnatural approach at the microscopic scale, artist Anicka Yi navigates the world of bacteria and environmental politics. Her work seeks to visualise and bring awareness to microbial matter through multi-sensory engagement, at the same time highlighting themes of power inequality and anthropocentrism (Figs. 6-7). Fundamentally, Yi's work aims to reshape our understanding of microbes as a natural and valuable part of a healthy ecosystem. Contemporary architectural propositions also manifest microbes in emerging material technologies and ecologies. One such example employs bacteria to self-heal cracks in concrete.[31] Others look to bacteria in the formation of biotextiles and even to bioluminescence. In the work of designer Teresa van Dongen, bacteria are harnessed to create electricity. Her *Electric Life* project takes the form of a 'bacteria battery' that transforms the naturally expended electrons of bacteria into an electrical current, enough to power a domestic light fitting (Fig. 8). A weekly feeding routine requiring little more than tap water, vinegar and nutrients is integral to the survival of the bacteria, yet demonstrates the potential of bacteria to be harnessed as a sustainable energy source and to strengthen human-nature bonds.

Rather than continue on the trajectory toward exclusivity and sterilisation, the aforementioned projects posit alternative realities for nature in architecture that strive for inclusivity and diversity. Key to this approach is an understanding of the microbiological and ecological systems at play in our environments, where there is still much further research to be done. While early experiments at the intersection of art and science demonstrate the advantages of working with, and not against, microbes, exploration within the discipline of architecture offers further possibility to understand the inherently environmental implications and opportunities brought about by their endemic presence. With a view to destigmatising the microscopic manifestations of subnature within our environments, we might in fact breed more encompassing and cooperative forms of nature and architecture, better for our health and our planet.

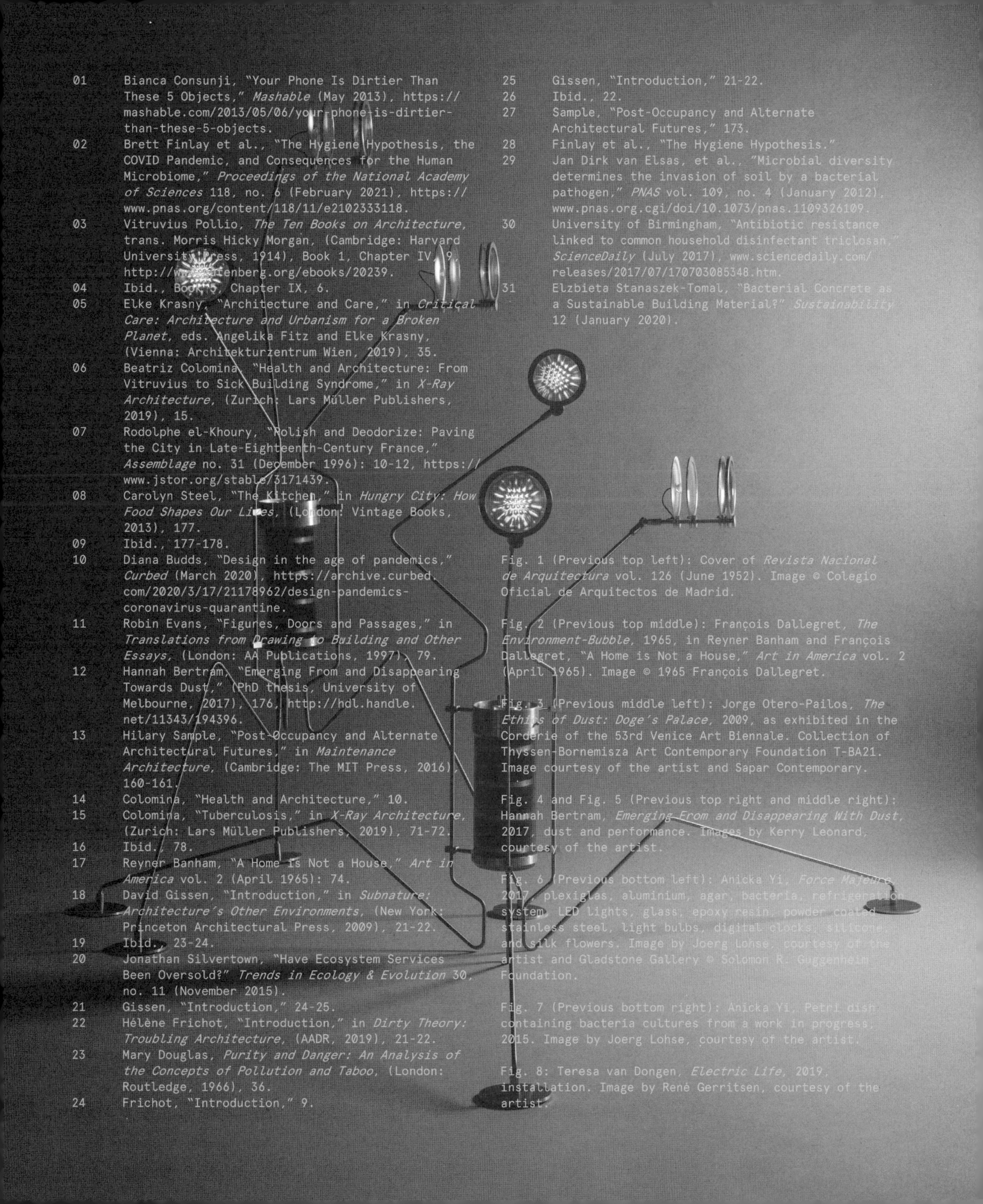

01 Bianca Consunji, "Your Phone Is Dirtier Than These 5 Objects," *Mashable* (May 2013), https://mashable.com/2013/05/06/your-phone-is-dirtier-than-these-5-objects.

02 Brett Finlay et al., "The Hygiene Hypothesis, the COVID Pandemic, and Consequences for the Human Microbiome," *Proceedings of the National Academy of Sciences* 118, no. 6 (February 2021), https://www.pnas.org/content/118/11/e2102333118.

03 Vitruvius Pollio, *The Ten Books on Architecture*, trans. Morris Hicky Morgan, (Cambridge: Harvard University Press, 1914), Book 1, Chapter IV, 9, http://www.gutenberg.org/ebooks/20239.

04 Ibid., Book 5, Chapter IX, 6.

05 Elke Krasny, "Architecture and Care," in *Critical Care: Architecture and Urbanism for a Broken Planet*, eds. Angelika Fitz and Elke Krasny, (Vienna: Architekturzentrum Wien, 2019), 35.

06 Beatriz Colomina, "Health and Architecture: From Vitruvius to Sick Building Syndrome," in *X-Ray Architecture*, (Zurich: Lars Müller Publishers, 2019), 15.

07 Rodolphe el-Khoury, "Polish and Deodorize: Paving the City in Late-Eighteenth-Century France," *Assemblage* no. 31 (December 1996): 10-12, https://www.jstor.org/stable/3171439.

08 Carolyn Steel, "The Kitchen," in *Hungry City: How Food Shapes Our Lives*, (London: Vintage Books, 2013), 177.

09 Ibid., 177-178.

10 Diana Budds, "Design in the age of pandemics," *Curbed* (March 2020), https://archive.curbed.com/2020/3/17/21178962/design-pandemics-coronavirus-quarantine.

11 Robin Evans, "Figures, Doors and Passages," in *Translations from Drawing to Building and Other Essays*, (London: AA Publications, 1997), 79.

12 Hannah Bertram, "Emerging From and Disappearing Towards Dust," (PhD thesis, University of Melbourne, 2017), 176, http://hdl.handle.net/11343/194396.

13 Hilary Sample, "Post-Occupancy and Alternate Architectural Futures," in *Maintenance Architecture*, (Cambridge: The MIT Press, 2016), 160-161.

14 Colomina, "Health and Architecture," 10.

15 Colomina, "Tuberculosis," in *X-Ray Architecture*, (Zurich: Lars Müller Publishers, 2019), 71-72.

16 Ibid., 78.

17 Reyner Banham, "A Home Is Not a House," *Art in America* vol. 2 (April 1965): 74.

18 David Gissen, "Introduction," in *Subnature: Architecture's Other Environments*, (New York: Princeton Architectural Press, 2009), 21-22.

19 Ibid., 23-24.

20 Jonathan Silvertown, "Have Ecosystem Services Been Oversold?" *Trends in Ecology & Evolution* 30, no. 11 (November 2015).

21 Gissen, "Introduction," 24-25.

22 Hélène Frichot, "Introduction," in *Dirty Theory: Troubling Architecture*, (AADR, 2019), 21-22.

23 Mary Douglas, *Purity and Danger: An Analysis of the Concepts of Pollution and Taboo*, (London: Routledge, 1966), 36.

24 Frichot, "Introduction," 9.

25 Gissen, "Introduction," 21-22.

26 Ibid., 22.

27 Sample, "Post-Occupancy and Alternate Architectural Futures," 173.

28 Finlay et al., "The Hygiene Hypothesis."

29 Jan Dirk van Elsas, et al., "Microbial diversity determines the invasion of soil by a bacterial pathogen," *PNAS* vol. 109, no. 4 (January 2012), www.pnas.org.cgi/doi/10.1073/pnas.1109326109.

30 University of Birmingham, "Antibiotic resistance linked to common household disinfectant triclosan," *ScienceDaily* (July 2017), www.sciencedaily.com/releases/2017/07/170703085348.htm.

31 Elzbieta Stanaszek-Tomal, "Bacterial Concrete as a Sustainable Building Material?" *Sustainability* 12 (January 2020).

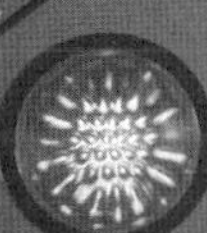

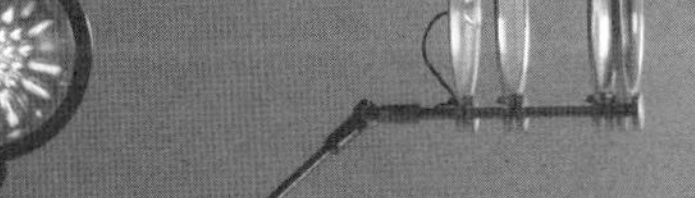

Fig. 1 (Previous top left): Cover of *Revista Nacional de Arquitectura* vol. 126 (June 1952). Image © Colegio Oficial de Arquitectos de Madrid.

Fig. 2 (Previous top middle): François Dallegret, *The Environment-Bubble*, 1965, in Reyner Banham and François Dallegret, "A Home is Not a House," *Art in America* vol. 2 (April 1965). Image © 1965 François Dallegret.

Fig. 3 (Previous middle left): Jorge Otero-Pailos, *The Ethics of Dust: Doge's Palace*, 2009, as exhibited in the Corderie of the 53rd Venice Art Biennale. Collection of Thyssen-Bornemisza Art Contemporary Foundation T-BA21. Image courtesy of the artist and Sapar Contemporary.

Fig. 4 and Fig. 5 (Previous top right and middle right): Hannah Bertram, *Emerging From and Disappearing With Dust*, 2017, dust and performance. Images by Kerry Leonard, courtesy of the artist.

Fig. 6 (Previous bottom left): Anicka Yi, *Force Majeure*, 2017, plexiglas, aluminium, agar, bacteria, refrigeration system, LED lights, glass, epoxy resin, powder coated stainless steel, light bulbs, digital clocks, silicone, and silk flowers. Image by Joerg Lohse, courtesy of the artist and Gladstone Gallery © Solomon R. Guggenheim Foundation.

Fig. 7 (Previous bottom right): Anicka Yi, Petri dish containing bacteria cultures from a work in progress, 2015. Image by Joerg Lohse, courtesy of the artist.

Fig. 8: Teresa van Dongen, *Electric Life*, 2019, installation. Image by René Gerritsen, courtesy of the artist.

UNTITLED

WORKING OUT THE WORK OF BUREAU ARCHITECTURES SANS TITRE

***Colby Vexler** text, **BAST** images*

Their work was already half present, an existing situation latent on site.

Intervention makes the other half present: demolition opens it up; renovation fixes it in.

Yet to only examine their built outcomes would be problematic, for their intentions lay as much in their construction—something that is never concealed. At the same time, examining the process does not reveal an overarching methodology because no smaller intentions lay in their work, but to make it work, and for that work to be at work within the working itself. Nothing slacks off, and yet everything appears simple.

Keep it, strip it back, paint it white, fix to it standardised industrial elements with raw finishes—self noted 'classic' moves for a young practice on a tight budget.

However, their work is certainly not ordinary. This is because it cannot be neatly posited within the history of architectural theories as their logic is neither the pure construction of the architect's desire or the filigree of contractors' vernacular, but an attitude toward commission—and the allocation of budget—which unifies such.

For this no individual name can take credit, nor could a single title or occupation—but a process of collaboration that goes against the convention of titling. In fact, even the work barely receives a title, or a name, just a letter and some numbers so it may be indexed, archived as a document of process, collaboration and construction techniques explored.

This is BAST—Bureau Architectures Sans Titre—for who at almost no point are architecture and construction delineated in their work.

As such, BAST suggest that architecture and construction are near synonymous. From conception to completion they are bound so tightly that their budgets and timelines cannot be compartmentalised. Their design begins with demolition and their budgets are always sympathetic to this—often spending more on the careful removal, cutting and opening up of the existing situation than on the addition of new materials—"except glazing of course."

A sense of rationality and practicality claim to govern this logic. They say that when "two ideas are fighting, the obvious one is picked." While signs and symbols mean little to BAST, their work is not at all anti-intellectual. Their projects demand disciplinary revision. Without clear titles, roles and obligations are elevated and extended on site. BAST put down their office tools and take sledge hammers to walls, and sometimes plumbers and electricians become designers. With this, a soft ideology emerges, one that demonstrates a much more nuanced criticality than formal manoeuvres could ever provoke on their own. As such, their work speaks with a certain profoundness that subtly taps into an essential disciplinary debate assessed by Vitruvius, Alberti, Le-Corbusier, Mies and the many other great interlocutors who sought to articulate the architecture-building complex.

Therefore their theory is their practice, and we see this at work on each of their sites of intervention:

[MØ3]

An existing masonry wall is punctured, twice. Two openings, equal in proportion, nearly exactly. A carefully considered operation on a wall unlikely to be perfectly straight. Concrete blocks are placed above each opening. They secure the voids below; lintels held together by delicately thin

—and neat—mortar.

Probably not a specified detail, but the signs of a contractor who works with care. Off-the-shelf, aluminium frame sliding doors are fixed to the inside face of the opening, strategically just too big to fit exactly within. No matter, now there is no need for intricate installation or weather proofing. Just caulk it. Money saved. The union of this intervention marks itself in white. Painted carefully to appear careless: no patches appear within its area, coating what was already roughly there, yet at its top edges it roughly fades into what was carefully put in.

[M19]

Surplus space is given utility. A robust-now-nearly petrified roof frame is fixed with a sink and tap. Plumbing wraps around the hefty column, as if to secure it—gently. Yet the sink and its drainage appear to not want to burden the column with their additional weight. They sit politely just in front. In any case, with a minimum, attic becomes more liveable.

[M20]

The former hard edge of an existing home receives surplus space. Retractable roof, concrete slab and a block wall suddenly houses a kitchen, living room, winter garden and terrace. Fixed to an existing exterior wall and resting on the new block-work, H beams provide the strategic minimum to cover and contain an under-utilised existing situation: a habitable area otherwise laying dormant.

[T12]

An old garage becomes an office. Façade alternates between an industrial, vertically-bi-folding door and thermal curtain—occasionally expressed as both. When the door is opened and curtain is drawn, privacy is insulated in the most peculiar yet simple way.

Four existing situations, four interventions. Each expressing their own delicate manoeuvres: aesthetically, technically, theoretically and in-directly historically. All claim to be governed by a rationality and logic undoubtedly settled on site. And yet still, by examining their processes and outcomes we do not arrive at an overarching methodology that brings together their disparate qualities.

Then, what defines the work of BAST?

A certain presence within each project's working out; a strategy that concerns itself equally with the existing situation and the intervention—and nothing else.

While BAST are labelled radical, austere or elusive even, their anonymity and untitled-ness mustn't be mistaken for a lack of accountability or responsibility—that is, to the discipline and its discourse. BAST are anything but non-theoretical. Their mere practice ensures contractors and associated parties equally share liability and ownership in the architectural work, they are not just delegated to construct it—a critical act in itself. But disciplinary critique is not their intention. Neither is an aesthetic signature. Concerns never seem to be unified by a singular, pre-determined pursuit. Instead great rigour and consideration is given to the parameters and conditions that emerge from every existing situation and each interventions. BAST observe, think, discuss, do and then reassess to think of their implications on the initial observations themselves. Yet this process is never linear or replicable as it is often detoured by an obsessiveness in particularities not generalities.

This is because, as I began, no smaller intentions lay in their work, but to make it work, and for that work to be at work within the working itself. This is something that is difficult to title or describe but is clearly present within each of the works of Bureau Architectures Sans Titre.

[M03]: Suburb House, Toulouse.
[M19]: Maison de Maitre, Noueilles.
[M20]: Chartreuse, Toulouse.
[T12]: Bureaux, Toulouse.
All images courtesy of Bureau Architectures Sans Titre.

TOXIC GROUNDS

MY CITY IS BLEEDING

Bernard Khoury

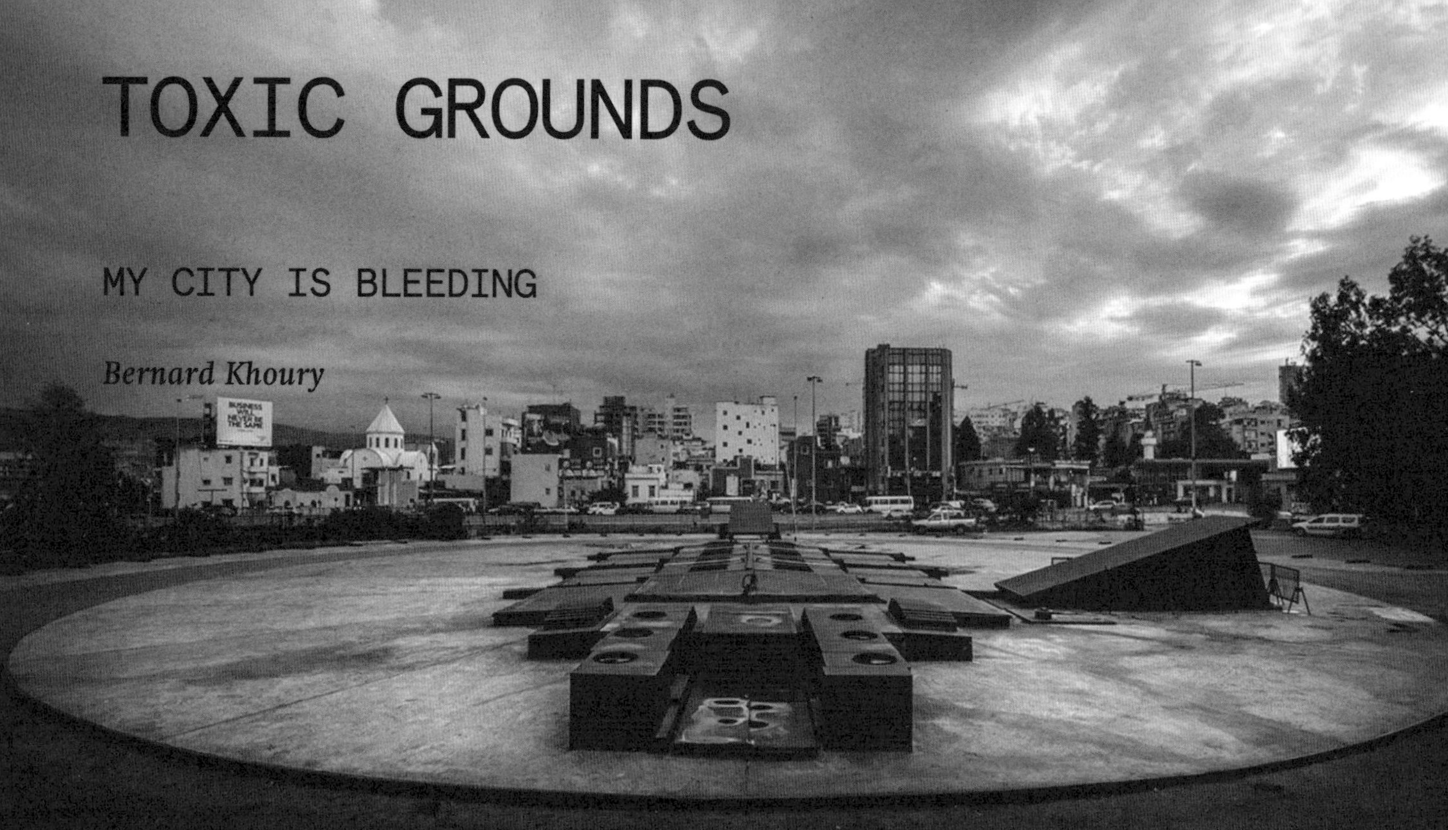

My city is bleeding, contaminating the Mediterranean Basin with its toxic fluids. On August 4th, 2020, Beirut took another major blow. Today, more than ever, its deeply scarred fabric is in desperate need of assistance.

As a practitioner, I have been drawn to problematic territories. Most of the grounds I have operated on were either highly sensitive zones, cities undergoing convalescence or regions in which the state and its institutions have failed to regulate or control the growth of the urban tissue. Beirut is a striking example of what I often call 'a wonderful catastrophe,' a city that, over the last few decades, has witnessed rapid and chaotic development. In the absence of federating and consensual political projects, our neighbourhoods have been shaped by individualistic and distinct gestures that do not cooperate with each other. These are often driven by defensive postures that are the result of the inability to predict the future of the surrounding context and the danger of what could be coming right around the corner.

In such conditions, you must be extremely alert. Engaging in any kind of speculation or assertive stance over the future settings of a project could be lethal. We have taken that risk in many of our schemes, which I would describe as voluntarily masochistic and at times consisting of suicidal propositions. There is no comfort zone on unstable grounds, where the most fundamental rules of urban planning do not apply. This is the result of the total moral bankruptcy, the incompetence and the corruption of Lebanese institutions. In such conditions, architecture must be a political act.

What could be at the outset an ordinary built program, can soon take on a whole other dimension. When the state does not provide the most common built typologies—parks, memorials, museums, opera houses, social housing—a residential development, a night club, a corporate office tower or a commercial building must be considered as projects that can hold a political charge. These private undertakings, which initially do not bear any heavy social or political accountability, can be the grounds for another kind of radicalism.

This is where architecture should take on another kind of political responsibility, in formulating a history that is non consensual and not necessarily affirmative. I did not choose my battlefield. I choose to act on distressed grounds, where meaningful and sympathetic efforts are most needed.

B018

Location: Beirut, Lebanon (1998/2018)
Project Type: Entertainment

B018 is a nightclub, a place of nocturnal survival.

In the early months of 1998, the *B018* moved to the 'Quarantaine,' on a site that was known for its macabre atmosphere. The 'Quarantaine' is located at the proximity of the port of Beirut. During the French protectorate, it was a place of quarantine for arriving crews. In the recent war, it became the abode of Palestinian, Kurdish and South Lebanese refugees (numbering 20,000 in 1975). In January 1976, local militia men launched a radical attack that completely wiped out the area. The slums were demolished along with the kilometre-long bordering wall that isolated the zone from the city. Over 20 years later, the scars of war are still perceptible through the disparity between the scarce urban fabric of the area and the densely populated neighbourhoods located across the highway that borders the zone.

The *B018* project is firstly a reaction to difficult and explosive conditions that are inherent to the history of its location and the contradictions that are implied by the implementation of an entertainment program on such a site. *B018* refuses to participate in the naive amnesia that governs the post-war reconstruction efforts.

The project is built below ground. Its façade is pressed into the ground to avoid the overexposure of a mass that could act as a rhetorical monument. The building is embedded in a circular concrete disc slightly above tarmac level. At rest, it is almost invisible. It comes to life in the late hours of the night when its articulated roof structure, constructed in heavy metal, retracts hydraulically. The opening of the roof exposes the club to the world above and reveals the cityscape as an urban backdrop to the patrons below. Its closing translates to a voluntary disappearance, a striking gesture of recess.

Opposite: *B018* exterior © Ieva Saudargaite

Yabani

Location: Beirut, Lebanon (2002)
Project Type: Entertainment

The *Yabani* project was built to house a Japanese restaurant and bar on a 285-square-metre site located at the edge of the Damascus Road on the former demarcation line that separated East and West Beirut. The traces of shelling of the recent wars are highly visible on many of the adjacent buildings in which refugees are still squatting.

The building incorporates a two-storey concrete structure below ground level and a 14 metre high steel tower above ground. The tower contains a mobile reception room that travels vertically within a circular glass perimeter from the street level to the restaurant level below ground. The guests' seating is laid out in a circular configuration around the transparent mobile reception which animates the centre of the plan. The vertical circulation of the guests' arrival and departure is intentionally overexposed as the reception becomes the point around which the seating is generated.

The restaurant interior is exposed to the sky through trafficable glass windows located at ground level. The patrons therefore enjoy their dining experience in total denial of their immediate, scarred urban surroundings. However, the *Yabani* also accepts its own absurd presence and its impossible relationship with the urban environment through its striking tower structure and the provocative relationship it establishes with its immediate surroundings.

Yabani describes a fraction of a society living in marvellous denial. Ruins of war and spectacles of desolation become a backdrop to the more impressive spectacle of a society being entertained. *Yabani* strives to be a monument for the entertainment industry, a building that claims a landmark status it cannot possibly assume.

Yabani exterior (Built 2002) © DW5 Bernard Khoury. Photo by Joseph Chartouni.

Derailing Beirut
Location: Rome, Italy (2010)
Project Type: Installation

Conceived for the MAXXI Museum of Contemporary Arts in collaboration with Yasmine Almachnouk.
Production: Georges Daou, Ryan Mehanna and A.C.I.D.

As an ultimate act of resistance to a falsified history in which we have become passive actors, are we capable of inventing the tools that can overturn Beirut's sensational stereotypes and denounce the innumerable fantasies attributed to it? We propose to draw an infernal circuit in which sensation-driven tourists seeking instant gratification are propelled in a predetermined course. As passive projectiles, the tourists are placed in a hermetically lethargic situation to ultimately be embedded in expected representations and clichés of our city. Beirut becomes an exotic amusement park destined to be consumed through representations of a history that escapes us, postcards that will, hopefully, be deemed historical waste.

Saïd, bearer of the rolling capsule, wanders the city awaiting the occasional tourist. His task consists of recuperating the device at the bottom of its course and hauling it back to its departure point. Before being assigned this duty, Saïd was a porter at Beirut International Airport.

French photographer Eric Lambert came to Beirut to document the circuit, which was jointly implemented by private investors and the Lebanese Ministry of Tourism. Soon enough, Lambert's fascination for Saïd's routine prevailed over the initial object of his research: the tentacular tracks within the cityscape become a mere background to the city that has yet again assimilated another discordant layer into its fabric.

Derailing Beirut, Saïd, bearer of the rolling capsule, wanders the city © DW5 Bernard Khoury.

Centrale
Location: Beirut, Lebanon (2001)
Project Type: Entertainment

Centrale is housed in a recuperated ruin of a 1920s residential structure that is under historical protection. It is in an area that was deserted during the civil war due to its proximity to the demarcation line that separated East and West Beirut. Near the site is the Beirut Central District historical quarters which have been subject to a rehabilitation scheme to restore the formal gestures of Ottoman, colonial and other influences to their 'original' state.

To implement the required space for the restaurant within the remains of the existing house, the internal partitioning walls of the building and the slab of the first floor were demolished. In the process of voiding out the interior of the existing structure, the outer envelope of the house was reinforced by placing horizontal beams that embrace the skin from the outer perimeter of the façade. This seemingly temporary process features in the final configuration of the edifice, with the steel beams used in the temporary reinforcement preserved. They now imply a new reading of the non-restored façade. Furthermore, we chose not to re-plaster the damaged façade, as would have been the case in a traditional rehabilitation. Instead, it is covered with a metallic mesh behind which the plaster finishing of the old façade remains in a state of decomposition. The mesh now enhances the poetic and temporal dimension of decay.

The construction process of the *Centrale* project relied heavily on the know-how of the local craft industry. Low-tech and non-standard techniques were particularly in use during the metal works. This is part of a more general concern we have with the making of architecture. It is a reaction to the prevalent construction industry that relies on standardised modes of production and an attempt to escape the typical process of construction by re-enacting traditional ways of making.

Structural beams inscribe a circular section encasing a 17 metre long bar above the main hall.
All *Centrale* images © DW5 Bernard Khoury. Photos by Joe Kesrouani.

Top and Bottom Right: The *Centrale* bar opens up through the rotating movement of the cylindrical envelope.

Bottom Left: The façade utilises horizontal beams and a mesh to embrace the outer perimeter.

SEISMIC ZAGREB

AND THE QUESTION OF 'HERSTEL'

Pınar Balat and Igor Sladoljev

In the early morning of March 22nd, 2020, an intense earthquake struck Zagreb, the capital of Croatia, claiming one life and displacing many. A preliminary damage assessment found staggering numbers of buildings, predominantly housing, to be unfit for use. The urban section of Zagreb, known as the 'foundational epoch' from late 19th to the early 20th century and referred to as Lower Town, incurred most of the damage. Close to 40% of the building stock in Lower Town was declared uninhabitable and now requires steadfast reconstruction.[1] It is here that Zagreb's urban character initially developed and became an emotional reference point where the benefits and hazards of reconstruction are to unravel. Much is at stake. Currently, Zagreb identifies as a European capital that shares the vision of a sustainable future; to think of the recovery of Lower Town as merely a means to mitigate the damage inflicted by the earthquake would be a wasted opportunity. As new ambitions are built on old stories of local identity, which myths can we use to frame, out of all possible futures, a desirable one?

To distinguish a place, we tend to think in terms of a local condition, prompting a system of shared beliefs that we interpret as identity. The 'local' quickly becomes a byword for a kind of uniqueness, a sum total of qualities that we want to protect or emphasise when facing delicate situations of preservation, restoration or reconstruction. The local does not emerge in a vacuum but often in response to an external influence it is exposed to, at a particular moment or over a long period of time. It regularly manifests itself in relationship to its opposite—the 'foreign.' Counterintuitively, the import of the foreign element can intensify the local condition by making it suddenly visible.

To illustrate this, let us consider Japan, an island once closed off from the outside world by the sea and by its own volition. Its people praise craft, particularly picture-making. When foreign prints and paintings found their way to Japanese markets in the early 1800s, they began to influence local print masters. By scrutinising foreign compositions, the print masters discovered novel visual storytelling methods to accompany to their traditional narratives. Before long, a little renaissance was in bloom. One day, there appeared a new import, a wonderous bright blue pigment. Its colour was the deep and rich blue of the sea, something an island nation, so profoundly defined by water, immediately identified with. In the hands of the most renowned local printmaker of the age, this extraordinary foreign pigment was crafted into a beloved image that offered one of the most complete portraits of the island to date. This image is known to the world as *The Great Wave off Kanagawa*, in which Japanese print master Katsushika Hokusai used Prussian blue pigment—manufactured in Berlin—to create what is perhaps the most quintessentially Japanese image of all time; an image that is endlessly reproduced.

The Great Wave off Kanagawa beautifully illustrates how the appropriation of something foreign can alter the local by enabling the creation of something new—the novelty, thereafter, is absorbed and becomes part of the local. It also shows that there might be blind spots in our understanding of the local condition, especially with regards to crediting the influence of the foreign element in the creation of that very condition. In order to better understand these concerns in relation to Zagreb's post-earthquake recovery, we promote a 'foreign-local' principle as a framework to help us interpret urban and social heritage so that we can retrieve the past specific to the requirements of this present.

Opposite: Zagreb's historic Lower Town and its 19th century urban block [L. Heilburn, Zagreb, 1926].

Tuškanac
Josipovac
Tuškanac

A hundred and fifty thousand people live in Zagreb, but from the way gossip stands in the street it is plain that everybody knows who is going to have a baby and when. This is a lovely spiritual victory over urbanisation.[2]

—Rebecca West

Zagreb, officially united into one city in 1850 by a royal decree conjoining two settlements—royal town Gradec and episcopal seat Kaptol—was the centre of the Kingdom of Croatia and Slavonia and directly under the rule of the Habsburg Monarch who governed from Vienna. Belonging to the Austrian Empire meant Zagreb was treated as peripheral with minimal control over its future growth. This excess of foreign influence restrained local autonomy, leading to conflicting ideations of local identity. The dominant semi-colonial past positioned locals as inferior, and Zagreb as modest, rejective of 'excess' and dependant. On the other hand, Croatia was one of the victorious kingdoms of Europe in the centuries-long battle against the Turkish. Unfortunately, according to Croatian sociologist Ivan Rogić, in the second half of the 19th century, there was no true social elite in Croatian society capable of opposing the Austrian Habsburg regime.[3] Owing to this, Rogić concludes, Zagreb was shaped to simultaneously satisfy both of its identities. First, it was the centre of the nation and the political unit whose outlines were defined by the Habsburg Empire. Second, it was the capital of an imaginary Croatia, which was simultaneously a former independent kingdom and a future independent country.[4] By the end of the 19th century, this condition had already manifested itself when the spatial contours of Zagreb's First Regulation Plan began to take shape. By the time the city published the Plan in 1865, Viennese officials had already provided several pieces of infrastructure for urban expansion: a building code, a cadastre plan and the railway line linking Zagreb to Vienna. The result was a robustly pragmatic grid carpet made of uncommonly large perimeter blocks, approximately 250 meters in length, laid over the existing settlement. This new city engulfed unregulated construction sites leftover from the agricultural land regulation. Prescribed in the plan was that block interiors would be cleared out in due course to become community courtyards. Alas, this clause proved impossible to enforce, partially due to Zagreb's lack of autonomy, which led to its bizarre urban condition referred to as 'parallel cities.' The outside of the perimeter block reflected Zagreb's aspiration to be an independent capital, while on the inside, the block interiors testified to what it essentially was at the time, a provincial town. This parallel urban condition can be seen as the direct spatial consequence of the social psychology described by Rogić's theory of parallel local identities.

The industrial modernisation of Zagreb contributed to rapid population growth. From 1850 to the end of World War I, the city grew from 20,000 to over 100,000 people, causing an insatiable demand for housing. Zagreb, which counted

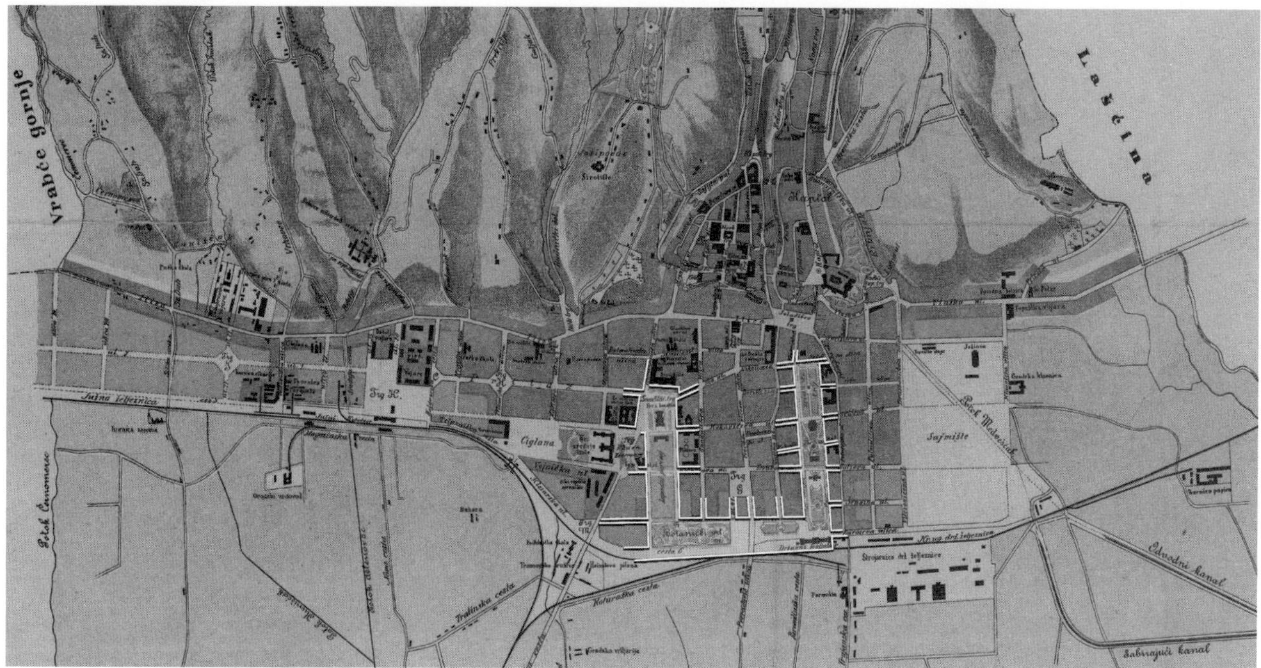

1,500 houses in the 1850s, had 6,500 buildings by the end of the century, over half of which were residential.[5] This unprecedented boom caused a surge in construction in the aftermath of the first devastating earthquake that struck Zagreb in 1880, precipitating new development opportunities. Simultaneously, it accelerated the formalisation of Zagreb's Second Regulation Plan, published in 1888. This plan was significant because it succeeded in organising property development while simultaneously introducing a framework of public spaces, omitted by the pragmatism of the First Regulation Plan. It formalised a sequence of parks and squares inscribed into the morphology of Lower Town, which later came to be known locally as the 'green horseshoe.' As a central public space, the 'horseshoe' was inspired by the Viennese Ringstrasse, yet the two public spaces had very different conception stories. If the Viennese Ring was the outcome of a meticulously planned transformation of former fortifications into a representative cultural landscape of the Empire, Zagreb's green horseshoe resulted from piecemeal urban tactics preventing increasingly valuable land from being developed into property. The praise attributed to city surveyor Milan Lenuci as the creator of the 'horseshoe' is proportional to the determination of foreign governance in rejecting any form of public urban design, which was seen as an unnecessary expense. Lenuci's achievement was in his ingenuity to hold off development on the empty plots within the 'horseshoe' by choreographing public activities and temporary structures. He spotlit the area, embedding it firmly in people's daily lives and memory as a public space. As property development slowly increased the city's budget, it became possible for new public buildings to replace the temporary structures and sports fields, much like the Viennese Ringstrasse. Those tactics were years in the making, but by the time Zagreb's Second Regulation Plan was drawn and published, the 'green horseshoe' was firmly fastened as its centrepiece. It remained the ultimate *gesamtkunstwerk* of Zagreb's foundational epoch and contributed in elevating the people of Zagreb to become 'modern citizens.' As the Croatian architectural historian Vladimir Bedenko writes, if the First Regulation Plan gave Zagreb its shape, the Second Regulation Plan framed its meaning.[6]

Although it would not be until the end of World War I that the green horseshoe would assume the form and program it has today, 'plot by plot' tactics championed by Lenuci had already begun to take hold over the imagination of architects

Opposite: Zagreb's new perimeter blocks as drawn up in the city's First Regulation Plan [Illustration by the authors. Base Image: Dragutin Albrecht, Nacrt Zagreba, 1864].

Above: Zagreb's 'Horseshoe' as drawn up in the city's Second Regulation Plan [Illustration by the authors. Base Image: Carl Albrecht, Nacrt grada Zagreba, 1989].

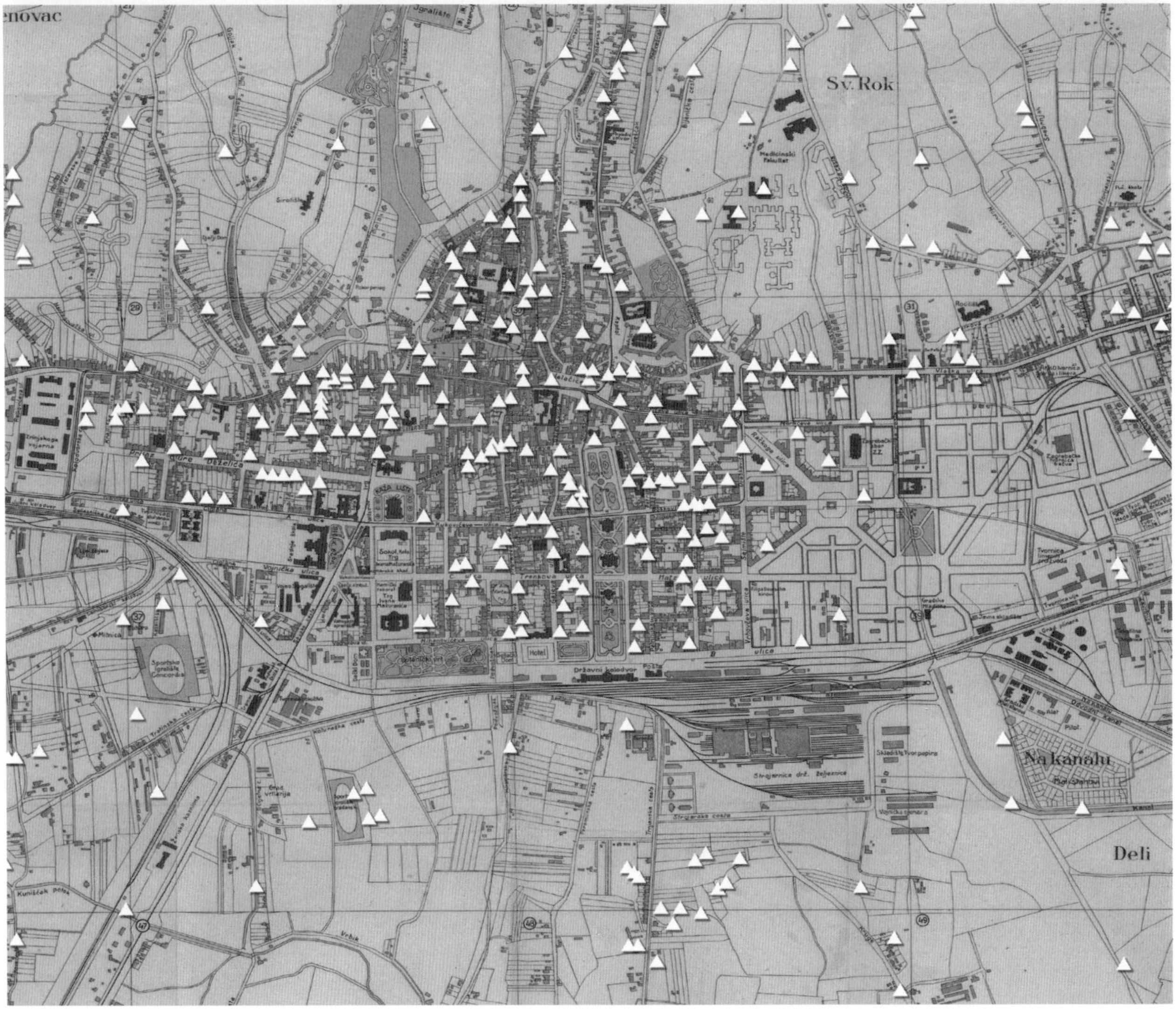

Sv. Rok
Na kanalu
Deli

as tools for city-making, developed in response to the lack of local sovereignty. The horseshoe's formation played a part in persuading the locals into opting for short term tactics rather than long term strategies—urban patching instead of urban planning—and effectively trusting the influence and scale of architecture rather than that of urbanism. This conditioning shaped the local know-how back then and has been relevant ever since. As a result, a special kind of 'urban-active architecture' emerged in Zagreb. Amidst the monotonous perimeter blocks of shoulder-to-shoulder houses, Lower Town became a zone of experimentation, culminating in the 1920s and 1930s, when a new generation of Modernist architects (most of which were foreign-trained), weary of the ineffective urban scale, sought to maximise public purpose with their architecture. Every plot became an opportunity for a micro-urban gain—setbacks created public squares; lobbies became streets and passages permeating the blocks; hybrid programs, such as cinemas and theatres, were introduced to extend the reach of the modern city. Cumulatively, the result was urbanism disguised as architecture, which was "the outcome of design processes and strategies developed to achieve rational results in conditions of instability and ambiguity."[7]

If it is indeed the condition of historical instability that forms Zagreb's urbanist *terroir*, then 'urban-active architecture' is one of its finest vintages—ready to be recalled, in the context of post-earthquake recovery, as Zagreb's 'know-how' par excellence. However, given that Zagreb entered a relatively long-term period of stability after becoming an independent European capital, the following questions arise: How can a city whose urban know-how is predominantly based on circumstances of instability adequately react to conditions of stability? And what do we mean by stability in the first place?

We cannot design cities, but we can devise structures which are stimulating.[8]

—Kees Christiaanse

A debate similar to the one taking place in Zagreb transpired in early 1950 post-war Amsterdam, where century-old maintenance problems and neglect had left the urban infrastructure dilapidated. Much like in Zagreb's Lower Town dilemma of today, Amsterdam's city centre needed a strategy for revitalisation and by mid-1950s two conflicting approaches led to a city-wide schism. Ambitions supporting the costly conservation of the historic inner city were challenged by initiatives advocating its modernisation and densification. The latter involved the replacement of traditional canal houses and small buildings with larger ones, as well as the replacement of entire canals with paved roads to support this increase in density.

We adopt Amsterdam as as an example of long-term stability:

> ...A powerful and assertive planning machine, specialised in urban expansion. Many inhabitants of Amsterdam were even frightened of this machine's power and 'mysterious elusiveness,' especially now that the focus had shifted to the old city centre.[9]

During the post-war period, it was clear that unless something was done fast, the heart of historic Amsterdam was at risk of disappearing. This urgency mobilised the social elite, who formed a *Comité* to take charge of the situation by publicly promoting the cause of restoring Amsterdam's historic inner city and devising an economic strategy that would be supported by the city council, through the generation of resources for conservation. The solution was to create a three-in-one hybrid entity: a combined 'public limited company,' a 'housing corporation' and a 'cultural heritage institution.' In this way, the initiative could take advantage of what all three had to offer in terms of legal benefits. Whereas the 'company' aspect operated as a developer, by buying, restoring and turning an interest for its investors, it could also enjoy the same fiscal benefits of a 'housing corporation,' such as exemption from corporation tax and transfer costs. As 'heritage institution,' supplementary funding could come from restoration grants. After a brief pilot, comprising two eligible canal houses, the scheme proved feasible, and *Maatschappij tot Stadsherstel N.V.* or *Stadsherstel* for short, was born. '*Stad*,' meaning 'the city,' is a reminder that the restoration and development of individual houses was not the company's ultimate aim but rather a means to a long-term city-wide ambition. While *'herstel'* is a synonym for the verb 'to restore,' it simultaneously means 'to heal' or 'to correct an error,' and thus "refer[s] to the future and the leaving behind of past wounds, wrong turns and misguided paths."[10]

Over 750 buildings restored during the 70 years after *Stadsherstel*'s founding testifies to the success of combining public purpose with business acumen. Although 500-year-old urban planning tradition and equally venerable, statecraft savvy social elite are not readily available to just any city, the *Stadsherstel*

Top Left: Damage after Zagreb Earthquake in 1880. [Ivan Standl, Masarykova Street after the earthquake on 9 Nov. 1880, 1880].

Top Right: Franjo Tahy, Damage after Zagreb Earthquake in 2020. [CC0 via Wikimedia Commons, 2020].

Bottom: Buildings declared 'unfit for use' by the City of Zagreb after the earthquake of March 22nd, 2020 [Illustration by the authors. Base Image: Author unknown (Gradski građevni odsjek). *Nacrt grada Zagreba*, 1923].

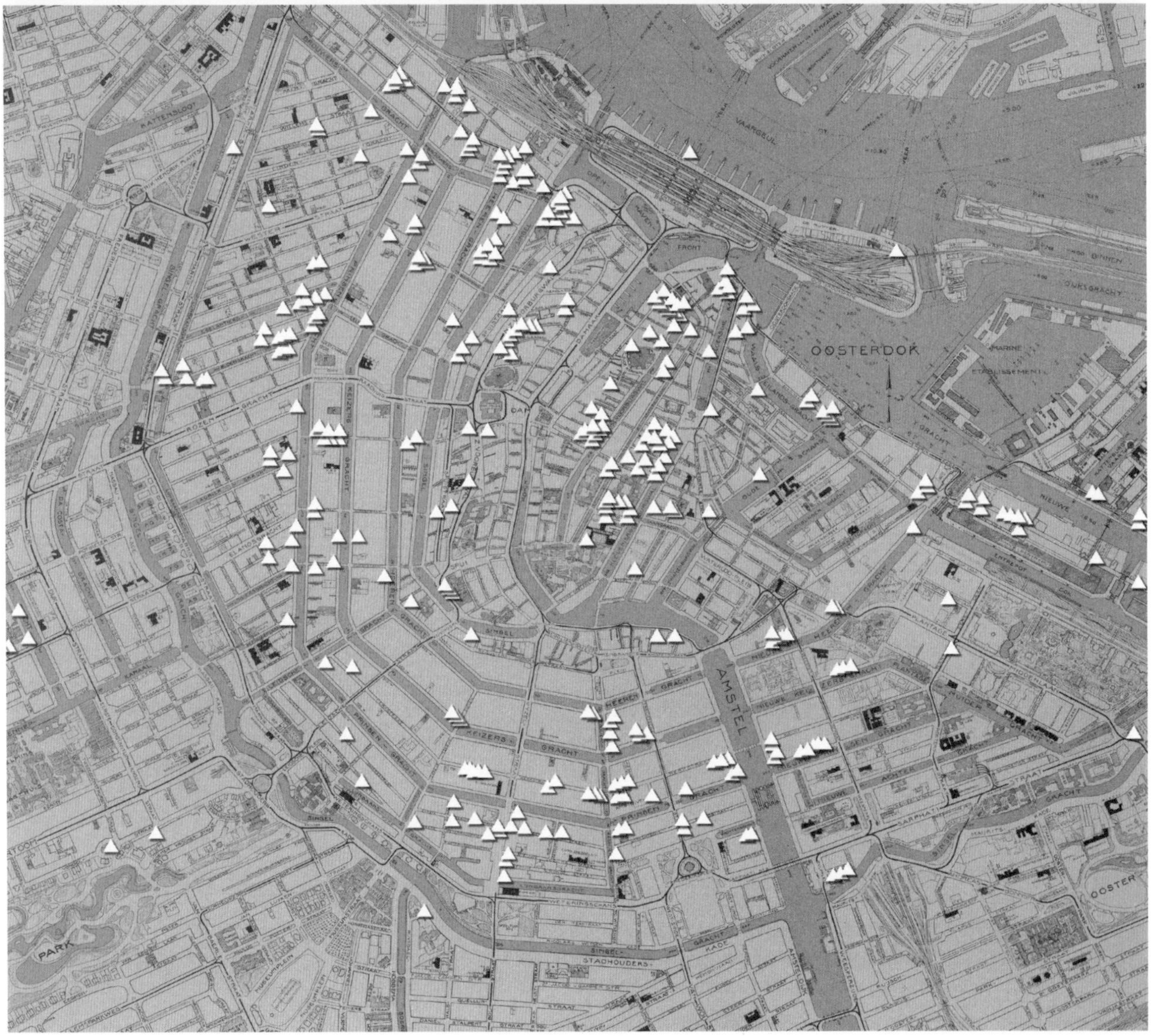

account is a relevant case study describing the systematic restoration of urban heritage in modern times. For Zagreb, Amsterdam's example might infer not a lesson in heritage restoration but rather the power of a robust public-private partnership as a bond that can ultimately improve a city's fortunes. The purpose of demonstrating long-term trust between the two, therefore, ranks above restoration itself. Private entities operating as agents of the public body is a scheme that could bring about Zagreb's own *herstel* (recovery), while simultaneously encouraging the emergence of responsible leadership in civil service as well as the public. The importance of endorsing an influential group of professionals, citizens and activists that should arise from both private and public fronts, as the Amsterdam example shows, is indispensable to a successful *herstel*.

Knowledge is information that can be globally shared, while know-how is embedded in people, organisations, and technical equipment—in the matter—and cannot easily be moved.[11]

—Markus Schaefer

In Croatia, 'transition' is a word attributed to the condition of instability, and is still used today on many occasions by local leaders. It refers to a change in political and economic systems as well as the shifting of national borders and identity. Given that over quarter of a century has passed since Croatia gained its independence and Zagreb finally became a fully autonomous capital, this rhetoric ought to be challenged as outdated, even harmful, if multi-generational agendas like Zagreb's post-earthquake recovery are to be accomplished. However, before long-term visions can be articulated, or new mechanisms to enforce them can be developed, it is necessary to recognise that Croatia's condition has changed, from instability to stability, as an outcome of its thirty years (and counting) of autonomy. As a recent European Union member stated, it is essential for Zagreb to shed its historically-fated modesty and begin to recognise itself as a European capital in its own right—one amongst equals. For this reason, the opportunity presented by the recovery of Lower Town must be seized and framed as methodical steps towards a future of innovative models rather than an endless project of reconstructing the past.

Top Left: A corner building in Amsterdam recovered by Stadsherstel - before reconstruction. Photographer unknown. Vijzelgracht, 1950.

Top Right: A corner building in Amsterdam recovered by Stadsherstel - after reconstruction. Photographer unknown, Vijzelgracht 1-21, Prinsengracht 646-666, ca. 1972.

Bottom: Buildings restored by Amsterdam Stadsherstel in the historic city centre of Amsterdam. Illustration by the authors. Base Image: Author unknown (Dienst Publieke Werken), Kaart van Amsterdam, 1929.

Foreign influence—that is, a historically dominant force translated into the local built environment—is illustrated by the mid-19th century reactive perimeter block typology of Zagreb's Lower Town, but also the urban-active architecture that emerged out of it. By retrieving the past specific to the requirements of the present, we argue that it is precisely this kind of local, urban-active know-how that should be protected, as something alive, useful and enduringly relevant. Figuratively speaking, by taking two steps back we can take one step forward, as the 'new local' of Zagreb might emerge once again through the selective appropriation of useful urban policies to be found in more traditionally stable capitals, elsewhere. Much like Mt. Fuji in Hokusai's *Great Wave off Kanagawa,* we anticipate the advent of Zagreb's own 'blue pigment,' as the city beings to resurface and enter a new age.

01 Gradski Ured Za Strategijsko Planiranje i Razvoj Grada, "Štete Uzrokovane Potresom U Gradu Zagrebu," Republika Hrvatska Grad Zagreb, 30 June, 2020, 7, https://www.zagreb.hr/userdocsimages/arhiva/statistika/2020/Potres_priop%C4%87enje_2.7.2020.%20a%C5%BEurirano%20Nives.pdf.

02 Rebecca West, *Black Lamb and Grey Falcon* (New York: Penguin Group, 2007), 47.

03 Ivan Rogić, "The Metropolitan Moves of the First Modernization," in *Project Zagreb - Transition as Condition, Strategy, Practice*, eds. Eve Blau and Ivan Rupnik (Barcelona: Actar, 2007), 39.

04 Ibid., 40.

05 Aleksander Laslo, "Between Two Building Codes," in *Project Zagreb - Transition as Condition, Strategy, Practice*, eds. Eve Blau and Ivan Rupnik (Barcelona: Actar, 2007), 91.

06 Vladimir Bedenko, "Die Gestaltung einer Hauptstadt : Zagreb von den Anfängen bis zur Gründerzeit," *Werk, Bauen+Wohnen*: Zagreb Agram 9 (2001): 22.

07 Eve Blau and Ivan Rupnik, "The Zagreb Block: Figure as Field," in *Project Zagreb - Transition as Condition, Strategy, Practice,* eds. Eve Blau and Ivan Rupnik (Barcelona: Actar, 2007), 108.

08 Kees Christiaanse, "Open Cities," filmed October 2009 at International Urban Planning: New Challenges in Global Metropolisation, KCAP, video, 14:37, https://www.youtube.com/watch?v=m4B1RI-6NDc&ab_channel=KCAPtube

09 Fred Feddes, "Stadsherstel: restoring order in the city," in *Recreating Amsterdam* (Amsterdam: Architectura& Natura, 2016), 27.

10 Ibid., 45.

11 Marcus Schaefer, *Switzerland: Deep Urbanism for an Age of Disruption* (Moscow: Strelka Press, 2020), 41, https://www.amazon.com/Switzerland-Deep-Urbanism-Age-Disruption-ebook/dp/B0889FNSF4.

THE SPACE OF POTENTIAL

PRESENCE, NON-PRESENCE AND POTENTIAL IN ALDO ROSSI'S ANALOGICAL CITY

Cameron McEwan

Potential signifies that which is not current, that which is not present.
— Paolo Virno[1]

The drawing always stops at a void which cannot be represented. For many reasons this void is both happiness and its absence.
— Aldo Rossi[2]

Presence is not only the material existence of architecture, presence is the discursive space of thought and the opening up of a space for thought. Presence is the space of potential. At a time when the humanities and the sciences are threatened by the irrationalism of thought, from climate change denial to the narrative of post-truth, and where there is a tendency in architecture to disavow its critical capacity, the present moment is a crisis of collective imagination—the social and historical production of forms and ideas through which a concept of the world may be articulated.[3] It is necessary to develop critical strategies, conceptual tools and knowledge practices to articulate modes of thinking and acting otherwise. McKenzie Wark has argued: "The common task is to produce a knowledge of the world made up of the differences between ways of knowing it."[4] The task of architecture and critique must be to interpret the world in order to change it.[5]

This article approaches the space of potential by linking architect Aldo Rossi's analogical city with political theorist Paolo Virno's ideas on potential, non-presence and presence. The first part of the article reflects on Rossi's analogical city by focusing on what Rossi calls "removal in space" and the "void" of drawing, which is interpreted in the register of non-presence and potential. The second part of the article details Virno's idea of potential and act using his lesser known book, *Déjà vu and the End of History*. Finally, in the third part, Virno's ideas are transposed onto Rossi's and read together. In doing so, the analogical city is articulated as the possibility for thinking about the city, the subject and the world otherwise, with the capacity to lead to a more egalitarian and critical architecture of the city.

The article operates in dialogue with a suite of montages, which explore the visual relationship between non-presence and presence, potential and act, void and figure. The montages develop formal operations, in particular erasure, repetition, demontage and remontage. An exchange is developed between Rossi's ideas and drawings, their transformation through the process of iterative montage and in relation to Virno, who helps to rethink the analogical city anew.

Analogical City

The analogical city was only a latent idea in Rossi's *The Architecture of the City*. It was captured in his argument that the city was an "historical text" embodying the "collective memory" of its inhabitants.[6] Thought takes form in the city and at the same time the city pushes back to condition thought. This reciprocal relationship was always present in Rossi's work. He argued that all cities lead back to the Greek *polis* as a paradigm of collective political life: "The memory of the city ultimately makes its way back to Greece; there urban artefacts coincide with the development of thought, and imagination becomes history and experience."[7] If all cities lead back to the *polis*, then all cities are connected to one another by a chain of association binding individuals and ideas to collectives, and to the spaces of the city. The city is an analogue of us and we are analogues of the city; the city is within our thoughts and bodies.

It is the preface to the second edition of *The Architecture of the City* when Rossi first concretely introduces his vision of the analogical city. He uses the example of a *capriccio* painting by Giovanni Antonio Canaletto.[8] In the painting, entitled *La*

Basilica di Vicenza e il Ponte di Rialto (1753), Andrea Palladio's Palazzo Chiericati and the Vicenza Basilica are positioned either side of a version of his unbuilt Rialto Bridge for Venice. For Rossi, the bringing together of existing elements from different cities to construct a new city embodies the possibility of analogical thinking as a "logical-formal operation." Rossi argues that Canaletto's painting constitutes an "analogous Venice formed of specific elements associated with the history of both architecture and the city."[9]

Canaletto's painting performs a critical strategy of refusal. The painting depicts neither Vicenza nor Venice. It does not depict Venice because the buildings that Canaletto paints are from Vicenza. It does not depict Vicenza because the scene is recognisably the Rialto in Venice with gondolas on the canal and a dense urban fabric behind the main buildings. The painting is an analogue of both cities and of neither, it is a counter-project against both cities. The analogical city can therefore be interpreted as a critical refusal of the existing city and the current urban condition, it is thinking beyond the present; beyond the status quo.[10] Against what Rossi called the "naïve functionalism" of the deterministic cause and effect relations of function to form, and the utilitarian logic of the city, the analogical city opens up a space for speculative possibility.[11]

Rossi reprises Canaletto's *capriccio* in subsequent essays. In 'An Analogical Architecture,' Rossi reflected on Canaletto's painting, citing an interest in the "removal in space" of Palladio's architecture: "The various works of architecture by Palladio and their removal in space constitute an analogical representation."[12] This "removal in space" creates a void and this idea is explored through Canaletto's *capriccio* (Fig. 1), which can be disarticulated in a series of iterations that incrementally 'remove' Palladio's architecture from the scene. The 'non-presence' of the void opens a space of potential where each building can be substituted or replaced for another: One palazzo substituted for another palazzo, a bridge is replaced by another bridge, a basilica for a basilica.

Later, in his essay 'The Analogous City: Panel,' Rossi focuses on "the relation between reality and imagination" in the analogical city.[13] He first summarises the reality of the city, reflecting on its uneven development, the housing question and "business-inspired destruction" of the city centre. He then returns to the painting by Canaletto. This time, Rossi interprets the painting as an alternative within reality, stating: "Without the capacity to imagine the future there can be no solution to the city as an essentially social fact."[14] The idea that the analogical city signifies an 'alternative reality' linked to imagining a different future shifts the conceptual structure of the analogical city into a critical project—it holds the possibility for imagining otherwise.

'The Analogous City: Panel' essay is illustrated by a collage of the same name, a collective work with Eraldo Consolacio, Bruno Reichlin and Fabio Reinhart. By disarticulating this collage, the principle typological forms are 'removed' to once again leave a void (Fig. 2). The space expresses a geometric figure—the square, the circle, the triangle, the line—while the void opens the conditions of possibility for an alternative presence. The logic follows the geometrical order prescribed by the removal in space of the object and the space left behind can be filled with something else, opening up numerous chains of association and possibilities for substitution. For example, the void left by the square may lead to the square grid of a typical Roman city plan, the walled enclosures of Beijing's Forbidden City, a Berlin höfe courtyard, a perimeter block, a tower or a simple monastic

Fig.1: Disarticulation of Giovanni Antonio Canaletto's *La Basilica di Vicenza e il Ponte di Rialto*, 1756. "Removal in space" opens the generative space of potential. All montages by the author.

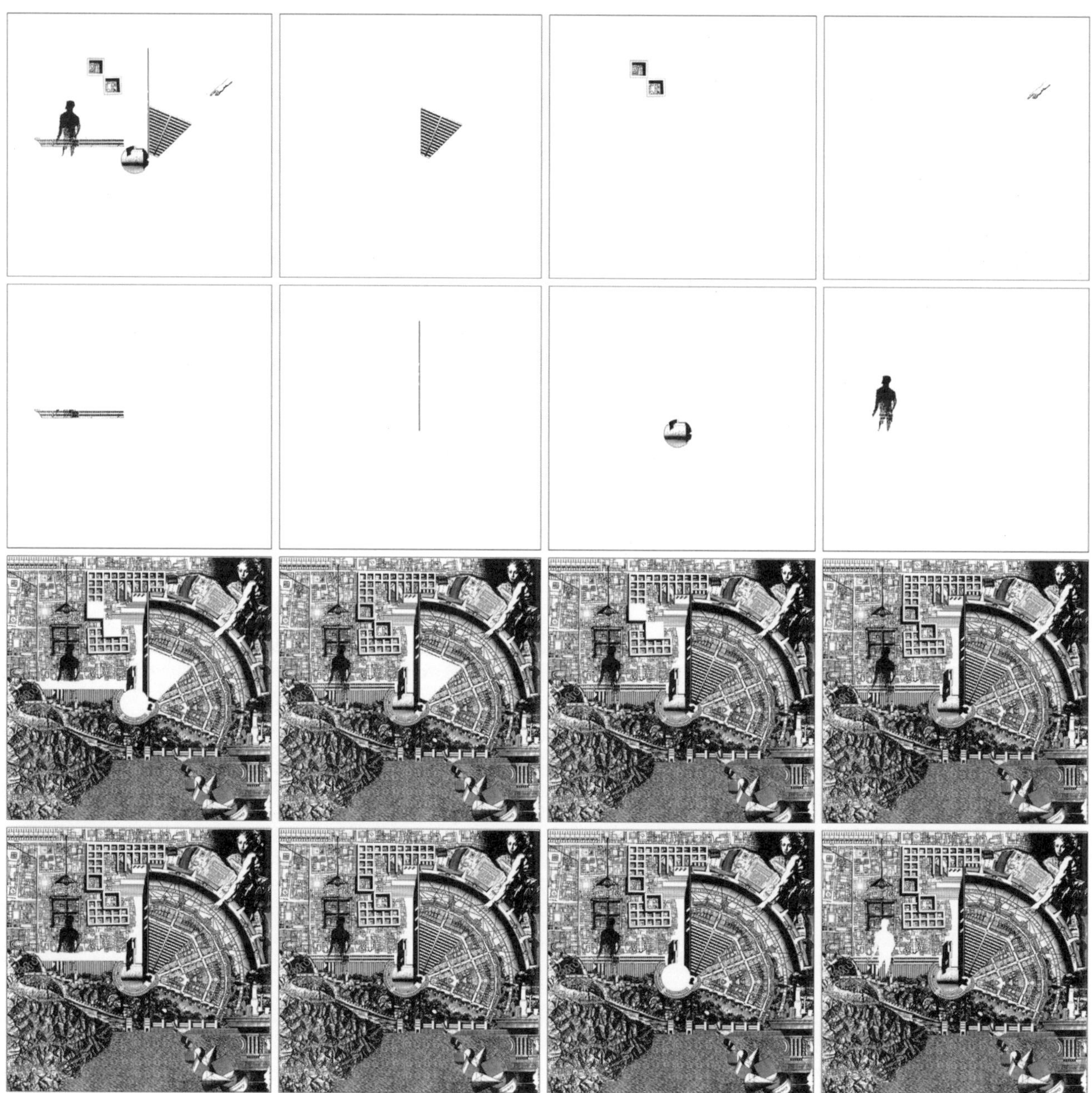

cell—scale telescopes from territory to room. Void is transformed into figure, interior to exterior and vice versa. Geometric typologies coincide with historical typologies and a formal grammar of syntax and association are staged to reveal the underlying geometrical order of the analogical city. The analogical city as a logical-formal operation; the analogue as non-presence, as removal in space and as a critical act suggest an alternative way of approaching Rossi's most diffuse and compelling ideas. Against those who consider the analogical city as nostalgic, irrational or autobiographical, this article argues that the analogical city is a project for imagining the city otherwise.[15] When Canaletto transposes elements from Vicenza to Venice, the 'space' left behind is a void containing generative possibilities. It is a space for thought, a constitutive gap that opens the way for thinking differently.

Potential, Non-Presence, Presence

Many of the themes that Virno puts forward resonate with the themes at play in Rossi's analogical city, such as ideas around collective memory, critical agency, critique of history and the question of language. For both Rossi and Virno, the human being who acts, thinks and imagines is central. Virno argues that the subject embodies the inexhaustible and indeterminate potential of language in *Déjà vu and the End of History*, interpreting the relationship between language, memory and materialist subjectivity to develop a model of critique that emphasises historical experience, radical imagination and the emancipatory potential of the subject.

Déjà vu and the End of History is divided into three parts that return on one another, inflecting the categories of potential, non-presence and presence. In Part 1, Virno focuses on the idea of déjà vu and critiques the end of history proposition that supported the dominance of capitalism as a mode of production and form of life. The associated deterministic implications of the end of history have served to close critical discourse and led to a concept of the world that is thoughtless and utilitarian. Virno refutes the narrative that history ends with capitalism and problematises the convention to understand history as a linear process. He proposes that history can be disrupted, split apart and put out of joint; likewise, so might capitalism. For Virno, déjà vu is a figure of thought that disrupts historical time and acts as a model of critique.

In a counterintuitive proposition, Virno argues that déjà vu is not an individual experience but a particular kind of collective experience that cuts through space, time and activates radical imagination. For Virno, déjà vu is an example of social memory because it is memory taking a "public character."[18] He argues that, momentarily, we become spectators of our own actions and consequently déjà vu is an act of "splitting time" in which reality is thrown into the past and there is a sudden simultaneity of past, present and potential future. Déjà vu is the "strangely familiar," the simultaneity of distance and closeness, it embodies "in one and the same event . . . the paradoxical coexistence of the real and the possible."[20] By disrupting linear time and complicating temporality, déjà vu can be understood as a conceptual model of critique because it opens the conditions of speculative thought and articulates the latent potential for an alternative future yet to materialise.[21]

In Part 2, Virno analyses the concept of potentiality and argues that potential is a non-chronological, permanent and indefinite past. Potential is in the same register as what Virno designates the "language faculty," which he describes as "language *in potentia*, or the power of language."[22] Potential is also placed in relation to act. While potential is the permanence of thought, history and the indefinite past; the act is a *now*, a present, a presence.[23] For Virno, acts do not fulfil potential. Hence, the present can always be *other*. The act does not translate the infinity inherent in the language faculty into actuality because the language faculty is the totality of thought; the totality of the indeterminate capacity to think, create and imagine. Acts never exhaust the infinity of potential. Consequently, there is always a gap between potential and act, which Virno calls a "temporal lacuna."[24] In the same way that déjà vu splits apart individual and collective experience, the coupling of potential and act are split apart to produce a gap, which is the disruptive void of critical thought.

Part 3 focuses on historical materialism, the concept of labour-power and extends Virno's discussion on potential towards a critique of capitalism. Marx is the fundamental reference point and Virno interprets Marx's idea of labour-power—the capacity of the worker to produce—as equivalent to "pure potential."[25] That potential is the accumulation of all mental and physical capacities embodied by the living individual to think and to act, to desire and imagine, to produce and to reproduce: "Labour-power does not indicate a circumscribed potential, but is rather the name common to the various different types of potential."[26]

Summarising the foregoing leads to the following framework:

1. *Act*: The perceived present, a presence;
2. *Potential Act*: The déjà vu of the remembered present, a non-presence that produces a void, which simultaneously separates and links potential and act; and
3. *Potential*: The indefinite past, which is the inexhaustible potential of the language faculty, indeterminate history and infinite thought; never fully actualised, non-present, but always permanent in the labour-power of the subject.

Analogical City and the Space of Potential

Virno's thought on the coupling of potential and act can be transposed onto Rossi's idea of the analogical city and spatialised. Potential opens a gap, it is the "space of thought," Virno's "temporal lacuna." Potential as this "space of thought" is equivalent to the "removal in space" of Palladio's architecture in Canaletto's *capriccio*. It is the void left over within which the space of imagination circulates. This space of potential is equivalent to the blank space articulated in the study of the *Analogical City: Panel* (Fig. 2), which condenses geometric types and historical types in relation to the figure, a collective subject and representation of labour-power. The figure is both present and non-present. The figure in Rossi's drawings is a linguistic subject and a signifier for the collective life of the city. Like the city itself, the subject is incomplete; always embodying inexhaustible potential that is never fully actualised. The white voids signify the potential for something else. They signify the possibility for reimagining architecture and the city.

Fig. 2 (previous page): Disarticulation of Aldo Rossi et al., *Analogical City: Panel*, 1976. Analytical montage of geometric types in relation to the figure as a collective subject. White voids signify the potential for thinking about the city otherwise.

Fig. 3 (above): Disarticulation of Aldo Rossi, Analogical City: Drawings [Selection], 1976-78. Analytical montage focusing on open doors as elements that signify the non-present subject.

In the *Analogical City: Panel* montage (Fig. 2), the relationship between figure and ground is also problematised, the ground being both present and not present. This undecidable nature liberates the space of imagination and opens the space for a critique of architectural categories and relationships such as figure and ground, space and object, geometry and typology, city and room. In other drawings by Rossi, hands, figures and faces are elements that signify the presence of a collective subject. They serve to disrupt and defamiliarise the existing order of architecture and the city. The open doors in Rossi's drawings suggest occupation where there is currently none, this void is a potential presence (Fig. 3). The figures who inhabit Rossi's drawings, and the elements that stand in for the subject—giant hands, open doors, oculus—affirm the human capacity to imagine and act in a collective world. The analogical city is a model of critical potential, which Virno argues is tied to the human capacity for imagining an alternative future presence. It is a political act of thought.

Imagining Otherwise

Radical transformation seems a long way off. Capitalism—as spectacle, as culture industry, as knowledge-economy—reduces the potential of labour to a commodity. Yet, for Virno, the potential embodied by the human subject is the source of all possibility. Virno's reflections on temporality, language, history and memory help to reframe Rossi's thought on the materialism of collective memory, the language of architecture, its urban types and spaces; and on the labour-power at play in the analogical city. Potential is in dialogue with collective memory and the linguistic subject, manifesting as voids in the city—spaces to think and act otherwise; places where the radical imagination may be articulated. 'Potential' frames a way of thinking about the architectural imagination as an indefinite past of critical projects, figures of thought and knowledge practices that lay dormant; present in the discursive space of thought, to be appropriated, reworked and transformed.

Potential is infinite thought and inexhaustible possibility. Opening the critical potential of the analogical city may provide the conditions to discover reasons and (ana)logics other than those of capitalist development.[27] Architecture must ultimately engage in the relations of possibility to articulate new visions of the world; to imagine new forms and new forms of living; and to articulate dignified spaces for individuals and collectives to act thoughtfully and with agency. Collective life, which is the social world of the planet, our built and natural environment, is not inexhaustible. Collective life and the potential embodied by the labour-power of individuals, exists in a world with material limits and depleting resources. Imagining otherwise and acting differently is more necessary than ever.

01 Paolo Virno, *A Grammar of the Multitude: For an Analysis of Contemporary Forms of Life* [2001], trans. Isabella Bertoletti, James Cascaito, and Andrea Casson (Los Angeles, CA: Semiotext(e), 2004), 82.

02 Aldo Rossi, *A Scientific Autobiography*, trans. Lawrence Venuti (Cambridge, Mass.: MIT Press, 1981), 24.

03 Naomi Oreskes and Erik M. Conway, *Merchants of Doubt: How a Handful of Scientists Obscured the Truth on Issues from Tobacco Smoke to Global Warming (London: Bloomsbury*, 2010); Berardi, *The Uprising: On Poetry and Finance* (Los Angeles: Semiotext(e), 2012); Sophia Rosenfeld, *Democracy and Truth: A Short History* (Philadelphia: University of Pennsylvania Press, 2019).

04 McKenzie Wark, *Sensoria: Thinkers for the Twenty-First Century* (New York: Verso, 2020), 4.

05 Nadir Lahiji, *Architecture or Revolution: Emancipatory Critique After Marx* (New York: Routledge, 2020).

06 Aldo Rossi, *The Architecture of the City* [1966], trans. Diane Ghirardo and Joan Ockman (Cambridge, Mass.: MIT Press, 1982), 128, 130.

07 Rossi, *The Architecture of the City*, 134.

08 Aldo Rossi, "Preface to the Second Italian Edition" [1969], in *The Architecture of the City*, trans. Diane Ghirardo and Joan Ockman (Cambridge, Mass.: MIT Press, 1982), 164-67.

09 Aldo Rossi, "Preface to the Second Italian Edition," 166.

10 The interpretation of the analogical city as a critical act of refusal could be expanded with reference to Mario Tronti, "The Strategy of Refusal," in *Workers and Capital* [1966], trans. David Broder (London; New York: Verso, 2019), 241-62; Paolo Virno, "Virtuosity and Revolution: The Political Theory of Exodus", in *Radical Thought in Italy: A Potential Politics*, ed. Paolo Virno and Michael Hardt (Minneapolis, Minn.: University Of Minnesota Press, 2006), 189-212. Tronti and Virno elaborate a strategy of engaged withdrawal focused around refusal, exit and exodus.

11 Rossi, *The Architecture of the City*, 46.

12 Aldo Rossi, "An Analogical Architecture," trans. David Stewart, *A+U: Architecture and Urbanism* 65 (1976): 74-76 (74).

13 Aldo Rossi, "La Città Analoga: Tavola / The Analogous City: Panel," *Lotus International* 13 (1976): 4-9 (5).

14 Rossi, "The Analogous City: Panel," 6.

15 The canonical disavowal of Rossi's analogical city is Manfredo Tafuri, *History of Italian Architecture, 1944-1985* [1986], trans. Jessica Levine (Cambridge, Mass.: MIT Press, 1989), 138. Tafuri was a supporter of Rossi in the 1960s and 70s; by the 1980s Tafuri concluded that Rossi's critical project and the analogical city in particular had succumbed to "a realm of images . . . whose source was De Chirico, frozen in spaces abandoned by time, . . . perversely bound to the unreal." Critiques of Rossi have too easily accepted Tafuri's conclusion and followed with refrains such as those mentioned in my text. There are also those who uncritically celebrated Rossi's "magical" thought, for instance, Vincent Scully, "Postscript: Ideology in Form," in *A Scientific Autobiography* (Cambridge, Mass.: MIT Press, 1981), 111-16. Also see Diane Ghirardo, *Aldo Rossi and the Spirit of Architecture* (New Haven: Yale University Press, 2019), 197. Although I take issue with Ghirardo's celebratory tone and assumption that her closeness to Rossi as friend, colleague and translator provides absolute authority, I agree with her statement that a "lesson of Rossi" is to "open rather than close ways of thinking about architecture."

16 Paolo Virno, *Déjà Vu and the End of History* [1999], trans. David Broder (London: Verso, 2015). Themes that run through *Déjà vu and the End of History* are further developed in Virno, *A Grammar of the Multitude*; Paolo Virno, *When the Word Becomes Flesh: Language and Human Nature* [2003], trans. Giuseppina Mecchia (South Pasadena, CA: Semiotext(e), 2015).

17 Francis Fukuyama, *The End of History and the Last Man* [1992] (New York: Free Press, 2006).

18 Virno, *Déjà Vu and the End of History*, 7.

19 Ibid., 8, 17, 32.

20 Ibid., 14.

21 Ibid., 32.

22 Paolo Virno, "Natural-Historical Diagrams: The 'New Global' Movement and the Biological Invariant", in *The Italian Difference: Between Nihilism and Biopolitics*, ed. Lorenzo Chiesa and Alberto Toscano, trans. Alberto Toscano (Melbourne: re.press, 2009), 131-47 (136).

23 Virno, *Déjà Vu and the End of History*, 72.

24 Ibid., 88, 117.

25 Ibid., 159

26 Virno, *Déjà Vu and the End of History*, 168-169. Italics in original.

27 McKenzie Wark, *Capital Is Dead: Is This Something Worse?* (London; New York: Verso, 2019).

STITCHING COOK CLOAK

OBJECTING: A NUANCED ENDEAVOUR

Katja Wagner

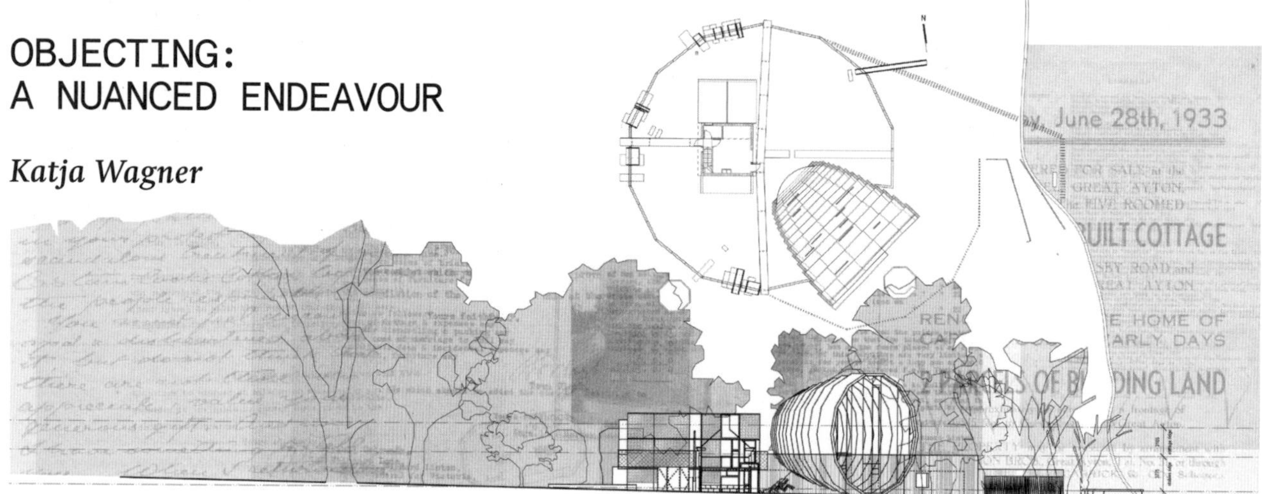

We are witnessing a time of far-reaching political upheaval and historical reassessment of power structures. In April 2020, social justice developments in the United States and United Kingdom precipitated renewed condemnation of colonial agents while also marking 250 years since the *Endeavour*'s landing at Botany Bay. Captain James Cook re-entered debate in a polychromy of penned, embodied and spray-painted rhetoric. Reversing the conventional roles of the discursive and constructed, civic spaces and urban voices became the frontline of postcolonial introspection.

It was in this context that I began to chart the polyvalent, overstitched and organic facets of Cooks' Cottage in Fitzroy Gardens. Through my thesis project supervised by Professor Philip Goad at the Melbourne School of Design, I investigated how modes of curatorial display calibrated by a language of observation, could articulate an architecture of enclosure that reframes Cooks' Cottage as a museological object and evokes deeper site histories. I became intrigued by the prospect of re-evaluating a complex field of symbolic and tangible presences, contesting boundaries and recasting their portrayal through architectural intervention in museological terms.

Opening the Archives

In mid–1933, plans were drafted and swiftly mobilised to unstitch an 18th century cottage from the urban fabric of Great Ayton in Yorkshire, for reinstallation into the Antipodean scenery of Melbourne. Home to the family of Captain James Cook, the dwelling was to be reconstructed as a constitutive token of British settlement within a series of events canonising 100 years since the city's declared founding. However, one would be mistaken to assume that the 87–year history of Cooks' Cottage in Fitzroy Gardens has been one of obliging silence, or its initial reception one of unchallenged accord. At the time of Victoria's Centennial Celebrations in 1934, decades had already passed since Federation and nearly two since the Gallipoli campaign, complicating gestures of axiomatic imperial remembrance. Even the media spotlight on the Cottage relocation featured British and Australian commentators alike raising questions over authenticity and contextualism which endure today.[1] Debate over the "impossibility of obtaining a site" solidified the radical view that "it was a mistake to uproot this old-world cottage with the object of transplanting it to a new country."[2] Indeed, when Russell Grimwade, an accomplished chemist and successful entrepreneur, presented 'Captain Cook's Cottage' in 1934, as "the repository for articles connected with the great man, so that his name will become revered by the rising generations of Australians,"[3] one wonders whether his collector's obsession with the antiquarian object and his devotion to nationalist legendry—magnified by a targeted media campaign to secure the Cottage—had eclipsed his better judgement.[4] Meanwhile, a similarly critical though somewhat cloaked chain of events unfolded in reaction to the nation's founding histories. As another centenary approached marking 100 years since the forced displacement of Indigenous Australians from central Melbourne in 1839, a burgeoning Indigenous rights movement led by William Cooper circulated a petition to instate a

representative of Indigenous peoples in Parliament.[5] In Fitzroy Gardens, a dismembered Scarred Tree and fragmented chain of ornamental water features remain as testimony to what was once a thriving seasonal wetland and ceremonial meeting place.[6]

Since the installation of Cooks' Cottage in Fitzroy Gardens, scholarly critique of the monument and museum, the politics of display and the legacy of colonial memory have been active forces for change. In central Europe, conceptualisation of the anti-memorial, counter-monument and *lieux de mémoire* (sites of memory) have precipitated several cogent responses to landmarks and buildings associated with the Holocaust and wartime atrocities.[7] In the US, monuments and museums related to colonial and racial histories have catalysed critical discussion and poignant response compelling cultural, social and legislative change.[8] These discourses have been influential upon the Australian postcolonial landscape, intensifying around commemorative time markers such as Australia's colonial Bicentenary of 1988.[9] Indeed, the corporeal fabrics of the gardens and Cottage bear witness to these shifts in an iterative semiology of plaques, statutory and vistas. A display curated in Cooks' Cottage stables is intended to represent Grimwade and Cook as complex historical figures. But compelling questions remain: what is the role of Cooks' Cottage in the broader cultural landscape, and how should its presence be physically confronted in Fitzroy Gardens?

Opposite: *Cook Cloak* southern elevation.
Above: Western perspective of the *Cloak* taken in situ.

Despite the contiguous web of debate, reflection and sentiment surrounding Cooks' Cottage, this object presents a unique challenge. As a relocated, occupiable relic, whose current context problematises rather than clarifies meaning, it is enriching to consider the practices of museum display. Indeed, the Cottage has always existed as "an antiquarian endeavour," and a didactic instrument of modern historical object-learning.[10] Russell Grimwade envisioned a "repository" and "Cook Museum," while *The Herald* described "a 'museum piece' rather than a picturesque or architectural ornament." This was echoed by the Melbourne T Square Club, which commended the structure to "be committed to the care of the Gallery Trustees . . . housed inside a building and not outside."[11] The science of *Wunderkammer* display—the 18th century private collector's cabinet of curiosities—is continued by Russell Grimwade's handmade eucalypt specimen cabinet as well as the interwar conservatory and glasshouses rising around Cooks' Cottage.[12] However, most importantly, understanding the Cottage as a framed specimen, suspends it in time to be recast as a relic or curiosity rather than remain an ambiguous symbol or fabrication.[13]

A Box, Warp and Weft

Towards this strategy of framed enclosure, Peter Zumthor's *Shelter for Roman Ruins* phrases a poetic envelope sleeved over an archaeological site in Chur, Switzerland. It has been described as architecturally bridging anachronistic monumentality and omnipotent contemporaneity to ponder the ruin at temporal distance.[14] Likewise, Carmody Groarke's *Hill House Box* enshrouds an historically monumental Charles Rennie Mackintosh residence in a silvery curtain and intricate observation structure. The house becomes a veiled artefact, or a "ship in a bottle."[15] Inversing this, Edmund de Waal's *Library of Exile* sculpts a habitable object within the museum environment as a transportive cloister for meditation upon displacement.[16] In addition, Peter Zumthor's 2011 Serpentine Pavilion folds a honeycombed wall around an otherworldly *hortus conclusus*, skylit by a charcoal compluvium.[17] By iterating the architectural vitrine, these points of reference canvas a position of critical introspection, and not only in theoretical, but in powerfully spatial terms.

The language of weaving as a medium of reconciliation between dialectic threads, suggests a further mediating dimension between pre- and post-Contact realities (Figs. 1-2). Throughout her practice, Anni Albers conceptualised the handloom as a tactile 'laboratory,' and her work resonates with notions of exile pertinent to Fitzroy Gardens' postcolonial histories.[18] The weaving traditions of Indigenous Australians and their three-dimensional objects, such as the eel trap, deepen this line of fingered inquiry. In parallel, James Cook's 'ditty box' embodies the object, containing vessel, and textile. Also the artefact most closely connected with the man himself, this small, initialled timber trunk would have encased pairs of supplies ('ditto') and personal possessions during his years at sea, among them needles and thread for stitched repair.[19]

Foregrounding a Response

With the intent to physically reframe the Cottage within its contemporary context, I defined a boundary condition enclosing the Cottage, its garden and adjacent underlying watercourse. This outline unfolds into an open cabinet of curiosities (*Wunderkammer*) hinged about the Cottage perimeter. In extension of this collecting sensibility and in response to the gardens, Grimwade and Cook, a conical seed archive is caught within this museological warp and weft. Among Grimwade's conservation interests was a fascination for botany, and in 1938 he commissioned a census of flora at the Mt Buffalo National Park. In addition, not far from the site at the National Herbarium is a repository of plant specimens collected by Joseph Banks and Daniel Solander on the *Endeavour* expedition, contained within a building also gifted for the 1934 Centenary.[21] Botanic seeds are valuable artefacts for the genetic information they store as repositories safeguarding the future of ecosystems and materials. The specimens deposited here as part of the Cottage vitrine document the pre-Contact ecological profile of the Fitzroy Gardens site.

Hence, pulling through this object-focused museological landscape is the continuous thread of layered observation. This language draws upon the magnifying and deeply penetrating instruments of scientific analysis and documentation familiar to Cook and Grimwade, in parallel with the fragmentary remains of an underlying Indigenous landscape, embodied most enigmatically by a ghosted central stream. In this way, the *Cloak* both veils and reveals successive cartographies, marking a stitched terrain of laden narratives in the manner of Mandy Nicholson's *Possum Skin Cloak* (2012). This tactile work of art for the University of Melbourne was crafted as a symbol of ceremonial welcome which indelibly charts, etched line into skin, iterative and intertwined student journeys in a medium which honours the culture and custodianship of the First Australians. In Fitzroy Gardens, the linguistically prominent 'Cooks' of 'Cooks' Cottage' shift from possessive subject to associative object, qualified cohabitant.

Stitching the Cloak, Inside Out

Framed by a sculpturally reinstated watercourse, *Cook Cloak* carves a series of viewing corridors through to significant landmarks visible from the site, including the Scarred Tree, Conservatory and Morton Bay Fig. Meanwhile, inwardly turned sightlines articulate facets of Cottage fabric within, among them an initialled lintel and the perceptual line connecting the Georgian windows of the eastern façade and elevated cottage garden with the watercourse as it passes through the site. To enter, the visitor circumnavigates the Cottage, arriving at its south-eastern coast, at which point the raised water feature becomes a recessed channel. Passing through a rope passage, the visitor steps between native grasses to arrive at the seed archive and fire pit, grounding their experience of this politically and historically loaded site in its material roots. Inversing the approach, the visitor descends a sloped incline onto a timber block deck, winding through the Cottage from its primary façade to access a network of suspended paths accessible at first floor level through a pair of articulated steel thresholds. As a whole, the Cottage vicinity repeats and refracts the prismatic geometry of European weaving traditions, like the handloom prop displayed in the Cottage's upstairs room, whilst the seed archive is earth-anchored and formally more reminiscent of concentric, Indigenous basket-weaving technologies.

Around the vitrines, the *Cloak* takes the form of a dual, woven and recycled rope curtain, transparent and operable within its open, galvanised frame—a fencing gesture recalling the hoarding within which the Cottage was reconstructed in 1934.[23] Objects are grouped according to function and their association with Cook. Beyond the sunken, polygonal ground plane, the *Cloak* splinters into a forest of steel fins stitching into the immediate context whilst shuttering a spectrum of narrow perspectival views between framed openings.

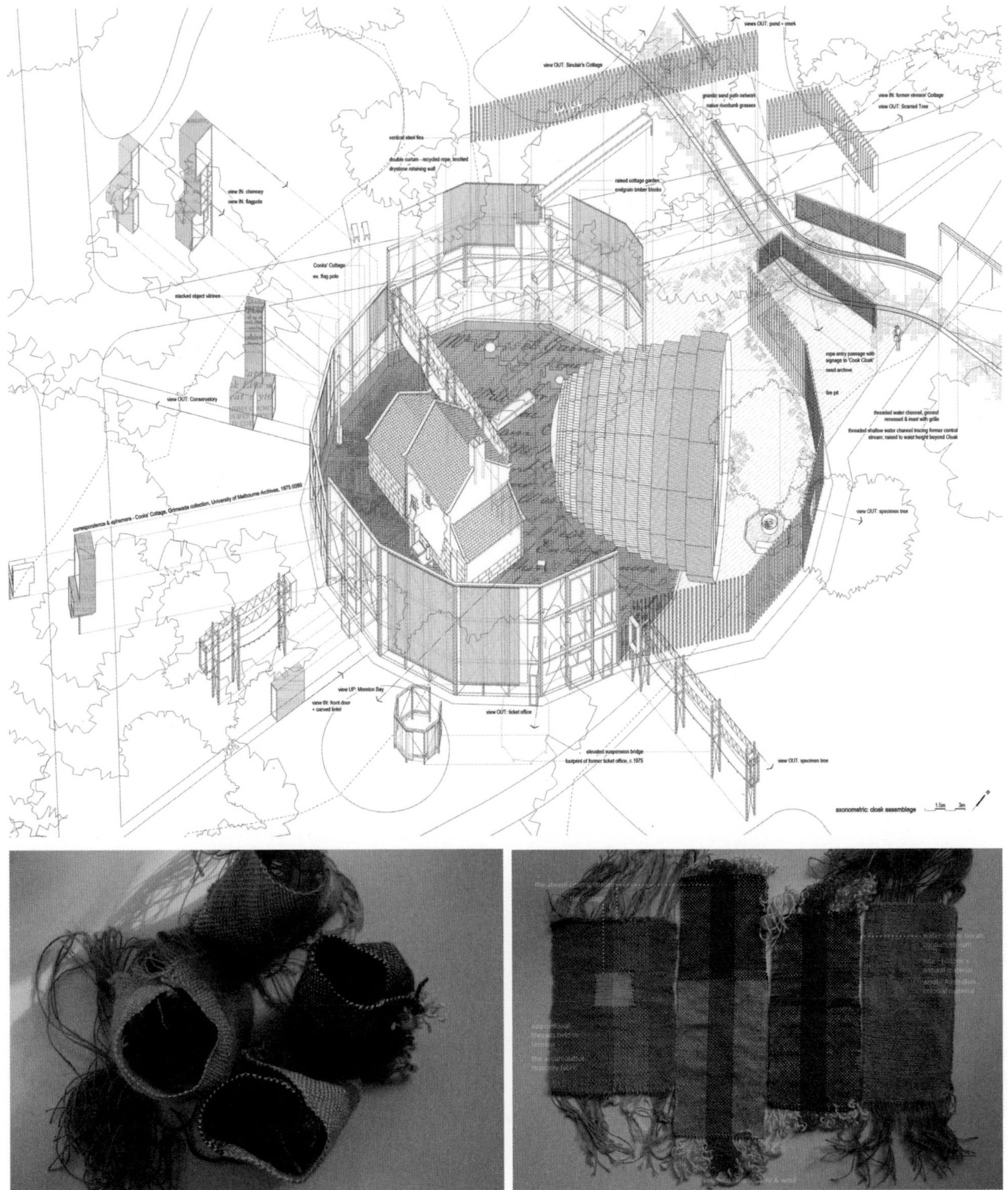

Fig. 4 (Above): Surveying the vitrine, unstitching the Cloak - fragmented axonometric.
Figs. 1-2 (Below): Woven samples, in jute and wool.

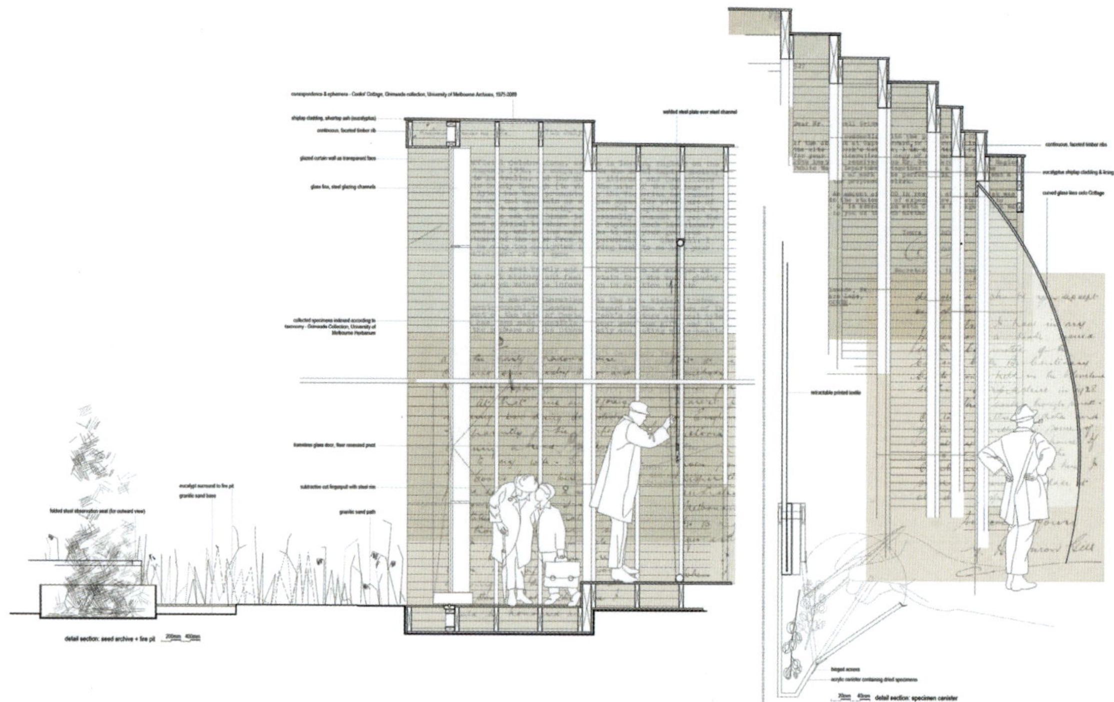

The vitrines themselves are a tessellated assemblage of stacked vessels or packing-cases which externalise the Cottage's domestic interior to recast it as an artefact. Higher-level objects are sighted on the viewer's approach, mirrored back to the ground plane or spied through the netting of suspended viewing platforms from which the Cottage contents and envelope can be observed by manner of a treetop walk or archaeological dig. This is the culmination of a journey through the Cottage interior, along which the viewer experiences the dwelling as a raw space. An ethereal Maree Clarke glass eel trap precedes a projected archival map surveying the 19th century course of the Birrarung tributary above. Outside, retractable didactic panels etch explanatory provenance details on glass, illuminated at night.

Anchored into a grassy mound, the seed archive is timber-framed and sheathed in shiplapped eucalyptus, encasing a palimpsest of textile screens printed with historic site imagery and weighted by glass canisters as taxonomically ordered seed repositories (Fig. 3). Moving through the tethered sails superimposes site elements whilst capturing a sense of its ephemerality and Indigenous roots. The textiles are vertically adjustable in response to the use of the terrain below, doubling as performance backdrop or proscenium. To the north, the seed archive acts as a magnifying lens through which to interrogate the Cottage at close range, whilst to the south, a glazed curtain wall opens up onto a further landscaped stage and fire pit. This circular gathering point is suggestive of the enclosing windbreak and communal hearth of Indigenous Australian sites, alongside traditional fire-centric land management practices and ceremony.[25]

Telescopic Lenses

Through the binding medium of this *Cook Cloak*, the woven *Wunderkammer* and seed archive act as agents of reclamation and exposure. By creating distance from its immediate context, the Cottage confronts its contemporary identity and by externalising its domesticated collection, enters into the rhetoric of its own display. In parallel, the seed repository resonates with the lost natural history of the site through objects which encapsulate the possibility of growth and renewal, whilst creating space for traditional ceremony and knowledge exchange. Experiencing the Cottage and observing it from an elevated position, the structure can be understood as an architectural accretion and the inner curtain of a larger and more complex display (Fig. 4). In spirit of the dialogic intent of the civic museum, ultimately these interventions aspire to stitch into the new era of cultural exchange and reflection which 2020 intensified. Empowered by the house not so much as a Cottage but a curatorially situated and haptically experienced artefact, the *Cloak* is pinned at the bifurcated focus of an open-weave, deeply rooted vitrine—a polemic physical presence is thus reframed, recast.

01 Lisa Sullivan, A Collection and a Cottage, exh. cat. (Parkville: Ian Potter Museum of Art, University of Melbourne, 2000), 7-9.

02 "The Cook Cottage," *The Age*, October 9, 1934, http://nla.gov.au/nla.news-article205873840.

03 Maryanne McCubbin, "Cooked to Perfection: Cooks' Cottage and the Exemplary Historical Figure," in *Journal of Popular Culture* 33, no. 1 (1999): 41, http://search.proquest.com.ezp.lib.unimelb.edu.au/docview/195367501?accountid=12372.

04 Hermon Gill, *Captain Cooks' Cottage* (Melbourne: Lothian, 1934), 15-17. http://handle.slv.vic.gov.au/10381/115001; H. N. B. Wettenhall, *Cooks' Cottage: JCG 1755, in memory of James Cook* (Melbourne: Joint Management Committee, 1979), 26, 33.

05 Aboriginal Victoria, "William Cooper," Aboriginal Victoria, last updated September 29, 2019, https://www.aboriginalvictoria.vic.gov.au/william-cooper; Francesco Vitelli, "Epic Memory and dispossession: the Shrine and the Memory Wars," *Mongrel Publications*, no. 1 (April 2005): 15.

06 Vitelli, "Epic Memory and dispossession: the Shrine and the Memory Wars," 15; City of Melbourne, "Fitzroy Gardens," Fitzroy Gardens Visitor Centre, accessed July 17 2020. https://www.melbourne.vic.gov.au/fitzroy-gardens/FitzroyGardens/Pages/History.aspx.

07 Pierre Nora, "Between Memory and History: Les Lieux de Mémoire," *Representations*, no. 26 (1989): 7-24, http://www.jstor.com/stable/2928520; James Young, "Germany's memorial question: Memory, counter-memory, and the end of the monument," *The South Atlantic Quarterly* 96, no. 4 (1997): 853-880, http://search.proquest.com.ezp.lib.unimelb.edu.au/docview/197290374?accountid=12372.

08 Society of Architectural Historians, "Part 1: Removal of Monuments from Public Spaces," moderated by Bryan Clark Green, 1:18:20. https://vimeo.com/438768223; Quentin Stevens and Karen Franck, "From Straightforward to Challenging," In Memorials As Spaces of Engagement: Design, Use and Meaning (London: Taylor & Francis Group, 2015), 34-60. https://ebookcentral.proquest.com/lib/unimelb/detail.action?docID=3570234.

09 Maria Nugent, "Historical encounters: Aboriginal testimony and colonial forms of commemoration," *Aboriginal History* 30 (2006): 33-44. http://www.jstor.com/stable/24046895.

10 McCubbin, "Cooked to Perfection: Cooks' Cottage and the Exemplary Historical Figure," 128.

11 Sullivan, *A Collection and a Cottage*, 10; McCubbin, "Cooked to Perfection: Cooks' Cottage and the Exemplary Historical Figure," 43.

12 Works of Art from the Russell and Mab Grimwade Bequest: the University of Melbourne Art Collection (Parkville: Museum of Art, University of Melbourne, 1989), vi.

13 Chris Healy, *From the ruins of colonialism: history as social memory* (Melbourne: Cambridge University Press, 1997), 32-39.

14 Anne Bordeleau, "Monumentality and Contemporaneity in the Work of Tarkovsky, Goldsworthy, and Zumthor," in *Chora 7: Intervals in the Philosophy of Architecture*, edited by Pérez-Gómez Alberto and Parcell Stephen (Montreal: McGill-Queen's University Press, 2016), 16-18, www.jstor.org/stable/j.ctt19jch8m.4.

15 Caroline Ednie, "Inside Carmody Groarke's Hill House Box in Scotland," *Wallpaper*, published 6 June 2019, https://www.wallpaper.com/architecture/hill-house-box-carmody-groarke-scotland.

16 Edmund De Waal, "Library of exile (installation view) 2019," Edmund de Waal artist's website, accessed August 9, 2020, https://www.edmunddewaal.com/making/library-of-exile#6.

17 Peter Zumthor Serpentine Pavilion 2011," Diversaire, published June 28, 2011, https://divisare.com/projects/170887-peter-zumthor-helene-binet-oscar-ferrari-serpentine-pavilion-2011.

18 Tanya Harrod, "Web Master: How Anni Albers Redefined Weaving as a Modern Art Form." Apollo, 188, no. 668 (2018): 99-100, https://search.ebscohost.com/login.aspx?direct=true&AuthType=sso&db=edsbl&AN=RN617343483&site=eds-live&scope=site.

19 Wettenhall, Cooks' Cottage: JCG 1755, in memory of James Cook, 7-9; Museums Victoria, "Ditty Bag," Victorian Collections, last updated July 31, 2020, https://victoriancollections.net.au/items/521602ef19403a17c4b9fb68.

20 The University of Melbourne, "Grimwade Collection," The University of Melbourne Herbarium Collection Online, accessed September 12, 2020, https://online.herbarium.unimelb.edu.au/collection/grimwade-collection#description.

21 Royal Botanic Gardens Victoria, "National Herbarium of Victoria," accessed September 12, 2020, https://www.rbg.vic.gov.au/science/herbarium-and-resources/national-herbarium-of-victoria.

22 The University of Melbourne, "Mandy Nicholson's Possum Skin Cloak," Cultural Commons NAIDOC week article, accessed November 11, 2020, https://culturalcommons.edu.au/mandy-nicholsons-possum-skin-cloak/.

23 Healy, *From the ruins of colonialism: history as social memory*, 37.

24 Maree Clarke, Ancestral Memory (2019), glass, steel, in: The University of Melbourne, Ancestral Memory, exh. cat. (Melbourne: The Old Quad, The University of Melbourne, 2019), p.15; archival map: Department of Crown Lands Survey (Vic), East Melbourne, c.1858-1888.

25 Bruce Pascoe, *Dark Emu* (Broome: Magabala Books Aboriginal Corporation, 2014), pp.120,166.

26 Rory Hyde and Alan Pert, "MSD at HOME with Rory Hyde: Design and Public Life," livestreamed discussion. September 3, 2020, 6-7.30pm.

Fig. 3 (Opposite): The seed archive - spaces of collection and connection.

All images by the author.

REROOTING TREES, BURYING SKYSCRAPERS

UNSETTLING THE FOUNDATIONS OF A SETTLER COLONIAL GEOSPHERE

Boyd Hellier Knox

Every spring, Melbourne's London Plane trees are injected with hormones to reduce their 'anti-social effects.' As the name of this seemingly nefarious tree would indicate, it is a species that is far from local. An import from Western Europe, the Plane was planted throughout Melbourne, for its significance as a member of a colonial kit-of-parts that sought to create a homage to the motherland. It is in this homage that an immersive and familiar codified space is perpetuated, with the architecture and objects of Melbourne coalescing as unified, highly legible work: a colonial *gesamtkunstwerk*. The *gesamtkunstwerk* of the colonial city is overwhelming in its immersion and permeance. This complete work does not stop at the boundaries of architecture and planning. It extends to and shapes a wider ecology, inclusive of flora, geology and the human. Its authorship by the coloniser is complex but deliberate, and its motivations plural. As the realisation of an ideology in physical space, the colonial city presents as a stubborn bulwark to processes of decolonisation. New pocket parks of native planting and A4 size plaques of pre-colonial history do little to belie its ubiquity.

On Melbourne's early 19th century Hoddle Grid, pedestrian-scaled manifestations of settler colonialism are found in the Victoriana street signs telling of Queen, King, or William Streets and in the colonial statues of explorers who exude dubious moral standing. These objects reinforce the aspirations of the colony as an extension of the coloniser, and the superiority complex evoked by this aspirational mimicry. Similar objects to those found in Australia may be spotted from Kenya to Hong Kong, Anguilla to Mumbai—places all grappling with the redefinition of their post-colonial identities. The unifying Hoddle Grid and its corresponding *gesamtkunstwerk* immediately displaced all pre-existing, pre-colonial epistemologies, creating a codified space that befits the objectives of the coloniser. While buildings and planning serve a central role in this new urban environment, it is often the objects imported into the grid that contribute to pervasive colonial urbanism.

Maps

Plan of the Melbourne Botanic Gardens - G.A. Yorston (1948).

Guide Plan to the Melbourne Botanic Gardens and Surroundings - W.J. Butson (1911).

Plan No. 26 (South Melbourne & Melbourne - Melbourne and Metropolitan Board of Works (1994).

Plan of the Government House Reserve, Botanic Garden and its Domain indicating the Principal Plantations - Drawn under direction of Dr. F Mueller by E.B. Heyne (1864).

Royal Botanic Gardens, Melbourne - Division of Survey and Mapping (1978).

Plan of the Melbourne Botanic Garden by William R. Guilfoyle - J. Noone (1875).

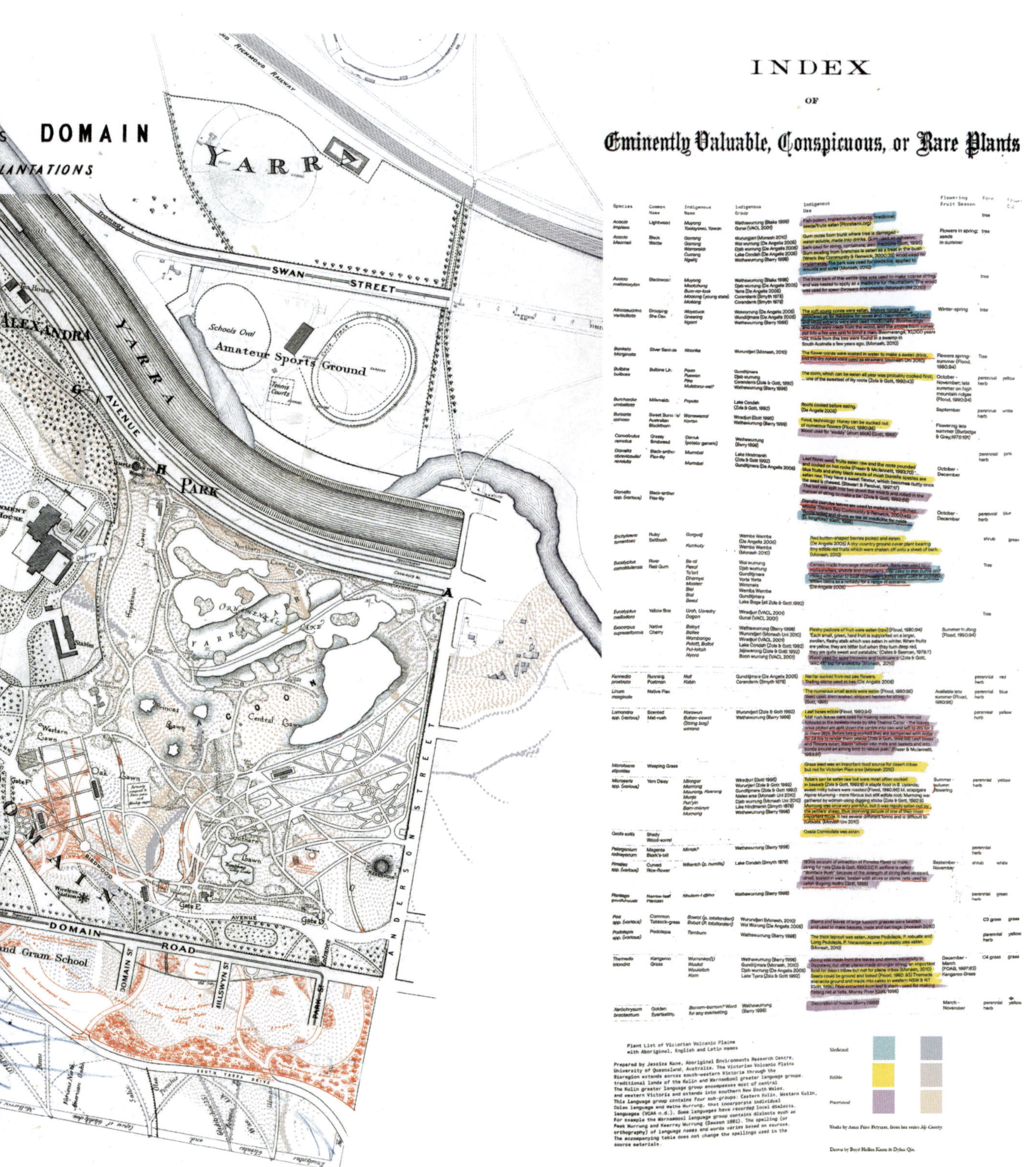

INDEX

OF

Eminently Valuable, Conspicuous, or Rare Plants

Species	Common Name	Indigenous Name	Indigenous Group	Indigenous Use	Flowering Fruit Season	Form	Flower Col
Acacia implexa	Lightwood	*Muyong* *Toolayowa, Yowan*	Wathawurrung (Blake 1998) Gunai (VACL 2001)	Fish poison, implements/artefacts, medicinal, seeds/fruits eaten (Florabank.org)		tree	
Acacia Mearnsii	Black Wattle	*Garrong* *Garrong* *Warraraik* *Currong* *Ngalij*	Wurungjeri (Monash 2010) Woi wurrung (De Angelis 2005) Djab wurrung (De Angelis 2005) Lake Condah (De Angelis 2005) Wathawurrung (Barry 1998)	Gum oozes from trunk where tree is damaged - water-soluble, made into drinks. Gum used as adhesive; bark used for string, containers; also medicine (Gott, 1995) Gum exuding from branches is eaten as a treat in the bush (Wreck Bay Community & Renwick, 2000:33) wood used for implements. The bark was used for medicine, applied to wounds and sores (Monash, 2010)	Flowers in spring; seeds in summer	tree	
Acacia melanoxylon	Blackwood	*Muyong* *Mootchung* *Burn-no-look* *Moolung* (young state) *Moilong*	Wathawurrung (Blake 1998) Djab wurrung (De Angelis 2005) Yarra (De Angelis 2005) Coranderrk (Smyth 1878) Coranderrk (Smyth 1878)	The inner bark of this wattle tree was used to make coarse string and was heated to apply as a medicine for rheumatism. The wood was used for spear-throwers and shields. (Monash Uni 2010)		tree	
Allocasuarina Verticillata	Drooping She Oak	*Wayetuck* *Gneering* *Ngarri*	Woiwurrung (De Angelis 2005) Wundjjmara (De Angelis 2005) Wathawurrung (Barry 1998)	The soft young cones were eaten. Mature cones were powdered up for medicine for sores and rheumatism, and bark and wood extracts were also used medicinally. Boomerangs and clubs were made from the wood, and the smoke from cones put into a fire was said to blind a man. Boomerangs, 10,000 years old, made from this tree were found in a swamp in South Australia a few years ago. (Monash, 2010)	Winter-spring	tree	
Banksia Marginata	Silver Banksia	*Woorike*	Wurundjeri (Monash, 2010)	The flower-cones were soaked in water to make a sweet drink, and the dry cones were used as strainers. (Monash Uni 2010)	Flowers spring-summer (Flood, 1980:94)	Tree	
Bulbine bulbosa	Bulbine Lily	*Parm* *Puewan* *Pike* *Mulotoru-weil?*	Gunditjmara Djab wurrung Coranderrk (Zola & Gott, 1992) Wathawurrung (Barry 1998)	The corm, which can be eaten all year was probably cooked first; ... one of the sweetest of lily roots (Zola & Gott, 1992:43)	October - November; late summer on high mountain ridges (Flood, 1980:94)	perennial herb	yellow
Burchardia umbellata	Milkmaids	*Popoto*	Lake Condah (Zola & Gott, 1992)	Roots cooked before eating. (De Angelis 2005)	September	perennial herb	white
Bursaria spinosa	Sweet Bursaria/ Australian Blackthorn	*Wonnewarra/ Korron*	Wiradjuri (Gott 1995) Wathawurrung (Barry 1998)	Food, technology. Honey can be sucked out of numerous flowers (Flood, 1980:95) Wood used for 'waddy' (short stick) (Gott, 1995)	Flowering late summer (Burbidge & Gray,1976:191)		
Convolvulus remotus	Grassy Bindweed	*Darnuk* (potato: generic)	Wathawurrung (Barry 1998)				
Dianella adrevicaulis/ revoluta	Black-anther Flax-lily	*Mumbal* *Mumbal*	Lake Hindmarsh (Zola & Gott 1992) Gunditjmara (De Angelis 2005)	Leaf fibres used, fruits eaten raw and the roots pounded and cooked on hot rocks (Fraser & McJannett, 1993:70) '... blue fruits and shiny black seeds of most Dianella species are eaten raw. They have a sweet flavour, which becomes nutty once the seed is chewed. (Stewart & Percival, 1997:17) 'The leaf was split into two down the midrib and rolled in the manner of string to make a tie.' (Zola & Gott, 1992:59)	October - December	perennial herb	pink
Dianella spp. (various)	Black-anther Flax-lily			Dianella caerulea leaves are used to make a high-pitched whistle.' (Wreck Bay Community & Renwick, 2000:45) 'Roots boiled and drunk as tea as medicine for colds (D. longifolia)' (Gott, 1995)	October - December	perennial herb	blue
Enchylaena tomentosa	Ruby Saltbush	*Gurgudj* *Kurrkuty*	Wemba Wemba (De Angelis 2005) Wemba Wemba (Monash 2010)	Red button-shaped berries picked and eaten. (De Angelis 2005) A dry-country ground cover plant bearing tiny edible red fruits which were shaken off onto a sheet of bark. (Monash, 2010)		shrub	green
Eucalyptus camaldulensis	River Red Gum	*Be-al* *Peeal* *To'ort* *Dharnya* *Moolerr* *Biel* *Bial* *Beeul*	Woi wurrung Djab wurrung Gunditjmara Yorta Yorta Wimmera Wemba Wemba Gunditjmara Lake Boga (all Zola & Gott 1992)	Canoes made from large sheets of bark. Bark also used to make shelters, shields and containers. [illegible] used to treat burns and mixed with water to treat [illegible] were used in aromatic steam baths as a remedy for a range of ailments. (De Angelis 2005)		Tree	
Eucalyptus melliodora	Yellow Box	*Urah, Uoredry* *Dagon*	Wiradjuri (VACL 2001) Gunai (VACL 2001)			Tree	
Exocarpus cupressiformis	Native Cherry	*Baloyt* *Ballee* *Wombarigo* *Palott, Ballot* *Pul-loitch* *Nyora*	Wathawurrung (Barry 1998) Wurundjeri (Monash Uni 2010) Wiradjuri (VACL 2001) Lake Condah (Zola & Gott 1992) Jajowerong (Zola & Gott 1992) Boon wurrung (VACL 2001)	Fleshy pedicels of fruit were eaten (raw) (Flood, 1980:94) 'Each small, green, hard fruit is supported on a larger, swollen, fleshy stalk which was eaten in winter. When fruits are yellow, they are bitter but when they turn deep red, they are quite sweet and palatable.' (Oates & Seeman, 1979:7) Wood used for spearthrowers and bullroarers (Zola & Gott, 1992:47) sap for snakebite (Monash, 2010)	Summer fruiting (Flood, 1980:94)		
Kennedia prostrata	Running Postman	*Nulf* *Kobin*	Gunditjmara (De Angelis 2005) Coranderrk (Smyth 1878)	Nectar sucked from red pea flowers. Trailing stems used as ties. (De Angelis 2005)		perennial herb	red
Linum marginale	Native Flax			The numerous small seeds were eaten (Flood, 1980:95) Seed used, stem soaked, stripped beaten for string (Gott, 1995)	Available late summer (Flood, 1980:95)	perennial herb	blue
Lomandra spp. (various)	Scented Mat-rush	*Korowun* *Bollan-cowat* (String bag) *wirrano*	Wurundjeri (Zola & Gott 1992) Wathawurrung (Barry 1998)	Leaf bases edible (Flood, 1980:94) Mat rush leaves were used for making baskets. The method followed in the baskets made by Mrs Thelma Carter - the leaves once picked are split down the centre into two and left to dry for 3 or more days. Before being worked they are dampened with water for 24 hrs to render them pliable (Zola & Gott, 1992:59) Leaf bases and flowers eaten. leaves woven into mats and baskets and into bands around an aching limb to relieve pain.' (Fraser & McJannett, 1993:51)		perennial herb	yellow
Microlaena stipoides	Weeping Grass			Grass seed was an important food source for desert tribes but not for Victorian Plain area (Monash 2010)			
Microseris spp. (various)	Yam Daisy	*Minngar* *Murnong* *Muurang, Keerong* *Munja* *Pun'yin* *Bam-mānya* *Murnong*	Wiradjuri (Gott 1995) Wurunjeri (Zola & Gott 1992) Gunditjmara (Zola & Gott 1992) Males area (Monash Uni 2010) Djab wurrung (Monash Uni 2010) Lke Hindmarsh (Smyth 1878) Wathawurrung (Barry 1998)	Tubers can be eaten raw but were most often cooked in baskets (Zola & Gott, 1992:8) A staple food in S. Uplands; sweet milky tubers were roasted (Flood, 1980:96) M. scapigera Alpine Murnong - more fibrous but still edible root; Murnong was gathered by women using digging sticks (Zola & Gott, 1992:8) Murnong was once very plentiful, but it was rapidly eaten out by the settlers' sheep, thus depriving people of one of their most important foods. It has several different forms and is difficult to cultivate. (Monash Uni 2010)	Summer - autumn flowering	perennial herb	yellow
Oxalis exilis	Shady Wood-sorrel			Oxalis Corniculata was eaten			
Pelargonium rodneyanum	Magenta Stork's-bill	*Mirrak?*	Wathawurrung (Barry 1998)			perennial herb	
Pimelea spp. (various)	Curved Rice-flower	*Wikerich (p. humilis)*	Lake Condah (Smyth 1878)	1830s account of extraction of Pimelea fibres to make string for nets (Zola & Gott, 1992:32) P. axiflora is called "Bootlace Bush" because of the strength of string Bark stripped, dried, soaked in water, beaten with sticks or stone, nets used to catch Bogong moths (Gott, 1995)	September - November	shrub	white
Plantago gaudichaudii	Narrow-leaf Plantain	*Nhulom-I djino*	Wathawurrung (Barry 1998)			perennial herb	green
Poa spp. (various)	Common Tussock-grass	*Bowat (p. labillardieri)* *Bobat (P. labillardieri)*	Wurundjeri (Monash, 2010) Woi Wurung (De Angelis 2005)	Stems and leaves of large tussock grasses were twisted and used to make baskets, mats and net-bags. (Monash 2010)		C3 grass	grass
Podolepis spp. (various)	Podolepis	*Tambum*	Wathawurrung (Barry 1998)	The thick taproot was eaten. Alpine Podolepis, P. robusta and Long Podolepis, P. hieracioides were probably also eaten. (Monash, 2010)		perennial herb	yellow
Themeda triandra	Kangaroo Grass	*Worronkoi(t)* *Wuulot* *Wuuloitch* *Kom*	Wathawurrung (Barry 1998) Gunditjmara (Monash, 2010) Djab wurrung (De Angelis 2005) Lake Tyers (Zola & Gott 1992)	String was made from the leaves and stems, especially in Gippsland, but other plants made stronger string; an important food for desert tribes but not for plains tribes (Monash, 2010) Seeds could be ground and baked (Flood, 1980: 93) Themeda avenacea ground and made into cakes in western NSW & NT (Gott, 1995) Fibre extracted from leaf & stem - used for making fishing net at Yelta, Murray River (Gott, 1995)	December - March (FOAB, 1997:83) Kangaroo Grass	C4 grass	grass
Xerochrysum bracteatum	Golden Everlasting	*Borrom-borrom?* Word for any everlasting	Wathawurrung (Barry 1998)	Decoration of houses (Barry (1998)	March - November	perennial herb	yellow

Plant List of Victorian Volcanic Plains with Aboriginal, English and Latin names

Prepared by Jessica Kane, Aboriginal Environments Research Centre, University of Queensland, Australia. The Victorian Volcanic Plains Bioregion extends across south-western Victoria through the traditional lands of the Kulin and Warnambool greater language groups. The Kulin greater language group encompasses most of central and western Victoria and extends into southern New South Wales. This language group contains four sub-groups: Eastern Kulin, Western Kulin, Colac language and Watha Wurrung, that incorporate individual languages (VCAA n.d.). Some languages have recorded local dialects. For example the Warnambool language group contains dialects such as Peek Wurrung and Keerray Wurrung (Dawson 1881). The spelling (or orthography) of language names and words varies based on sources. The accompanying table does not change the spellings used in the source materials.

Medicinal

Edible

Functional

Works by Anna Price Petyarre, from her series *My Country*

Drawn by Boyd Hellier Knox & Dylan Qin.

London Plane trees are just one such object of the colonial-*gesamtkunstwerk*. Highly resistant to pollution, London Planes can withstand the toxic and exploitative practices of colonial industry through their constant shedding of bark. Similarly, their sleek leaves easily cast-off urban grime. Planes may also be heavily pollarded, or aggressively pruned, in order to accommodate infrastructural elements such as power lines. Most salient however, is the London Plane's evocation of the Picturesque—read 'civilised'—gardens and streets of Western Europe, where they accounted for over 60% of London's urban trees during the 1920s. The assumed superiority of imported flora superseding indigenous flora is recounted in a pompous Francis Myers anecdote on a Sydney garden in 1886. Of the giant pine species he wrote "as the tree of a foreign forest, towering over all those of native growth, it stands symbolical of the established supremacy of immigrants of foreign sap over the old native race."[1]

Melbourne's Plane trees are in the process of being removed. Currently comprising 70% of the CBD tree population, they are unable to respond to the powerful impacts of climate change in Australia.[2] Though remarkable in its hardiness, this Northern Hemisphere native struggles with the increasing occurrence of 45-degree days. Once seemingly invulnerable, the tree finds itself a victim to one of the greatest consequences of the maladaptive thinking found in the colonial mindset.[3] When the recreation of an ideological image is prioritised over a connection and response to place, it is the ecology that suffers through maladaptation and impropriety.

London Plane trees are just one example of flora co-opted as colonising object. These, and many other imported plants populate Melbourne's Royal Botanic Gardens. The gardens' picturesque approach is anthropocentric; it orients planting to the human gaze. Plants in the Gardens are part of a collection, with their collectability indicative of their object status. Such objects are assembled into a curated, groomed ecology for the viewing pleasure of a colonising audience. In contrast, Indigenous Australian ways of understanding Country position flora as subjects of reciprocity; Deborah Rose Bird describes Country "as a place that gives and receives life."[4] If care is given, care will be returned. Plants are valued for their medicinal, spiritual, functional and edible properties, with knowledge passed on between generations through oral histories. Flora figures in Indigenous belief systems, with oral histories such as the 'bush yam dreaming' associated with a diet staple, reflecting the dignity and respect offered by Indigenous Australians to that which provides sustenance.[5]

This palimpsest (previous page) is a conceptual analysis of Melbourne's Royal Botanic Gardens, that explores intersections between Indigenous and colonial relationships to flora. Combining seven maps of the Royal Botanic Gardens from between 1864 and 1994, the work highlights a constant restyling of the colonial Gardens to the fashions of the time. Carefully positioned rose gardens, lawns and ornamental lakes are indicators of flora rendered as object, and appeal to the ideals of the colonial society. Overlayed is an artwork by Indigenous woman Anna Petyarre, from her series *My Country*, accompanied by an index of native flora. These trees and plants speak to the harmonious and reciprocal relationship that First Australians have with the landscape, a stark contrast to that of the settler. Plants are sorted into three categories—medicinal, edible and functional. The foundation for this categorisation was from a list prepared by Jessica Kane, of the Aboriginal Environments Centre at the University of Queensland.[6] Utilising this species list, the artwork functions as landscape plan, re-painting the Picturesque landscape with the richness of an ancient understanding of Country.

The outcome is a work that is a disarray of dots, paths and text notes. While the planting populates the landscape, it is still the solidity of colonial-era buildings, earthworks and objects that appears to dominate. In this way, the work is folly, with any mission for a 'reconciliation through plants' far too little and far too late. Non-Aboriginal Australians planting natives in their settled Gardens will not undo processes of invasion and dispossession.

Given the deeply lasting and powerful scale, harm and time of the settler colonial project in Australia, this work advocates for an attitude of criticality and truth telling in establishing new avenues of discourse. Such a strategy involves questioning the historical continuum of settler logic that has come to characterise much of Melbourne today. Libby Porter speaks to the continuation of the colonial project through urban development, stating that it is one of the "structure[s] that underpins all subsequent and future acts of settling."[7] This continuation is evidenced through the rampant commodification of land, an ingrained practise that has escalated rapidly since colonisation. Perhaps the greatest material development in the world of land as property, is that of verticality. Where Plane trees were motifs for the 'civilising' power of the colony, towers and skyscrapers are symbolic of the contemporary capitalistic city.

Questions of Context, Conditions of Interior

MSD Thesis Design Outcome

Just as the colonial toolkit of Plane trees, street names and settler statues are paradoxically both global and local, so too are the hallmarks of the capitalistic city. Glass curtain walls, Uber ranks and maximised floor area ratios are some of the icons of the multinational endeavour. It is a globally familiar urban ecology, illustrative of a financial system often detached from physical place. Just as the commodification of land in the wake of colonialism ruthlessly carved out winners and losers, so too does this new moment in city making. Indigenous practitioner Sarah Lynn Rees speaks to the denial of history and environment in contemporary cities, that leaves us "without any sense of place, culture and identity."[8] The arbiters of this city are predominantly capital and market forces. It is in this urban ecology of dubious standing where critical questions of contextuality and urbanism may be asked, and where tentative responses may be unearthed in the geology, archaeology, as well as ecology of the site.

In Melbourne, the looming presence of the capitalistic city is most felt in the blocks north of Latrobe Street, where a rapidly developing ensemble of nondescript towers dwarf those found in Hong Kong, Tokyo or New York.[9] They speak to a capital motivated moment in city-making, divorced from the obligation to cater to the resident, the visitor and the non-human. In responding to this largely placeless context, an approach grounded in geology and ecology offers relevance for delivering an architecture and city, driven by criticality, introspection and curiosity. To engage with this matter is to grapple with the site on a vastly different scale, both temporally and spatially. Geology does not simply chart rock formations or technical specificities, but moments and fragments on a timescale that is largely incomprehensible. Indeed acknowledging, harnessing, and building in earth stretches back to the earliest moments in human settlement. This is a construction technology that transcends time and borders, but is deeply in touch with place.

Failing to be viably commercialised, earth building largely stands outside the capitalistic building industry. That is despite earth housing providing for 30% of the world's population, often constructed by those who then dwell there.[10] In 1950s Melbourne, earth building took on an association with the bohemian counterculture, offering individuals and families the opportunity to construct their own dwellings. These houses existed outside the dominant aesthetic and societal structures of the time, engaging with a respectful relationship to the land which stood at odds to the exploitative practises of the coloniser. My family have something of an affinity for earth building. My grandfather, Alistair Knox, was a significant Australian environmental architect, well known for his work building mud brick houses. Using materials excavated or found on site, his projects were inextricably contextual. Occasionally reading his books while writing this text, I was continually struck by the continuity of thought, both socio-politically and architecturally. In the present climate, the thinking that drove much of this movement has significant value and relevance, through the embedded understanding that the ground that one stands upon is much more than a simple surface or stage.

These questions of context, geology and ecology drove my 2020 Masters thesis proposal, titled *Questions of Context, Conditions of Interior*, supervised by Professor Alan Pert. The project was situated at A'Beckett Urban Square, one of the few remaining unbuilt plots in this part of Melbourne's CBD. While any visual trace of a geological history has been surfaced by concrete and bitumen long ago, the remaining ground plane stands in sharp relief to the overwhelming vertical surrounding. This break in the skyline is soon to be lost to a 24-level mixed use tower designed by Denton Corker Marshall, speaking a familiar commercialised language of patterned panels. The tower typology carries significant ethical, environmental, social and architectural baggage as a result of its role as the preeminent architectural typology of capitalism. However, it was understood in this project that to propose anything other than a tower for this site would be a disengagement with the realities of site, real estate, and capital, as well as the existing proposal.

The subsequent thesis proposal is for a tower driven by a sense of civic generosity, developed through a forensic study of the site's archaeology and geology. The tower projects 100 metres above ground, and 100 metres below ground. All excavated soil remains within with envelope of the building, as it is presently tainted by arsenic, lead and mercury from historical industries. In the tower, this toxic matter remains within the envelope, rearranged, nullified and instrumentalised within its new sarcophagus. During this process, the placement of soil generates a positive form. Its removal leaves a negative space and a new interior. This interaction between a once untouched ancient geology and the unchecked toxicity of an early, growing Melbourne is emblematic of contemporary discourse on colonialism, place and environment.

Furthermore, in a quiet but deliberate manner, this project usurps the colonial Hoddle Grid. The tower is oriented two degrees askew of the grid, with its orientation determined by the dominant line of pedestrian approach and an unused laneway, thereby undermining the strictly perpendicular city plan. A planting scheme developed from the Royal Botanic Gardens analysis (see title page) carries through to this site, where the organic forms of native flora are emplaced.

Although the site's ecology was deeply questioned, it was not until the pragmatics and realities of construction were considered that the nature of this quasi-tower's built form became clear. Earth is a material that we learn to understand as children, at beaches, playing in the mud or in sandpits, rendering its properties utterly unambiguous to the human experience. Hence, gravity informs the form and construction of this tower. Likewise, the tower's construction methodology never allows soil to enter or leave the site; the site's geology is simply rearranged vertically. As geological matter is excavated, it is moved to the topside, and repurposed as formwork for the main hall. While the mining operation is inescapably anthropogenic, the mounded geology, through its material tendencies and angle of repose, determines the form of the tower. This natural settling point is then held in place by a combination of geotextile fabric, soil nails and shotcrete—rough and candid detailing.

This commentary advocates for the significance of practitioners in acknowledging geology and ecology when designing for place. It is in the spirit of Libby Porter's musings: "when Country sits at the heart of our thinking, then place, land, earth, water, sky and rock come to story not as resources and inert matter to be struggled for, but as vital place."[11] Through a critical investigation of the city, from its trees and skyscrapers to its bedrock and soil conditions, one may begin to piece together the myriad manners in which existing power structures may either be obliviously perpetuated, or slyly evaded. Ultimately, the final built proposal does not masquerade magical solution to pervasive forces; rather it probingly Questions—as per its title—an established Context, and humbly yet persistently aims to re-arrange something subversive, unsettling and down to earth.

Title page: Palimpsest map of the Melbourne Botanical Gardens.

Opposite: *Questions of Context, Conditions of Interior.* All images by the author.

01 Kylie Mirmohamadi, "'Wog plants go home': Race, ethnicity and horticulture in Australia," *Studies in Australian Garden History* 1 (2003): 93.

02 Melissa Davey, "Melbourne's plane trees to be replaced by species resistant to climate change," *The Guardian*, October 2019.

03 Val Plumwood, "Decolonising Australian gardens: gardening and the ethics of place," *Australian Humanities Review* 36 (2005): 3.

04 Deborah Rose Bird, *Nourishing Terrains: Australian Aboriginal Views of Landscape and Wilderness* (Canberra: Australian Heritage Commission, 1996).

05 David Roth, "Bush Yam Dreaming Yarla," *Japingka Gallery*, July 2019.

06 Maurio Baracco & Louise Wright, "Repair: Australian Pavilion," 16th International Architecture Exhibition, La Bienalle di Venezia 2018.

07 Libby Porter, "From an urban country to urban Country: confronting the cult of denial in Australian cities," *Australian Geographer*, 49:2, 239-246.

08 Sarah Lynn Rees for IndigenousX, "Our cities reflect the denial of history. Blak design aims to change that," *The Guardian*, July 2018.

09 Leanne Hodyl, 'Melbourne high rise densities much greater than world's highest densities,' *Planning News*, 41(2) (2015), p.16.

10 Laurence Keefe, *Earth building: methods and materials, repair and conservation,* (London: Taylor & Francis, 2005).

11 Porter, "From urban country," 244.

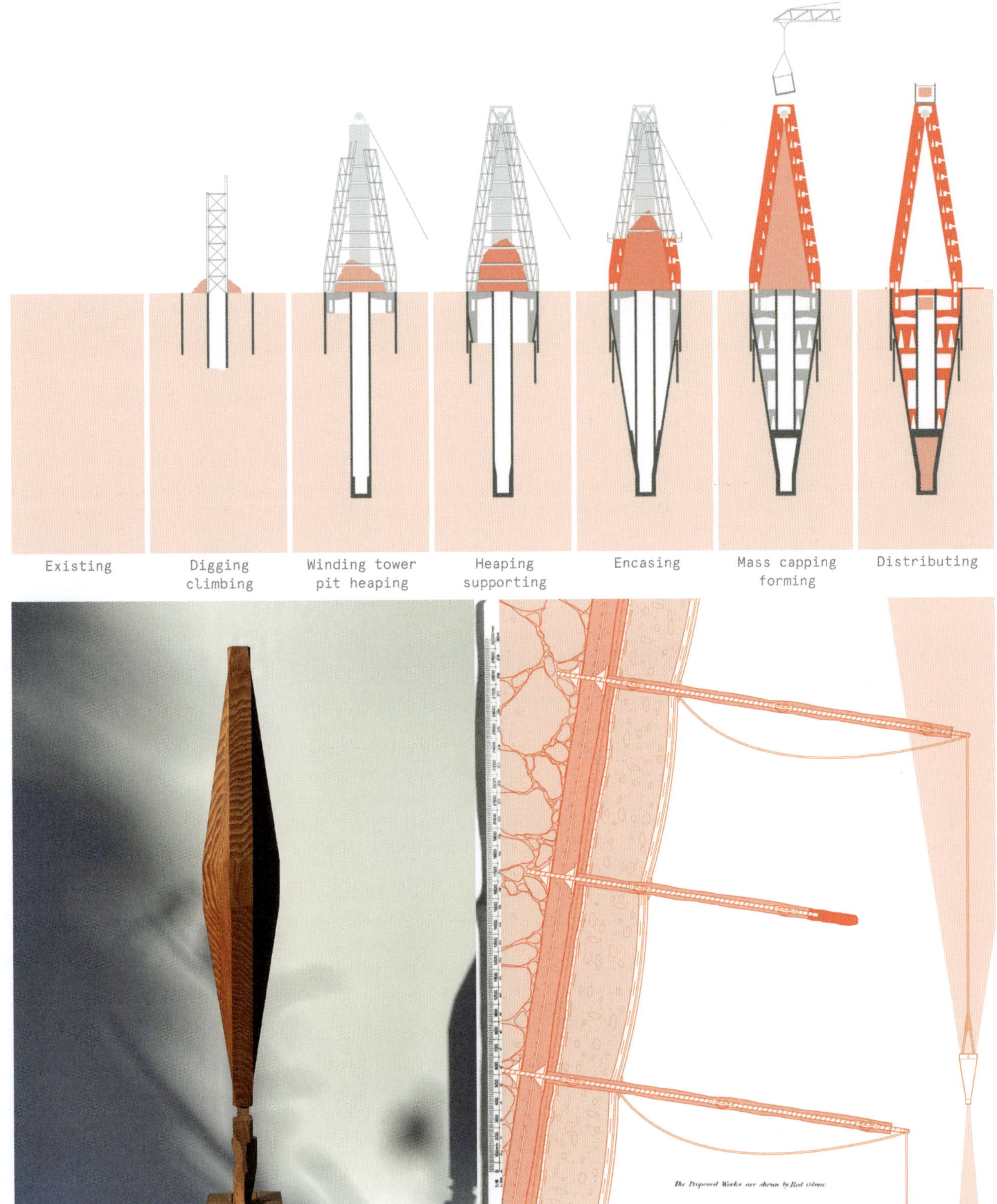
Existing
Digging
climbing
Winding tower
pit heaping
Heaping
supporting
Encasing
Mass capping
forming
Distributing
The Proposed Works are shewn by Red Colour.

TOUCHING SPACE

ON THE WORK OF PARTNERS HILL

Timothy Hill

Timothy Hill established Partners Hill in 2013 while based in London. Returning to Australia in 2014, the firm has since received extensive national and international recognition for their design work, which emphasises construction finesse and the potency of the plan. The following is transcribed from a conversation between Timothy Hill and Inflection *editors on the work and approach of Partners Hill.*

To the Touch

An especially Australian concept that we still have not overcome is that something is 'better' if it is rudimentary. For the interiors of the *Longhouse*, we aimed for something exquisite, but it is absolutely unlike the Australian idea that a country house is only legitimate if it is roughed up; a sort of bush fantasy.

One thing that is particular about our detailing is that it is very unevenly distributed. One 'cannot have party food all the time.' This is reminiscent of Aalto buildings, which are very uneven. Huge amounts of the *Longhouse* are very droll, but there is a lot of concentration on the moments that are going to matter. We focus a lot of very memorable and intense experiences at the points where people are endlessly going to have to encounter as they move through and use the building.

The other critical moment is where you touch the building. We organise a lot of detailed incidents around elements such as staircases and doors, where you are always in contact. At the *Install House*, there are two slightly different colours across the walls. The lower colour is generated by a layer of wax over what is extremely matte paint, the former is the layer you are inevitably going to come into contact with. While matte paint looks essential and fantastic in older buildings, if you touch a matte wall it is revolting. The waxed datum is very comfortable to touch and very viable to clean. This contrasts with the layer above which is its antithesis, a delicate, untouched, light reflective paint surface leading the atmosphere of the room.

The objective is to engage the imagination. Imagination tends to fail if all you are trying to do is impress—if the detailing is dominant then it is unengaging. What makes people exercise their imagination is inviting them to make acts of comparison; large with small, rough with smooth, public with private, in with out, landscape with constructed. By designing a space with unevenness and contrast, people can have that astonishing encounter with 'difference.' They start to actively imagine and feel fundamentally included in the space.

Above: *Longhouse* exterior by Partners Hill, 2019 Australian House of the Year, *Houses Award*. Photo by Rory Gardiner.

Buildings Inside Buildings

When approaching heritage, we are not just approaching a building, we are approaching an orthodoxy. Our primary approach is to be self-conscious, to understand what the building is on behalf of people and time—which is quite different from being compliance minded. We do not privilege a particular moment in time when considering a building's post-settlement heritage.

For example, *Install House* is one of the oldest 'buildings' in Australia. It was built in 1811, but because the house has a very sensible Georgian plan, it has had about 30 uses and the plan has served those uses. It had a major renovation in 1835, another one in 1870, and then another one in 1975. Our approach was to say that it has actually been of great service to an enormous number of people through time and therefore it would not be reasonable to preference one particular moment through our interventions. We do not ask, "should it be the 1811 version? Should it be the 1870 version?" Instead, we try to include and involve the things that have happened in the building throughout its life. It would be grotesquely egotistical to think that what we are doing now is somehow the most significant thing that has ever happened to the building.

At the *Install House*, we still have the doctor's hand warming basins from the 1970s, we have a ridiculous steel structure that stands in the middle of the kitchen—placed in 1975 to pour a concrete slab over the beautiful 19th century veranda for bathroom floors. We have kept it all because it is part of what has happened in the place. The most important thing is that the plan keeps demonstrating how versatile the building is. We have been able to use it simultaneously as a townhouse an office, a gallery and a shop. It is where people live, where people stay, where we host functions . . . in that way it is very important that the agility of the plan remains its triumph. In recognising this, we actually have not touched the building. Instead, by making a suite of installations, we have just transformed the experience of it.

At Partners Hill, we often make buildings inside buildings, or change the routing, or deal with things that are illogical as illogical, rather than follow the tactic of 'cleaning it up' or making it ordered. I view it as decency. Who are we at this moment to think that we have more authority than all of the people who have come before us?

Above: Located in nipaluna/Hobart on the lands of the Muwinina people, *Install House* incorporates contrasting wall paint layers into the 200-year old building. Photo by Shantanu Starick.

Demands on Place

It would be selfish and completely against the heritage of making places for buildings to be over-particularised for the person who commissioned them. A person is commissioning a 'place within a place,' and it is peculiar to think that someone may direct it completely as their own personal object. When the great Florentine families were building their *Palazzi,* they were patrons, but they also wanted to make sure that it was excellent for the city, not just that it reflected them and their taste.

I have found that as people move through life, they exert very different demands on place. My effort has been to make a house not specific to family use, since the family is a short-lived period within most people's lives. The capacity for a 'house' to be other things as life changes and as the members of the household change, must include being able be to serve as many purposes as possible—there is a big difference between a 'family' and 'household.' This has been an affirming outcome of COVID-19; that people have been reminded that this massive investment, a home, could do a lot of other things.

My response concerns prioritising the organisation of the plans, while being sympathetic and studious. The plan is the element that determines the involvement of the site, the construction, the apparentness and coexistence of the landscape as well as the reconstruction of an imagined context. It is also the plan that decides if there is going to be flexibility over time, it designates experiences and exchanges of in and out, the effects of light and foremost the capacity for the occupant to adjust for different circumstances.

Above (left): Remnant steel column within the *Install House* now captured as part of a versatile kitchen prop by Partners Hill. Photo by Michael Wee.

Above (right): The *Longhouse* reconciles the desire of its owners to establish a boutique farm, cooking school, reception venue and home with an existing property holding. *Longhouse* is located in Elevated Plains, Victoria, on the lands of the Dja Dja Wurrung people of the Kulin nation. Photo by Rory Gardiner.

Logic and Deduction

There was no inspiration for the *Mermaid Multi-House*. If you are inspired, you can make dreadful mistakes. Instead, we must be very, very studious—a building is going to stand for a long time. And it is not one's own money. The last thing we should do as architects is to be inspired or, worse than that, be creative.

We know that if you need to spend a long time in a building, it is important to have a 'memorable place.' I have found that if you overlap the 'memorable place' with a lot of other functional things, such as organising thresholds or giving extra vantage points to rooms—it is amazing. All of the things that you never imagined would happen in a space, will probably happen there.

The *Mermaid Multi-House* needed to be vastly multifunctional as a multigenerational household, so we already had a fundamental logic to expand on. The next step was to deduce what organisation would make the occupation memorable, even though the site has no prospect or views. It is a classic non-architect site—I love these sites. After decades of architects doing houses with views and after seeing so many justifications for plans organised around views, I can assure you that views wear off. Just go for a walk and look at how many curtains are drawn. But there are other things to enjoy. For example, by putting a pair of double height arcades together, the edges of the connected rooms could all be ventilated and lit from two sides at least, and most of the rooms are in fact lit from three sides.

A great thing you need to do when designing a building is to try and make the ordinary rooms good. Once you start to deduce all of these spatial connections, it is just an act of patient, lateral deduction. No inspiration, but a lot of obligation. We try to conduct ourselves deductively. We ask, after a studious glance and with a listening ear, what is really happening around us?

Above (both): *Mermaid Multihouse* is located in Mermaid Beach, Queensland, on the lands of the Yugambeh people. Two slightly different sized and planned occupations stand divided by a party wall to cater for multigenerational living. Generous arcade-like outdoor spaces act as innovative and multifunctional climate modifiers. Photo (left) by Shantanu Starick. Photo (right) by Alex Chomicz.

OH BB BB!

A COLLECTIVE REVIEW OF SIBLING ARCHITECTURE AND ADAM NATHANIEL FURMAN'S BOUDOIR BABYLON

Helen Rix Runting, Claude Dutson and Janek Ożmin

For this Inflection *article, Timothy Moore of Sibling Architecture and artist Adam Nathaniel Furman proposed for theorist Helen Rix Runting to conduct a review of their collaborative installation,* Boudoir Babylon. *Mirroring the design process in its discursive format, Runting sought academic Claude Dutson and architect/artist Janek Ożmin to engage with ideas of queering architecture through a collective review of the project.*

"Come in single, leave as a throuple" was the cheeky tagline given to *Boudoir Babylon* by its designers. This spatial installation and interior scenography occupied the ground floor Gallery Kitchen space at the National Gallery of Victoria during the NGV Triennial, from December 19th, 2020–April 18th, 2021. The project is the result of a commissioned collaboration between Australian architecture practice Sibling and the London-based designer Adam Nathaniel Furman, and comprises of a central structure—part column, part catwalk, part amphitheatre seating—a series of freestanding screens that divide and structure the space around this central piece; and a surface graphic, which is applied to the walls, floor and ceiling of the space. Furman describes the work as a response to "a commission to queer the Museum's 400-square-metre café and surrounding space,"[1] placing queerness at the conceptual centre of the work. Sibling describe the project in norm-critical terms as seeking to "challenge and rethink norms of how people come together and socialise."[2] The installation uses bold pastel colours, psychedelic patterning, glory-hole perforations and iconographic references to abstracted bodies and genitalia. The design is described by both architects as taking its point of departure from the three typologies of the boudoir, the salon and the nightclub.

In this text, we address Babylon Boudoir as a restless object and stage for an act of remote, collective criticism. The work is herein referred to (affectionately) as BB. We meet BB, and each other, on a simultaneous evening and morning in May 2021, in the geographically untethered platform space of a 'Zoom room.'

Exchange

HR: I can start by saying that I did actually visit BB in person: it was a few weeks back, I passed it in a mad dash through the NGV Triennial on a stolen afternoon. A good friend and I had snuck off from work. The Triennial was packed with people and with affirmative, bubbly, beautifully packaged stuff. Walking through the car park afterwards, it was like we had been in a shopping mall all afternoon—you know that sense of being exhausted, full and as a result a little empty? BB occupies the café, a space that is accessed from the ground floor lobby. It is a transition zone, adjoining the door to the big, juicy Jeff Koons sculpture and thus the entrance to the whole Triennial. In order to spend time with the installation, you have to stop in your tracks, right in the middle of this really hectic, high-volume cafeteria-lobby space. Having arrived in Melbourne only a couple of weeks before from Europe, this city with ostensibly no COVID and no social distancing at the time, I was a little . . . revolted by the sheer number of bodies that completely covered the thing: cranky old couples with overpriced sandwiches, the design crowd with glasses of wine, hanging out and staring at each other and children running around, everywhere. I wanted to get nearer, but my instinct was also, "get me out of here!" I think that is (pandemic) testament to the success of this piece. It is irresistibly popular.

The NGV is essentially made up a series of white cube galleries; and the Triennial is the event which uses those spaces to show 'what art can do.' BB is literally—physically—an entry point into that conversation. In Nina Power's essay 'Towards a Feminism of the Void,' she stakes the claim that men have been dominating the 'void' in art for so long, that feminism—as the critique of these binary structures that leave to the feminine only the role of being the negative pair of the masculine—needs to reclaim 'nothingness' and particularly to do so from all of those male phenomenologists and philosophers.[3] But whilst BB refuses to act fully as an art object—its qualities as an architectural interior, a room, prevent this—it also refuses

Boudoir Babylon occupied the Gallery Kitchen at the NGV Triennial. Photo by Tom Ross.

to act as a void. The column in the centre prevents this, it fills this space. It is certainly not performing the vagina of Niki de Saint Phalle's *She – A Cathedral* (1966) or Åsa Jungnelius' design for Hagastaden subway station in Stockholm, *Snäckan* (2019–2021).

JO: Yes, I don't think you can take the central vertical piece as a phallus, in a Freudian sense—it is more a totem than a phallus. This is a design that stages from one point: from being a stage, it goes vertical. And then we have vagina and anus. It goes: vagina, haemorrhoids, anus, as you move around it, but no penis. In a heteronormative-masculine territory, anus is something that few talk about, and the penis is also often hidden or relegated to a graphic. In contemporary film and media, penis is coming forward now, a little bit more, I think. This specifically relates to the vulnerability of the male ego which is traditionally protected. But generally, penis is hidden. So, it is selectively queer in its representation of body parts—the penis is hidden, and the other two organs are displayed. Why? Why is that?

I am being a bit vulnerable about this. On the one hand, it is not the responsibility of the queer community, of queer designers, to be educating heterosexual people at any level about anything. On the other hand, there is something really interesting and risky about staging body parts. The question, again, is what are the politics of those body parts as represented in the installation?

CD: Then it is worth commenting on the glory holes. Are they at the right height? That is the moment, when you go into a bathroom and you are like "there's a hole … right there." And these holes seem to be at elbow height. If this was going to be subversive, should they not be at the right height?

JO: This is a standard tactic of capitalism: there is a subculture identified, and then it is transported into the mainstream through *fun*, so the glory hole is definitely a subcultural design object and then it is brought in as this colourful thing that you pass a hot dog through. I think that is very important. The ergonomic critique might sound odd, but it is telling: if it is not at the right height, it falls into a standard trap of design transfer from subculture to mainstream and loses its subversive qualities. Once it is not ergonomically correct, we are in *No Logo* territory.

The boudoir, the salon, the nightclub are all cited by Timothy as having informed the design. This is an ambitious and tough palette of references to work with and I appreciate the difficult task they have set themselves. My understanding of the boudoir, based on its various descriptions, is, firstly, that it is a place that women go to be 'moody'—you know, it is set up for a retreat out of a performance in a wealthy family environment—but it is also a space of seduction, where it is appropriate for women to take control of a sexual encounter, as opposed to the other way around. There is power in the

boudoir. Even the chaise lounge couch is half-couch, half-bed: there is a whole series of seductive elements in there. So the boudoir is about power and seduction, and about revealing the body in a certain way, and about an inversion of power. And then you have the salon, the tearoom, where politics outside of patriarchal masculine structure, another politics and another action, is formed. These are really feminist spaces. And then we get to the nightclub: the nightclub of the post-70s. Now suddenly, we are into something that I understand as queer, that has 'queer' as an identity at its centre. While the other two I would have identified as something that has feminist power at its centre. That is tough, because if the installation is about inverting power relationships, then what are we talking about? Is that background just an image? An image of a space is not the same thing as how it operates as an apparatus of power.

CD: I would like to propose a slightly different queer reading of boudoir and salon. The boudoir I am really seeing in BB is the one that celebrates movie stars and their dramatic moments, when they are on their own—people like Betty Davis, Joan Crawford—there is a lot of imagery of these stars that comes from the boudoir. I do see a queer reading of those spaces here.

It is worth unpacking the term 'queering' a little further, because I feel that the term is expected to do a lot of work here. If we look to theoretical reflections that relate to this piece—for instance, Hannah McCann's essay 'Queer I: Seeing Queerly'[4] or, indirectly, Timothy Moore's conversation with Simona Castricum 'The Trouble with Queering Architecture'[5]—queering is understood as a technique of subversion, and that seems to be pretty universally accepted. But, at the same, it is also expected to create kinship. These are the two things that queering is supposed to do, that BB is expected to do. Simona comments that queer is not about normalising queer, but about making the normal strange, and thus seeing queer possibilities. And I think that BB does this.

But what about kinship? As a queer person, you have this moment of *coming out*. And you have a coming out story. But then you realise that you are going to be coming out repeatedly. You have this significant moment, and then you realise that you will be doing this for the rest of your life: you will have to do this big reveal *every day*, and often when you least expect it. In contrast, we might also talk about *flagging*: this is a way of indicating to other queer people that you are queer, and this goes on under the radar. Kinship does not come from the coming out moment—it can do, but not often—usually, that comes from flagging. And BB definitely does a lot of queering, but does it flag? Maybe it does, maybe the totems flag, but flagging is a really visual act that is only to be read by your community, and it is not to be read by anyone who does not know those languages. In a way, BB is a coming out moment—a "tah-dah!" in front of the people coming to the Museum, who did not realise there was going to be something so . . . homosexual there.

JO: In masculine cultures, and through masculinity studies, there are many tropes: the jock, the nerd, the hero. I do not know if you can say that they flag, but they signal using clothing, body posture, phrases and expressions, interests (sports, products, cars) and we seem to be familiar with them. But thinking through BB, our conversation is making me realise that we are not confronting a homogeneous queer culture, but a super-specific representation of queer. You have a male design team that hides the penis, perhaps playing down their collective identity as specific authors. Should we talk about a queer-masculine queering here? Queer is not homogeneous. So what are the specific traits in the installation that make it masculine-queer not feminine-queer?

CD: In the previously mentioned conversation between Timothy and Simona, Simona points out that trans people still face hostility in simply using a public toilet. Within the queer community, people can be at such different levels when it comes to basic human rights and lived experience. The only thing that I disagree with Simona on is that I think the queer community has always done both: always created spaces for celebration when things were really shit. Going out and being hedonistic is not the end result of advocating for human rights: you know, the Stonewall Riots started in a bar, so I do not think it is a hierarchy of needs. Partying can also be a political act, as long as it does not leave others behind. So, even if I do not recognise my own queerness in BB, I am sympathetic to it. I get that it is doing something on behalf of me, even if it is not speaking directly to me. That being said, butches, trans men and women, and gender non-conforming people would not be immune from harassment in bathrooms within the gallery building . . . which could come from the same people who just enjoyed the queer aesthetic.

HR: Sean Griffiths, infamous post-modernist and, along with Sam Jacobs, founder of the London-based practice FAT, wrote an opinion piece on *Dezeen* a few years back titled 'Now is not the time to be indulging in postmodern revivalism' in which he says: "We didn't do pomo because we liked it. We did it because we hated it. We were trying to challenge our own tastes."[6]

Opposite: Boudoir Babylon uses bold colours, psychedelic patterning, glory-hole perforations and iconographic references to abstract bodies and genitalia. Photo by Sean Fennessy.

I think that BB also has to be positioned within the context of London-based postmodern revivalist architecture, which Adam Nathanial Furman is definitely a part of, along with Yinka Ilori, Camille Walala and Morag Myerscough, among others. Based on those comments, I am curious about how and whether this work challenges 'good taste': It is pretty luscious, despite the transgressive iconography. It is not out to shock or seduce as much as to titillate and flirt, right?

Pop culture, and pop architecture, takes on a different cast in a present saturated with social media. In this conversation, we continue to project into the actual space of the National Gallery of Victoria, to imagine what it is like to be standing in front of this work, but I wonder what might happen if we accept that we are meeting it as a set of images, on computer screens, on Zoom, in a pandemic? What does it do to architecture to become a set of images circulating on *Dezeen*, with a set of names attached to it, which is 'read/looked at' by an audience who in turn scroll idly through a 'feed' that is part of a broader media landscape, maybe on a Sunday morning, maybe in their pyjamas, maybe in bed, maybe hungover? Suddenly, the audience becomes a very different set of people than perhaps the ones that we imagine inhabiting a gallery space.

CD: If you look at some of the images of the work—because I am only encountering this through images—it looks like a TV set, and I think a lot of that is the lighting. It has this very, very bright lighting. I do not know if that is how it felt to you, Helen, but for me, a boudoir, a salon and a nightclub would all be very dark. They would not have this rack of lighting? And that, for me, is really strong. Timothy does describe the work in terms of 'scenography,' so I do not think that this is a mistake, but I do think that the real performance of bodies in salons and boudoirs and clubs is very different from a TV performance of those interactions. It is like that moment when you are in a club and the lights come on. Suddenly, it is bright and all of your sweatiness is revealed in this very cold, stark way, and you just get out as soon as you can, into the early morning. I keep looking at this installation and thinking, how would this be experienced if there was much lower lighting?

It is like that moment when you are in a club and the lights come on. Suddenly, it is bright and all of your sweatiness is revealed in this very cold, stark way, and you just get out as soon as you can, into the early morning. I am reminded of that feeling, thinking about your description of kids climbing on it . . . I keep thinking about this nightclub that I used to go to in the 1990s that was a Spanish tapas restaurant by day called 'Gaudi' and a gay club by night called 'Turnmills.' It was a sweaty, sleazy gay club and there were these bizarre moments where you would walk around the spaces and see twisted ironwork and Gaudi-esque styling and you would think "wow, people actually sit here and have meals here?" This is a club that started at 5 a.m. on Sunday and ended at 1 p.m.—an inversion of space that is usually experienced very differently. I keep looking at this installation and thinking, how would this be experienced if there was much lower lighting?

JO: And this is a workplace . . . This is a café. The café is the corporate space of the gallery. It is often where they sell the objects, the books are there, it is the kind of passive income for the gallery—it is like you say, overpriced sandwiches. That demands that we ask: What about the curator's role in this location decision? Why was it not the commission for a pavilion at the entrance of the museum and not an interstitial space between a 'Jeff Koons thing' and sandwich kiosk? This appears to have happened a few times, in the previous Triennial it was 'marginal ethnic'; this time it is the queer. It is as if they are saying "we have got this in between space, what do we fill it with? Oh yeah, representations of the margin." The curator might be commissioning 'an act of queering' as a way of challenging the norm, but then they are forcing it into an interstitial space which is difficult to do anything with. That is not very generous, is it?

HR: I am thinking about Katherine Shonfield's essay "Why Does My Flat Leak?" where she talks about the host as a 'joint' (or the joint between prefabricated elements as a host, to be precise), which in a mass-produced and standardised world has to do a whole lot of work in absorbing forces.[8] BB is expected to do a fair bit of shock absorption, in this space, as a 'joint' or inflection point between Koons and the lobby. Women are constantly forced to be a host in domestic space; here, we have a public space, where 'the queer' is allocated a hosting function, made to throw a party. The massage parlour, the nail salon . . . there are so many examples of this. I guess I am suggesting that BB is performing a fair bit of affective labour.

CD: It reminds me of the installation, *The Double Club* by Carsten Holler, a split bar, which was really putting to work African identity for an artgoing public. It was shown in London and then became *The Prada Double Club in Miami*. You could go there and consume on one side this Congolese club, but also on the other side a Western club. It described itself as an attempt at cultural cross-pollination without fusion.

JO: . . . and the bar was in the middle. The money is in the middle. You can go to either side, but your money is all the same to me.

Reflection

The activity of architectural criticism covers a diverse set of practices that have traditionally sought to in one way or another to assess or evaluate architecture. Within the 'InstaDezeenDaily' media landscapes of semiocapitalism, beyond its evaluative or situating functions, architectural criticism takes on a productive cast, constituting yet another form of content production that augments the building or work by performing a branding function.[9] Reviews not only plump and fatten online platforms, generating hype and presence around an architect or project; they also provide the internet's sprawling archives with legibility, establishing hypertextual 'filing' protocols allowing images of projects to be tagged, traced, reproduced and circulated. Never innocent, architects play into and with this system, staging the dissemination of their works by bating audiences with content-rich backdrops for social media posts.

As critics, how are we to conceptualise of our role in this new media landscape and what can we contribute beyond extended captions for social media scenographies? We might begin thinking through these questions by drawing on the comments of Danish architecture critic Morten Birk Jørgensen.[10] Writing about the process of judging an architecture award ("Arne of the Year"), Jørgensen argues that the value of architectural criticism lies in the process of evaluation: in its necessary failure to establish solid truths, the situating and evaluating tendencies of professional critique come into conflict with the taste-driven metrics of popular reception.[11] It is the debates between colleagues in architecture offices, the disagreements that arise between members of a jury and a public, and the remote possibility that an argument about architecture might ensue at a bar in Copenhagen on a Friday night that makes the exercise worthwhile. "While collective criticisms are common practice in architectural educational institutions, spaces for collective professional criticism seem limited in the industry," he notes.

This opens up a tantalising proposition that we have engaged with here: Why not embrace the stage sets of media architecture as spaces for framing collective reflection about architecture more broadly? To think through what a work like *Boudoir Babylon* might do and be and mean and say for queering architecture, we also have to inhabit it, project ourselves into it, fight about it, claim it and care about it, perhaps more than it was designed to be cared about. Our exchange suggests that a queer architecture might demand responses other than those that the outdated practices of traditional architectural criticism might offer—queer architecture challenges singular points of view, implicitly retires a number of tired disciplinary hang-ups and demands a new language, forcing us to take our time and linger on the surface, just a little longer than is comfortable.

01 Adam Nathanial Furman, "Boudoir Babylon," https://www.adamnathanielfurman.com/projects.php?pc_id=89.

02 Sibling, "Come in as a single, leave as a throuple: Boudoir Babylon," http://siblingarchitecture.com/projects/boudoir-babylon.

03 Nina Power, "Towards a Feminism of the Void" (November 9, 2017), https://ninapower.net/2017/11/09/191.

04 Hannah McCann, "Queer I: Seeing Queerly," *NGV Triennial* 2020-2021 Catalogue (Melbourne: National Gallery of Victoria, 2020), 138-152.

05 Simona Castricum and Timothy Moore, "The trouble with queering architecture: Simona Castricum and Timothy Moore in conversation," in Jess Berry, Timothy Moore, Nicole Kalms and Gene Bawden, eds. *Contentious Cities: Design and the Gendered Production of Space* (London: Routledge, 2021).

06 Sean Griffiths, "Now is not the time to be indulging in postmodern revivalism" (October 30, 2017), https://www.dezeen.com/2017/10/30/sean-griffiths-fat-postmodern-revivalism-dangerous-times-opinion/.

07 See for instance: Marcus Fairs, "Colourful 'New London Fabulous' design movement is challenging minimalism, says Adam Nathaniel Furman," *Dezeen* (May 26, 2020), https://www.dezeen.com/2020/05/26/new-london-fabulous-design-movement-adam-nathaniel-furman.

08 Katherine Shonfield, "Why Does Your Flat Leak?" in *Walls Have Feelings: Architecture, Film and the City* (London: Routledge, 2000).

09 The "semiocapitalism" thesis argues that capitalism has undergone a fundamental mutation and that we now confront a series of entirely new relations of production and exploitation. This theoretical position empathises the effects of shifts in the nature of labour in the post- Fordist mode of capitalist production. See: Helen Runting, *Architectures of the Unbuilt Environment*, PhD. Dissertation (Stockholm: KTH Royal Institute of Technology, 2018), https://kth.diva-portal.org/smash/get/diva2:1202641/SUMMARY01.pdf.

10 See: "Damn Critics!," accessed June 17, 2021, https://javlakritiker.com/en/landing-page.

11 Morten Birk Jørgensen, "Byens Bedste Bygningskunst," *Magasin for Bygningskunst og Kultur 1* (2021), https://bygningskunstogkultur.dk/nr-1-2021/byens-bedste-bygningskunst.

Claude Dutson is an academic and lecturer at Royal College of Art. She trained in Architecture at the University of East London (2005) and the Royal College of Art (2008), completing a PhD (RCA) by practice in Architecture in 2016. Claude has a background in Media Studies and her work investigates architecture, technology and labour from a feminist critical perspective. Claude's work is published in a number of journals internationally, and she is currently writing a book on the architecture of Silicon Valley (due 2023).

Janek Oźmin is an architect, artist and Doctoral Candidate based in Stockholm, Sweden. His Doctoral research project examines the suburban garage and the penthouse apartment as two critical sites related to the production of masculine subjectivities. His commissioned work bridges art and architecture and includes sculpture and landscape art, and he has exhibited work in the Royal Hibernian Gallery, Dublin, and at Arkdes/Moderna Museum, Stockholm.

HIDDEN FIGURES

UNCOVERING WOMEN ARCHITECTS OF COLOUR

Sarah Akigbogun

Once upon a time, I wanted to road trip through France to see Le Corbusier's *Villa Savoye*. My student colleagues and I often talked about it in the studio as we worked. Corbusier was a 'hero,' the father of Modernism. It is not a trip we ever made. Today, I would instead like to do a road trip across America, in search of the lost and hidden work of some of the women architects of colour whose stories are mysteriously absent from historical records.

The issue of racial diversity, combined with gender, has become a recurring question in my mind, one that has moved slowly to the foreground. It is a question that I have been probing over the last couple of years as I search for and document the stories of women of colour who are present in the architectural profession, in the United Kingdom and beyond. People of colour are largely missing from the memories of making westerns cities and from wider global narratives about architecture, but this void is particularly evident regarding women of colour. With few notable exceptions, the records are scarce. Why is this? Why are their stories seemingly hidden? In the historical fabric of the built environment, who gets to leave a trace?

XXAOC

As a practicing architect and educator in the UK, much of my time as a student and in practice has been framed by a lack of historical references for the work of people of colour. The issue became stark for me when I found myself working as the only Black female architect in a thousand strong practice—a common experience for Black professionals. In UK architecture, fewer than 1% of architects are Black and female and, as of 2019, the number of Black women on the register was 107. 107 out of 42,000 architects.[1] The reasons for this are complex, but structural inequality plays a role, as does the cost of education and high dropout rates: The percentage of Black and mixed-race architects who complete the seven-year training is only 3.7% of the total number who qualify in the UK.[2] Low pay and poor working conditions also hinder access and progress; so too does discrimination.

At the start of 2019, I embarked on my search for women architects of colour with a crowd-sourced film project titled XXAOC. Over time, the project has evolved into an online database to record the work and profiles of these women, filling in the blanks in our mainstream data sources to learn from, engage with and inspire others. The project has become one partly of excavation and partly one of archiving for posterity, and the last two years have altered my perspective immeasurably.

My journey began virtually on January 13th, 2019 with a tweet that was intended as a tentative probe to the world. I expected the odd 'like' and hoped for a few retweets; often when talking about the subject of racial diversity it is like shouting into the void. This time responses came thick and fast, and the suggestions sent came from and referenced women from all over the globe. I had completely underestimated just what interest there might be in this topic and in a sense, the response provoked me to redefine the project. Since that first tweet, I have discovered many historical figures I had not previously known of and also interviewed inspiring contemporary women such as Dr. Sharon Egretta Sutton and Elsie Owusu, who are trailblazing architects based in the US and UK respectively. Some historical figures, such as Amaza Lee Meredith, Ethel Bailey Thurman, Beverly Lorraine Greene and Minette de Silva are in the public domain—thanks to diligent archivists and researchers—but they are far from part of mainstream discourse. As such, their work and their existence have not been visible nor accessible to inspire future generations.

In the case of Meredith, De Silva and Sutton, much of their work is ground-breaking; De Silva fuses the cultural influences from her western education while Sutton is an academic, vocal campaigner and activist. Learning about these women, alongside the more familiar architectural 'heroes,' might have changed the perspective of a young Brown girl studying architecture in the UK.

I would love to travel through Virginia to see *Azurest South* by Amaza Lee Meredith and the work of Ethel Bailey Furman, who built more than 200 churches and homes. I want to understand more about these structures and about how these African American women were able to build them, despite their context. However, like much of the work of Black women in the built environment, many do not exist anymore—neither physically nor in architectural historical records. *Azurest South*, built by Meredith in the 1930s, is an exception, a rare surviving legacy—a building designed and built by a Black woman, in the deep American South, at a time when segregation still limited the opportunities of many. Most of the historic figures I have come across have been American, but during the course of thinking about my film and whilst doing my early research, I started to wonder who the pioneering women of colour in architecture were in the UK. A search that began as simply trying to tell the stories of female architects of colour has become one about also trying to find them. This has meant looking at the intersection of conditions that have created the void in our records.

Searching for Female Architects of Colour

As you drive through the campus of Virginia State University, past the manicured lawns and red brick faculty buildings, on one of these lawns lies *Azurest South*, home of the Virginia State University National Alumni Association since 1986. You may just glimpse the single-storey building, with its striking green stripe along the roof edge. It is one of a few remaining built traces of Amaza Lee Meredith's work as an architect.[3] Its presence is celebrated by a 'historical marker,' a signpost just ahead of the building which reads:

> Lynchburg native Amaza Lee Meredith was one of the nation's few African American female architects in the mid-20th century. Her self-designed residence is a rare Virginia example of a mature International Style building . . . [4]

Amaza Lee Meredith was born in 1895 and lived during a time when Jim Crow laws still enforced racial segregation in southern US States, disenfranchising the Black population, restricting access to education and stifling economic progress. Miscegenation laws also made interracial marriage a crime in Virginia and meant that her parents, Samuel Peter Meredith, a white carpenter, and her mother, Emma Kennedy, a Black woman, faced legislated discrimination.[5] Determined to marry, Samuel and Emma crossed state lines in segregated trains in order to travel north where their marriage could legally take place. In the years following their marriage, Samuel's company struggled to survive and in 1915, he committed suicide.[6]

Despite this tragedy, in 1922, the young Amaza became valedictorian at her school and would begin her life-long commitment to teaching, starting her career as a maths teacher in rural America. Later, she would move north to Brooklyn, New York, to train formally, gaining a degree in Fine Art from Columbia in 1930 and a Master of Arts in 1934, after which she founded the Arts Department at Virginia State University. A polymath who designed, invented and made art that was exhibited in the Virginia Museum of Fine Arts, New York and North Carolina, it is evident from her life's work that she had an interest in architecture. However, her race and sex meant that studying architecture formally was not an option. Despite this, she went on to build *Azurest South*, producing all the drawings for its design and construction, as well as supervising the build. She was also instrumental in a form of development activism through the creation of *Azurest North*, a leisure resort for Black families, built as a way of circumventing Jim Crow laws that denied African Americans access to the beaches in the affluent Hamptons. *Azurest South*, completed in 1938, is her best-known work, and with it, Meredith secured her legacy as an architect.

Looking through the lens of segregation, we can understand in part why so little work was created and preserved by Black architects in the US, despite the presence of a large Black population. At the time Meredith was practicing, there were

Opposite: Sarah Akigbogun.
Photo courtesy of Morley Von Sternburg.

only 59 Black people practicing as architects and only 47 as draftspeople.[7] This is, regrettably, no surprise. What is more intriguing is how those who left a trace managed to do so. In this America, the work of Black architects was largely invisible to the world of white clients, who held much of the power to commission public projects.[8] Virginia State University, a historically Black college, was a rare setting where Meredith was able to carve out a place for herself. Here, she created both a physical space in the form of the home she designed and lived in with her partner, Ms. Edna Colson, and as a teacher and founder of the Fine Art program at the university. Meredith is one of several women of colour whose ambition to become a licensed architect was thwarted by the system within which they lived, which effectively 'pre-erased' their legacies. Yet, by gifting the building to the university upon her death, Meredith evaded this erasure and created a lasting presence for posterity.

In contrast to Meredith, Beverly Lorraine Greene, born 20 years later in 1915, was permitted to study Architectural Engineering. She was the first Black woman in America to graduate from the University of Illinois with this degree and the first African American woman to register as an architect in 1942.[9] It is notable that the first Black American woman to make the US register should have come out of Chicago, Illinois, a state that was one of the first to repel segregation laws, thereby removing one of the structural barriers in education that would have prevented many Black and mixed-race people, such as Meredith, from entering the built environment professions. Segregation meant that many African Americans were poorly educated in underfunded schools. Greene was also the daughter of middle-class parents, her father being a lawyer, and it was the practice of those in a position to do so to send their children north, to cities such as Chicago, where they could receive an education and with it the possibility of social and economic progression.

Pioneering women architects of colour. From left to right: Amaza Lee Meredith (courtesy of Virginia State University); Beverly Lorraine Greene (courtesy of the Beverly Willis Architecture Foundation); Ethel Bailey Furman (courtesy of the Library of Virginia); Minnette de Silva (courtesy of PAP); Norma Skelek; Georgia Louise Harris Brown (courtesy of the Beverly Willis Architecture Foundation).

Despite the privilege of her middle-class background, Chicago was not without its problems for Greene. Discrimination and barriers still existed, even for one determined enough to become the first Black female registered architect. One of these barriers was the Chicago press, which ignored much of the work of people of colour and therefore made it a struggle to gain commissions.[10] This led Greene to relocate to New York and apply for work on a housing project for Stuyvesant Town in lower Manhattan, before gaining a scholarship to embark on her master's degree.

Greene had a keen interest in the dramatic arts and after gaining her master's degree, she went on to work on an impressive array of projects with architects Edward Durrell Stone and Marcel Breuer.[11] She worked on at least two celebrated theatres with Stone: the theatre at the Arts Centre for the University of Arkansas in 1951, and in 1952, the Arts Complex at the Liberal Arts College, Sarah Lawrence. In 1955, Greene also assisted Breuer on the most well-known project she would be part of, the UNESCO United Nations Headquarters in Paris.[12]

Architectural history often only recognises the work of the lead architect, the *auteur*, and the traces of other designers are lost. It is likely that Greene struggled to create work in her own right and would have been overlooked without diligent investigation by researchers, who over the years have sought to record the African American presence in architecture. Greene died young, at only 41, and we will never know where this promising start may have led.

Born 11 years after Greene, in 1926, Norma Sklarek would succeed in rising to the level of Director and would be one of the first African American women to lead a large architecture firm. Her career is well-documented, but it is worth noting that she existed in a world where it was rare for women, much less women of colour, to even be named as part of projects:[13]

> It was unheard of to have an African American female who was registered as an architect. You didn't trot that person out in front of your clients and say 'This is the person designing your project.' She was not allowed to express herself as a designer . . . [14]

Ethel Bailey Furman, born in Virginia in 1893 to upper-middle-class African American parents, also travelled north for her education, in her case to New York, where she studied architecture privately. Back in her home of Richmond, Virginia, Thurman found that she would not be accepted as 'the architect of record' on her own projects, forcing her to submit her work under the name of male contractors. Though she is believed to have designed some 200 churches and residential buildings in Virginia, her presence is masked by the signatories she had to hide behind. She was obscured, erased, her work unpreserved and, for a long time, unacknowledged. How many other Black women's work might have been hidden in this way?

Aspects of these women's stories are repeated in other places around the globe. Black women in architecture were often impeded, if not by systemic discrimination on the grounds of race, then by gender, and very often by both. Like other women, they were not attributed as contributors to architecture. Sometimes, their work was not visible because it occurred in unrecorded realms off the radar to historians, critics and writers.

Although there is little trace of Black women in the United Kingdom narrative before the 1970s, we know of the presence of female students of colour in UK schools of architecture from pictorial evidence, fragments and tantalising clues that exist from the 1950s. In one such photo, there are three unidentified women in a lecture at the Architectural Association. What follows is a fictional speculation, set in the past and present, that acts as a cultural probe based on my own research into the processes that lead to erasure. Some of these speculations arise out of interviews I have conducted for the XXAOC project. They are coloured by my own experiences and casual conversations with young women architects of colour: "Why am I always the only one? It was a struggle, they didn't get me," and in my case, "so, are you an architect?" It is a question I have been asked all too often when starting in new offices. For me it is the work-based equivalent of, "so where are you from? No, where are you really from?" A question that will be familiar to many other second- and third-generation migrants.

A Studio of Her Own

London 1954

In those days, she would often walk from her flat to *The School*, winding from north to south through the expanse of the city and across the river. Sometimes men would whistle or shout their appreciation. Sometimes other things were said, but either way, she was never invisible.

Nor was she invisible when she arrived at *The School* in 1954. Pushing open the heavy Georgian front door, she felt the weight of its history. Carved into the wall of stone flags were the names of the 'greats' who had crossed that threshold—almost entirely men. Sometimes, she would run her fingers along the smooth, cold surface to the point where they stopped, wondering if a name like hers could ever make it onto this surface.

From day one, it was clear that it would not be easy for her to leave a mark—the front door would not be the only thing she had to push against. She raised her hand. Perhaps he had not

meant to ignore her, but in a room of enthusiastic students, he always chose the boy to speak. Her role it seemed was to listen, not to speak. To receive knowledge, not to share it.

She had dearly wanted to work with buildings since she was a child. Her parents were diplomats and the house was often filled with politicians and conversation. It must have been floating around those rooms, listening to these conversations, hearing about the plans for her city that first made her decide to study architecture. Her home, Lagos, was going through great change at the time; more and more of the country was becoming urbanised and new ways of catering for modern life needed to be found. She had won a place at an Arts College in Lagos and when she was offered a visit to *The School* and its new department as part of her course, she seized the opportunity.

At *The School*, there were lectures by famous architects happening all the time. She eagerly absorbed new theories and was fascinated by the functionalist aesthetic of Modernism and the International Style. The ideas of lightness, structural efficiency and minimal ornamentation were interesting, exciting even, but a little voice in the back of her mind wondered where she would fit in if there was to be no individuality or cultural expression? These were things she and her peers discussed in heated exchanges at the bar. She was told that she was 'old fashioned' for wondering how the symbolism of her culture would fit the Modernist aesthetic. This new architecture was a response to modern life. If 'they' wanted to keep up, there was no room for whimsy, ornament, fuss. There was no room for their way of life.

Women architects of colour interviewed for the XXAOC Project. From left to right: Shiromi Pinto; Stephanie Edwards; Charlene Campbell; Remi Connoly Taylor; Jacqueline Bleicher; Selasi Setufe and Neba Sere. Photos courtesy of the author.

Conversation was typically feverish on the day *The Famous Architect* came to *The School*. His lectures were highly anticipated and she wanted the opportunity to raise some of the questions she and her friends were discussing: Would whitewashed walls work somewhere like Nigeria? She positioned herself near the front. Today, her questions would not be overlooked. She was the only one in traditional dress, a conscious choice to be seen. *The Famous Architect* wanted a picture of himself and the overseas students, they were urged to move further forward. *The School* had wanted to capture this moment of knowledge exchange, knowledge transfer. They had been some of the few women in the room, and the only Brown ones—she was happy to show that they were there.

London 2019: The Search

For Abi, the search had started because of a quiet curiosity that had grown louder, a questioning of why there were so few architects who looked like her documented in the UK's architectural history. After all, there had been a continuous recorded Black and Brown presence in the UK since as far back as the 16th century. It had been a slow awakening for Abi, moving through her education and work seeing no one else that looked like her, she finally began searching. There were a handful of records for Black American female architects dating back to the 1900s, but in the UK, there was nothing prior to the 1970s. Who was the first Black female architect in the United Kingdom? Why do we not know her story? Why is there a void? It soon became apparent to Abi that the idea of 'Black' did not even exist in the UK records until 50 years prior to her search. A deeper excavation would be required.

Slowly, as people started to hear about what Abi was doing, leads began to appear and a chance conversation with another researcher led to her finding out about *The School* and how students came from Africa and the West Indies to study with *The Famous Architect*. She found herself in the archives of *The School*, reading through papers *The Famous Architect* had

donated. Goosebumps. She leafed through the faded sheets and the carefully compiled pages of drawings, papers and then, there it was. The photo. A black and white photo. A white, male lecturer speaking. Pointing. Four Black people, three of them women. All looking up. Attentive. A pencilled note on the back dated the picture. 1954. It identified him. But the women, who were they? This was a whole new line of enquiry, opening up bigger questions about the global narrative around architecture and the role of Black women in it.

One of the women, in particular, caught Abi's eye. She was closest to *The Famous Architect* and in part traditional African dress, an air of confidence about her. The fabric had a slight shimmer to it and looked like the heavy cloth sometimes worn for important occasions. Had she expected to be in the photo? And where might she be from? Ghana? Nigeria?

In the 1950s and 60s, Nigeria and other African countries were on the cusp of independence. Modernists were like architectural missionaries, spreading with zeal the word of functionalism, truth in materials, clean aesthetics and white walls. At that time, colonialist countries saw West Africa as a potential market, taking their ideas to them. Training them to be architects and urban designers was part of the mission. This woman may have been part of that story, but who was she? All of the women were unnamed, presumably considered minor players in the sweep of architectural history. She knew that not only were the women in the photograph likely to have been buried behind the work of others, they were also unlikely to have been celebrated in the press even if they had received commissions.

Abi looked in the places where the Black presence was recorded, through scholarship records and immigration papers. A faint paper trail led her to a local records library and finally to an advert in a local paper from parents seeking a guardian for their daughter who was moving to the UK for her studies. It was just an advert in a local paper, but could this be her? After all this searching, might there be some answers?

London 2019: The Daughter

The photo had arrived in the post, as part of a magazine article soon to be published, if she agreed. How strange to see her mother as a young woman, wearing her traditional dress, looking up at the lecture board at *The School*. It seemed odd that someone would be interested in her mother now, after all this time. The photo had arrived with a letter from a young architect, a woman, Black and British born, Abi. She wanted to interview her about her mother. What did she want to know? How had she even found her? What could she tell this young woman about her mother's career?

She, the daughter, would tread the same path as her mother. She had walked through the same doors at *The School*, walked past that same wall of names and had convinced the interviewer, who sat black-suited across the table from her, to give her a place. "I want to go back home," she had said, "I want to go back to build schools . . ." She did want to return someday, perhaps. However, she had only said it because if she gave any hint that she wanted to stay, she might not get a place at all. If she indicated that her dream really was to make a life in the UK and start a studio here, in the country that she had actually spent most of her time being educated, they would see her as competition for 'locals' and her application would be denied. "You'll go back to Nigeria to build schools? Very good," he had replied.

It was the early 1970s, not long after 'The Rivers of Blood' speech by Enoch Powell and just after the time of the 'No Blacks, No Dogs, No Irish' posters in shop windows. She had lost count of the number of times the police would stop her in her little car as she drove from Kings Road to Notting Hill and sometimes Brixton, where riots would later take place in the 1980s. She found a community, a tribe at *The School*. They were an outsider bunch:

hippies, homosexuals and Blacks. The studios were where they mixed. She had loved the late-night drawing sessions, the not-so-early morning coffees. Always black, no sugar. Parties in flats across London, West and East. Dinner parties, with conversation in English and French, dances to afrobeat and reggae. There were post tutorial drinks in Soho bars and conversations about revolution, independence and changing the world. At that time, in that place, the world had seemed full of opportunity.

The differemces were small, imperceptible at first—she had even felt herself thriving. She spoke well, she was told, but tutorials were a political minefield. She was too outspoken and her ideas were too radical, too bold. Her clothing was too bright. They did not get her. Sometimes it was as though she needed a translator despite speaking plain English.

Doing well and navigating these sessions was a performance. Occasionally, she wore bright fabrics—her mothers—particularly for presentations. She would bring a dash of colour into the whitewashed rooms. She could not enter without being noticed anyway, so why hide?

Above (left): Elsie Owusu, interviewed for the XXAOC Project. Photo courtesy of the author.

Above (right): Sharon Egretta Sutton performing at Tanglewood with a Brass Quintet (1963). Photo courtesy of Morley Von Sternburg.

The promise she showed did not seem to bear fruit, promotions did not come. Her mother had said, "come here to Nigeria," so she settled into a back-and-forth life working in both London and Lagos. In London, activism became the focus. She knew that, in her time, her mother had felt restrained in both worlds: in London, because of her race; in Lagos, because of her sex. She wondered, did her own work represent a progression?

Prompted by the young interviewer, she found a box with a few more fragments of her mother's career, some of her drawings. Her mother had contributed to many design projects in Nigeria, though she was seldom able to lead, and these were the record of that. She remembered the patterns on the walls at the West African University her mother had helped design. As a child, she had visited the University while it was being built. These were the manifestations of an exchange of culture and knowledge, and her mother had been part of that conversation. She could picture her now, working with local women, particularly those in the difficult situation of finding themselves alone, widowed and with land to manage. She would help them build on the land, she enjoyed the exchange with the local craftsmen and would try to pass on some of the things she had learned at *The School*. What she was really doing was helping these women manage their assets, protecting them from family members who would claim undeveloped land. It was a form of economic empowerment, but there were few records, few pictures. Many of the buildings no longer existed and she had considered her role too small to document. The box contained the only traces of her mother's legacy.

The Search Continues

As a Black woman in architecture, your skin immediately marks you out as different, bringing with it all sorts of issues. For Norma Sklarek, it meant that she could not hitch a lift to work with a white male colleague who was always late:

> It took only one week before the boss came and spoke to me about being late. Yet he had not noticed that the young man had been late for two years . . . My solution was to buy a car since I, the highly visible employee, had to be punctual.[15]

Up until starting my search, the issue of how skin colour might affect my own progression through the profession was not one I had confronted directly. I had naively assumed that having grown up in the UK and having parents educated under the UK system, I would be accepted as such. Even so, I had been prepared for the fact that my name might be a hindrance. In my case, when discrimination did occur, and I am certain that it did at various points in my journey, it was difficult to determine whether the reason was race or gender. I have had many workplace encounters where, with the benefit of hindsight, I can see that some form of discrimination was probably at play. For example, having colleagues exclude me because they thought I was a member of the "IT team," being told that "I didn't fit" or a colleague saying "I don't know why they gave this task to me, you are clearly better at it." However, usually, it is less direct, somehow one is just left with the aftermath. Judgements are made silently, in an instant, like fleeting shadows impossible to arrest.

On June 7th, 2020, the bronze statue of Edward Colston, a former top official in the Royal African Company, was pulled down in Bristol. This removal happened during one of the many anti-racism protests which followed the killing of George Floyd on May 25th, 2020 in Minneapolis. It was an event that ricocheted around the globe and was a reminder to the world that racism is still part of the present, not just the past. For many, it is an everyday reality, robbing people of opportunity and presence. Many of us are reminded of the historic and ongoing imbalance of power by the built structures and monuments that surround us, such as Edward Colsten's statue. These conversations are a beginning.

The XXAOC project was, for me, a way of cutting through all of this, finding different narratives to inspire and be inspired by. Through it, I have found not only individuals—the aforementioned Sharon Egretta Sutton, Elsie Owusu, Minette De Silva, Amaza Le Meredith—and the many practitioners I have interviewed, but also collectives doing incredible work. There is still much more to do to build recognition and awareness for the contributions of women architects of colour in the built environment, as well as to engage with systemic under-representation in architecture today. However, I find hope in the new generation starting to break through, building on the activism of previous generations whose legacy is in the paths they have laid for others. My own perspective has shifted immeasurably, and I hope that as the search continues, the XXAOC project will become a valuable resource for others.

01 Architect's Registration Board 'we keep a Register of all architects in the UK. We hold E&D data for around half - 26,422 registrants. Of those, 107 women identify as African, Caribbean, any other Black background, White & Black African or White & Black Caribbean' Twitter 1:32 AM - 17 Jan 2019.

02 Mirza & Nacey Research, *RIBA Education Statistics 2016/17* (RIBA Architecture, 2018), Report Table 21: Ethnic group of students.

03 "Amaza Lee Meredith (1895-1984)," https://www.hmdb.org/m.asp?m=130078.

04 Ibid.

05 "Amaza Lee Meredith (1895-1984)," Virginia State University Alumni Association, https://www.vsuaaonline.com/azurest-south/amaza-lee-meredith-1895-1984.

06 "Amaza Lee Meredith," https://www.livingplaces.com/people/amaza-lee-meredith.html.

07 "Amaza Lee Meredith (1895-1984)," Virginia State University Alumni Association, https://www.vsuaaonline.com/azurest-south/amaza-lee-meredith-1895-1984. This is according to census data. In the United Kingdom, race has only been recorded for the last 50 years, so this information is not available.

08 Dell Upton, *Architecture in the United States*, (Oxford, New York: University Press), https://archive.org/details/architectureinun0000upto/page/273/mode/2.

09 "Beverly L. Greene," https://blackhistory.news.columbia.edu/people/beverly-l-greene.

10 Jolene Nolte, "Beverly Loraine Greene's Brief And Groundbreaking Career," Atomic Ranch, 2021, https://www.atomic-ranch.com/architecture-design/beverly-loraine-greene.

11 "Beverly Loraine Greene," https://distributedmuseum.illinois.edu/exhibit/beverly-loraine-greene.

12 "Beverly L. Greene University of Illinois Archives," https://archon.library.illinois.edu/?p=digitallibrary/digitalcontent&id=3153.

13 "Norma Merrick Sklarek," https://pioneeringwomen.bwaf.org/norma-merrick-sklarek.

14 "Norma Merrick Sklarek dies; pioneering African American architect," https://www.latimes.com/local/obituaries/la-me-norma-sklarek-20120210-story.html.

15 Ibid.

TRANSOCCUPATION

March Studio

This project is simultaneously an investigation into a 1:1 plywood box truss (the segment) and a 1:10 structural system for a tower (the whole). The work continues a wider body of research undertaken by March Studio where materials, technology and structure are used to explore disorderly form in order to propose new opportunities and architectural typologies. In the case of Transoccupation *(overleaf), we propose a new, interchangeable residential tower that is more akin to a vertical village than a typical extruded tower model.*

4" x 2" Nest

Transoccupation is an evolution of an earlier piece from 2009, *4"x 2" Nest*. Made of a 20-tonne stack of 4"x 2" ordinary builder's hardwood, *4"x 2" Nest* embodies a rudimentary habitation for one person. Fabricated entirely from one material, its construction is elemental. The rotated stacking method is inherently familiar, and not dissimilar to a log cabin or a pile of firewood. It appears initially as a solid, impenetrable mass and only when one finds the entrance does one understand that the structure is habitable. *4"x 2" Nest* sits in a vague zone between form and function, nature and the fabricated, structure and architecture. It occupies a territory that our studio finds inherently more interesting than the refined and the predictable.

Transoccupation, like its predecessor, employs the repetition of one element and variation of length to create apparent randomness. The blurring of the whole through simple two-directional movement, is a technique that we are relentlessly pursuing at a range of scales and in a range of materials. The ambition of the project is to generate an architecture that, despite the realities of client, brief and budget, has a chaotic, yet entirely constructable quality.

Like a half-built building, free from the mundane, our work strives for the same elemental construction tectonic. Through exposed structure and expression of materials, we reveal and celebrate the beauty of architecture beyond mere product specification and conventional construction techniques.

Left: 4" x 2" Nest, by March Studio.

Above: Section 8, by March Studio.

Section 8

We first tested the combination of repetition with rudimentary construction techniques in 2005, on a 'temporary' project called *Section 8.* Occupying a carpark in Melbourne's Central Business District, *Section 8* consists of 100 recycled timber pallets, two shipping containers, 140 linear metres of fibreglass sheet (trimdeck profile), seven HB350 steel trusses, 39 HJ150 steel purlins, 14 100mm SHS 5mm steel posts and six cans of white aerosol road paint.

Days after completion, the project graced the front cover of *Architecture Australia* but was not credited to our then fledgling and relatively unknown studio 'DireTribe.' We were advised that the project made the cover not for its architectural merit but rather, according to the editor, because it was an urban condition that had apparently just sprung up of its own accord overnight. After we presented planning and building permit drawings showing the contrary (that the project had in fact been intentionally designed) *Architecture Australia* published a correction the following month.

What fascinated us the most was that not only had the project successfully embedded itself into the city, it had *become* the city. Whether it was due to our naive detailing or lack of budget, the project gained an authenticity that many architectural projects struggle to replicate. This untamed expression was more familiar to the habitation found in nature than an orchestrated architectural process.

14 years on, *Section 8* became an institution and undisputed success. Even today, the land is more profitable serving beers than any other building type. What is successful inhabitation and why are people attracted to this kind of environment over another, even in mid-winter?

Transoccupation

Unlike most architects, who obsess about creating perfectly curated environments, we see the opportunity and beauty in the noise and chaos of everyday life. The unpredictability offered by a user-driven modular approach is attractive for the way in which it economically fosters spontaneity.

Transoccupation is driven by its inhabitant's programmatic requirements. The building's volume and appearance are dependent on the choice and actions of the people who inhabit it. Inhabitants are invited to reconfigure their dwelling based on personal preference. Its modularity enables repetition with difference—reconfiguration and endless variation.

As a purely residential model, *Transoccupation* speculatively houses an upwards of 500 people, albeit less if other programmes are added (shops, schools, parks, swimming pools). Inhabitants are offered an empty module with various cladding options. Plumbing locations are restricted to base points, and the length of the dwelling cannot exceed the maximum path of travel back to the fire stair (30 metres). *Transoccupation* adopts a superstructure as a base within which timber truss containers are placed. Base services incorporated into the superstructure include plumbing stacks, staircases and elevators.

Since each module is a rigid, independent structure, it is plausible to replace parts of the building or to move them. The tower therefore has the ability to evolve over a period of time—to dissipate or grow according to external forces. This plug-in construction methodology allows a project's developer to stage the building process, committing at first only to the infrastructure and not the entire building. Nomadically, it allows inhabitants to take their dwellings with them, to another superstructure, or to be placed in a field, in the snow, or beside the beach. The result is continual flexibility and reconfiguration.

Each dwelling is a variation of a standard CLT box beam structure. With steel and concrete production being some of the most energy-consuming and CO2 emitting industrial activities in the world, we look to a 100 per cent renewable material and continuously developing techniques. Through high-grade assembly plants, stronger glues, and laminating methods, timber structures can be built higher than ever before.

'Trans' has abbreviated roots in 'transformation'—to change from one thing to another—and 'occupation' means, of course, the action of living in, or using a building or place. *Transoccupation* evolves from our earlier projects (such as *4" x 2" Nest* and *Section 8*); it also grows, reconfigures, and acclimatises. Despite its speculative nature, this project has come to both inform and characterise the guerrilla, adaptive nature of March Studio's praxis.

Right: Transoccupation, a speculative project by March Studio.

CHRONOTOPE

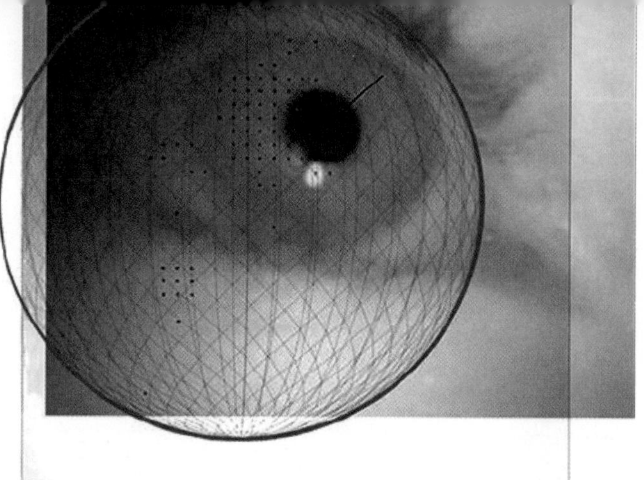

DIGITAL CRAFT AND EMBODIMENT IN ARCHITECTURE

Daniela Mitterberger

The term chronotope is derived from two Greek words, khrónos (time) and topos (space).[1] In literary theory, chronotope describes how different combinations of time and space are represented in language and discourse. Applied to design, it specifies the influence that a unique place and time can have on architecture and its domain of relations, and vice versa.[2] Chronotope, therefore, reinforces the idea of architecture as an indissociable network, a unit of interactions. It challenges the idea of architecture as a discrete and isolated object tuned to maximum efficiency and makes space for an aesthetic of interconnectedness, imperfection and unpredictability.

Being 'present' and interacting 'live' during the fabrication process is essential to achieving a chronotopic architecture. This presence can be physical or virtual, as 'liveness' can no longer be defined by human attendance nor specific physical and temporal relationships.[3] Liveness and presence are therefore linked to the human's affective experience as well as novel technologies that are able to respond to input in real-time, in a feedback loop that we initiate. Following two chronotopic projects that utilised real-time operations, *Psychotropic Topologies* by MAEID and *Augmented Bricklaying* by Gramazio Kohler Research, this article focuses on how digital tools are being used in new ways to support and elevate creative craft practices. In both projects, humans are augmented to enhance intrinsic cognitive and physical capabilities to solve specific fabrication and design parameters. By illuminating the role of 'human-making' in digital craft, chronotope underlines the importance of human intuition, tacit knowledge, dexterity and decision-making in developing innovative digital design and fabrication processes.

Chronotopic Architecture

The concept of chronotopic architecture is closely related to the term 'event' in physics and relativity theory.[4] An event is the instantaneous physical state or occurrence associated with a definite location and time, defined by a point in spacetime, and while chronotope only contains 'time' and 'space' in its direct translation, it also refers to all actors present during an event. The framework of a chronotopic event can therefore be described in terms of space, time and actor: space is defined by three spatial coordinates (p = x, y, z), time can be described by one coordinate (t) to specify the moment in which the event occurs and the actor can be described by one coordinate (h). These five coordinates form a five vector description associated with a chronotopic event—two chronotopic events can either happen at the same time but in different spaces or at different times in the same location.[5] Therefore, two separate chronotopic events will never be identical, as either time, space or actors must change. Architecture, in such a context, becomes hyperlocal and hypertemporal, making every chronotopic event, and architecture, unique. This concept contrasts with normative definitions of architecture that define space as an objective form, or that associate architecture with discrete qualities defined by clearly identifiable and individuated objects.

Currently, digital design methodologies or machine-produced objects and architecture do not yet visualise these spatial, temporal and human relationships. 'Human-made' objects, in comparison, very much reveal this additional information. In this context, 'human-made' does not imply entirely handcrafted pieces but rather processes that are not fully automated. The physical outcome still depends on the human craftsman who controls and executes the fabrication.

Another opportunity for a chronotopic architecture to occur is through the application of a material as an 'active' agent. This 'active' material can change according to environmental conditions during fabrication, revealing the passing of time and its location during the process. Objects manufactured exclusively by machines, without a human craftsperson nor an 'active' material, exhibit the remarkable yet expected characteristics of perfect sameness, a similarity which no worker could reproduce by hand. The accuracy and reproducibility of machine work might be one of its most essential advantages, ultimately increasing efficiency and saving labour time. Yet, it does not offer any surprises nor discoveries on the side of the client—once you know one object or architecture, every other object from the same production line will look the same. To quote Timothy Ingold: "The separation of design from making has resulted in a built environment that has no 'flow' to it. You simply cannot design an improvisation or an adaptation."[6]

In David Pye's *The Nature and Art of Workmanship*, the author offers two concepts of craft and workmanship: the "workmanship of risk" and the "workmanship of certainty."[7] While executing the "workmanship of risk," the quality of an outcome still depends on the maker's judgment, decisions and care during the process, even though machines and devices are used. The client can read multiple layers of information on the piece, similar to a cartography of events that happened during fabrication. The craftsperson might have been tired, inspired, excited or distracted for a short amount of time and resultingly, what should be a perfectly straight line might have a shake, or a collection of patterns is surprisingly but beautifully arranged. In "workmanship of certainty," the quality and aesthetic outcomes are already predefined before the production starts. By changing risk processes to certainty, machinery can increase productivity because the dexterity and care required to form the product are reduced.

To find a balance between certainty and risk, the craftsperson can be equipped with tools which regulate human input within specific quality standards, while still allowing them to apply decisions during manufacturing. Hand gestures might be filtered through different machines but the craftsperson can still create a truly unique outcome. Chronotopic architecture supports a 'workmanship of synthesis' that reveals the temporal and spatial categories of a fabricated object or space. Such spaces redefine the notion of 'site-specific design' by linking the human presence with the time frame of construction as well as its specific location.

Embodied Computation

The importance of a new 'workmanship of synthesis' that amalgamates the analog (human input) with the digital (machinic output) can be observed in various other fields, such as bio-art, digital art and electronic music. This demonstrates that the merging of the digital realm of data with the realm of the human body allows the human and body, as an agent, to become part of the production and design process. This interaction can be conscious or unconscious, supporting a more process-based design methodology that focuses on the entire operation of fabrication and design, rather than solely on an end product. Consequently, designing becomes metabolic rather than a mechanical and linear procedure, concentrating on the performative and temporal aspects of design and fabrication to enhance creative and generative possibilities. Similar 'event-driven' qualities can be found in physical craft, which relies on the visual, tactile thinking of the craftsperson during the entire fabrication process. According to Terry Knight, 'craft' is defined by its performative aspect and its embodied improvisational and time-based qualities. The ability of the body to sense, feel and interact with the world is known as embodiment, and Knight questions how we may include such qualities in the digital design and fabrication workflow.[8]

Current digital design methodologies strictly separate the design and fabrication realm, primarily following a linear workflow. Data is saved to a file and fed consecutively to an output device such as a 3D printer or robot. The machine and the tool in these processes are still 'the things we think about' rather than 'the things we think with.' Therefore, to enable digital methods to incorporate chronotopic events, we need to redefine the relationship between humans and machines and develop novel interactive strategies of computation and production.[9] We must recalibrate machines as extensions of ourselves, as partners with whom we must work closely.[10] In doing so, we may uncover unintended and critical potentials that add to the qualities of a design. Such a process connects the digital design outcome and fabrication procedure with the designer's and craftsperson's cognitive and physical involvement, which results in a process that includes the intuition and dexterity of both designer and craftsperson.

This interaction between human and machine aims to exceed traditional automation and rationalisation paradigms, enabling the combination of 'the peculiarities of the human' with 'the advantages of the machine.' To achieve chronotopic architecture, we must investigate this new relationship in terms of technological, societal, economic and aesthetical aspects. It is necessary to integrate novel sensor systems and actuators into the work environment to augment the craftsperson during design and fabrication. Furthermore, sensor technology incorporated into the fabrication realm can process information and translate user input registration to enable embodied computation.

Augmented Bricklaying

Augmented Bricklaying, a project by Gramazio Kohler Research, is an example in which the 'craftshuman' has been expanded with sensor technology.[11] The project is currently the largest architectural building project constructed in situ with an augmented reality fabrication interface, using 13596 individually rotated and tilted bricks. Gramazio Kohler Research collaborated with incon.ai to develop the custom-made dynamic optical guiding system to design the façade.

Above: Augmented Bricklaying at Kitrvs winery @ Gramazio Kohler Research.
First Page: Tracking of a physical input, such as gaze, to stimulate computational reactions © MAEID.

The Kitrvs Winery is situated in Pydna's mountainous environment, and the wine produced in the surrounding vineyards is processed and stored in the newly built structure. The client was inspired by the Gantenbein Winery (2008), constructed using a robotic production method in Switzerland and also by Gramazio Kohler. As Kitrvs Winery is in Greece, it was neither sustainable nor economical to send robots from Switzerland, nor to prefabricate the façade in Switzerland and ship it to Katerini. Furthermore, the client wanted to include handmade bricks and traditional brick building techniques with mortar into the design process. Robotic systems are efficient and economical when it comes to repetitive processes such as bricklaying, but involving malleable materials—such as mortar—and handcrafted components—such as handmade bricks—can be difficult to automate. Therefore, the focus shifted from purely robotic fabrication to machine-instructed fabrication, namely, augmented reality. This system would support masons to operate with improved spatial precision while still promoting their skill and experience in mortar handling by eliminating additional physical templates or guidelines. Instead of a holographic augmented reality system, the position of the bricks was tracked in real-time.[12] This system's technological innovation uses visual-inertial object tracking features and real-time feedback to precisely relate what has been physically built back to the digital model. With the help of machine vision and edge detection algorithms, the physical location of a brick is compared to the position of a brick in the digital model.

The façade design also needed to reflect the new potential of this system for architects. The semi-transparent parametric façade design, informed by a Perlin noise field, creates a morphing pattern resembling light flowing across a liquid surface. Gaps between the individual bricks also allow for ventilation and reduce the impact of the powerful Greek sun while taking advantage of the physical ability of a craftsperson to vary the height of applied mortar between bricklayers. Mortar, which is traditionally used as secondary material in the construction of fair-faced brick walls, became a prominent feature of the façade. *Augmented Bricklaying* takes a human-centered approach to the concept of an automated construction site by reintroducing skill and dexterity into digital manufacturing processes. As a result, *Augmented Bricklaying* may be viewed as a means of overcoming the inherent chronotopic limitations of robotic automation while also broadening the reach of digital fabrication through a socially sustainable approach to digitalised building construction. *Augmented Bricklaying* also shows how important it is to augment the craftsperson with novel user interfaces. Within digital architecture and design discourse, many projects aim to move beyond the restrictions of a screen-based, graphical user interface (GUI) to allow for real-time embodied interaction. Nevertheless, most digital fabrication and design processes are still based on a GUI and do not offer interactive computational workflows. The relationship between the designer/architect/craftsperson and the machine—whether the computer, the robot or the 3D printer—is still anonymous and distant. 'Digital craft' is a phrase often applied to work fusing made-by-hand and made-by-machine methods. However, rarely do architects discuss the aesthetical implication of such a fusion. In addition to the new sensor and actuator systems—intuitive user interfaces, real-time feedback and bi-directional manufacturing systems—successful chronotopic architecture requires developing novel, feedback-based digital design models which use an interactive algorithmic logic enabling synchronised digital and physical manipulation. This computational logic introduces the concept of 'real-time' into architectural design. Conventional design strategies support a linear workflow with a straightforward task set, whereas interactive algorithmic modelling allows the user to change and adapt the design model during fabrication. The physical human presence becomes an irreplaceable part of the digital design setup.

Psychotropic Topologies

By linking the physical presence of the designer with the digital model, *Psychotropic Topologies* discusses a potential newfound aesthetic in the digital design process. The project was part of an Architectural Association Summer School framework, taught in 2020 by Tiziano Derme and myself in collaboration with Andrea Reni at the Melbourne School of Design. Students were asked to imagine and generate a digitally embodied space that physically reacts to the user and thus adapts its virtual spatiality in response to their inhabitants' and visitors' needs and presence. The project's goal was to create new cyber-physical transfer methodologies that combine the digital realm of data and design with the domain of the body. The concept of the studio was also envisioned as a potential digital prototype for an architecture that can react to its occupants in real-time, a theory discussed in research branches such as 'Co-Corporeality,' which investigate active and responsive biomaterials.[13] Through this research, diverse biomaterials and sensor systems were developed in close collaboration with chemists and microbiologists, resulting in small-scale, reactive architectural prototypes. The virtual sibling, *Psychotropic Topologies*, constructed a comparable experience by drawing parallels between digital representation and physiological data obtained during the user's daily confinement routine.[14] Real-time tracking of the designers, in this case, the students, linked their physical presence with the digital modelling process. Sensor systems and machine vision such as real-time eye tracking, facial recognition, emotion detection and pulse sensors were used to influence the design

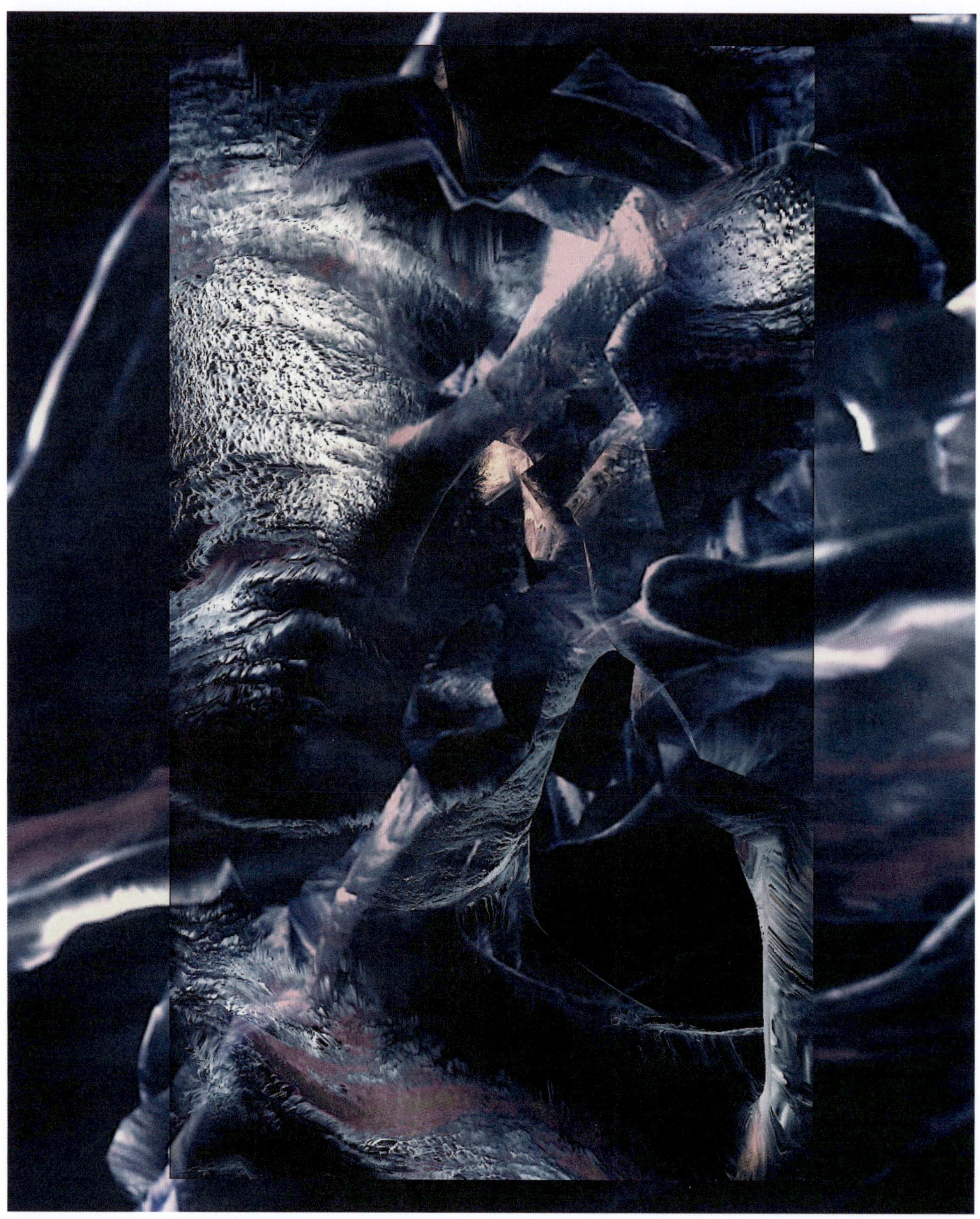

Chronotope

outcome via conscious and unconscious data. Students were able to design with their gaze, their pulse and their expression. Data was partially collected and partially real-time, tracking the changes of the human body over time.

This connection between human inhabitant and physical environment was first conceived in JG Ballard's text 'The Thousand Dreams of Stellavista,' which narrates the story of a psychotropic building.[15] The house affects its resident's mental state, shifting the subject-object dilemma to a 'quasi-object' and 'potential-subject' storyline. The perception of this house as 'alive' and as a living system is best described as a digitally mediated relationship between several individuals rather than the performer/audience model.[16] In 1982, two Chilean biologists, Humberto Maturana and Francisco Varela, described living systems capable of reproducing and maintaining themselves as units of interactions existing in an environment and closely linked to an observer.[17] The observer is therefore defined as an entity specified by their own domain of interactions. Living systems cannot, from a purely biological point of view, be understood independently of the environment with which they interact, nor can the environment be independently defined by the living system that is occupying it. Therefore, living systems are characterised through successive interactions in a constantly changing environment. When we translate these concepts from literature and biology back into architecture, we achieve a built environment that is non-deterministic nor objectified but instead focuses on process and interaction. Architecture becomes a manifestation and amalgamation of humans, time and space.

Chronotope questions the traditional concept of the human as an isolated and physically limited entity capable of only observation and experience. In addition, chronotope demonstrates that physical and digital environments cease to be ontologically and physically separate. It shows how the weaving of human and machine can result in objects and spaces that embody the creator's attributes as well as the machine's imprint, challenging the idea of a fully automated and standardised architecture. The combination of the craftsperson's attributes and the machine's imprint rethink the cultural boundary between technology and humanity, the interaction between human and machine, while powerfully refocusing on the dynamics of technology-in-use.

01 The term was initially coined by M.M. Bakhtin to show how literary genres operate with configurations of time and space.
02 H. R. Maturana, "Neurophysiology of cognition," in *Cognition: A multiple view*, ed. Garvin P. (New York: Spartan Books, 1970), 3-23.
03 Philip Auslander, "Digital Liveness: A Historico-Philosophical Perspective," *PAJ: A Journal of Performance and Art* 34, no.3 (102) (2012): 3-11, DOI: https://doi.org/10.1162/PAJJ_a_00106.
04 A.P. French (1968), Special Relativity, MIT Introductory Physics Series, CRC Press.
05 The mathematical model of the five vector builds up upon the event model of Relativity, which is defined by a four coordinate description, see W. Rindler, *Introduction to Special Relativity* 2nd ed. (Clarendon Press Oxford: 1991).
06 Timothy Ingold, "The textility of making," *Cambridge Journal of Economics*, 34 (2010): 91-102.
07 David Pye, *The nature and art of workmanship,* 1968.
08 Terry Knight, "Craft, performance, and grammars," in *Computational Studies on Cultural Variation and Heredity* (Springer, 2018), 205-224.
09 Daniela Mitterberger, "Is Body Architecture?" in *ADATO #1_2020 Architecture and Medicine* (2020), 44-53.
10 M Ejiri, "Towards meaningful robotics for the future: Are we headed in the right direction?" in *Robotics and Autonomous Systems* 18, no.1-2: 1-5, https://doi.org/10.1016/0921-8890(95)00083-6.
11 D Mitterberger, K. Dörfler, T. Sandy, et al. "Augmented Bricklaying," in *Construction Robotics* 4 (2020): 151-161, https://doi.org/10.1007/s41693-020-00035-8.
12 G. Jahn, A. Wit "[BENT] Holographic handcraft in large-scale steam-bent timber structures," in *Ubiquity and autonomy*, eds Kory B, Briscoe D, Clay O (Austin: Acadia Publishing Company, 2019), 438-447.
13 Co-corporeality: https://cocorporeality.net.
14 http://newpaper.space/portfolio/psychotropic-topologies/?fbclid=IwAR3IfL6fVia9VUrE8UagVV5VsHgD_68PVBNeNTXxf1p1Rao-3OkrKwZlG1o.
15 J.G. Ballard "The Thousand Dreams of Stellavista," in *Vintage Classics* (2001).
16 P. Auslander. *The Performativity of Performance Documentation, PAJ: A Journal of Performance and Art*, 28, no.3 (2006): 1-10, http://www.jstor.org/stable/4140006.
17 R. H. Maturana, J. F. Varela, "Tree of Knowledge: The Biological Roots of Human Understanding," in *Shambhala*; Revised, Subsequent Edition (1992).

Augmented Bricklaying
Gramazio Kohler Research, ETH Zurich.
Collaborators: Dr. Kathrin Doerfler (project lead), Daniela Mitterberger, Dr. Timothy Sandy, Foteini Salveridou, Fernando Cena, Lukas Stadlmann, Lefteris Kotsonis, Eleni Alexi, Dimitris Ntantamis.
Consultancy: Dr. Nebojsa Mojsilovic, Structural Masonry, ETH Zurich.
Selected experts: Dr. Tobias Bonwetsch, ROB Technologies. AR-Tracking-System from incon.ai.

Psychotropic Topologies
MAEID [Büro für Architektur und transmediale Kunst] Daniela Mitterberger, Tiziano Derme.
Collaborator: Andrea Reni.
Students: Madeline Bosaid, Hongrun Che, Daniel Fielding, Joyce Huang, Xuan Lin Li, Shijin Liu, Gaby Miegeville-Little, Mason Mo, Yaonan Xiong, Luyao Zhang.

Image: *Psychotropic Topologies* by Madeline Bosaid and Mason Mo © MAEID.

THE UNDERGROUND SEEN

Domenic Trimboli

Traversing the city streets, we might imagine below our feet a world of tunnels, cables and pipes amongst the earth. More often than we may realise, however, our urban terrains are also built directly over human remains, long erased from cultural memory. There is a burial ground beneath Sydney's Town Hall and another under its Central Station; in Melbourne, the Queen Victoria Market was once the colonial city's first public cemetery. Historically, the erasure of a city cemetery has typically been justified as the "necessity of progress" for the Capitalocene, and maybe even a welcome visual relief as new cemeteries were generally located well outside urban centres.[1] That is, of course, before urban growth inevitably caught up to these, and the cycle repeated. *Presence* here is therefore about asking—how have former cemeteries influenced urban spaces? and how have our attitudes changed towards former cemeteries, as well as their successors?

Thinking about former cemeteries beneath the city elucidates the way society has come to translate an austere, all too transactional dichotomy, between 'life' and 'death' within designed spaces. This narrative dualism asserts that one is light and the other dark; that the sky is divine but the ground is more likely to lead to purgatory or the Mad Hatter's tea party. As art historian Alexis Boylan contends, there are even unspoken rules about how a parent ought to 'curate' the colours to which their child is exposed as they develop, by which dressing a child and painting their room in black remains an ostensibly macabre choice.[2] We tend not to question these things. They are simply internalised as a convenient warding-off or aversion to a universal presence of death itself. While there is validity in locating the roots of this dualism via theological readings of biblical concepts such as '*vanitas*' or 'God is light,' even these ancient sources have had a depth and richness of artistic representation and interpretation—in, say, 17th century art—that a contemporary audience might find confronting. Architectural design and representation of memorialisation and burial spaces is no less guilty of perpetuating this kind of mythology. For example, the 18th century French architect, Étienne-Louis Boullée, says of his sombre and melancholic funerary monuments: "This type of architecture, formed by shadows, is a discovery in the art which is mine alone…"[3] For all the dark, monochromatic evocativeness that characterises his speculative renderings, this is undoubtedly a bold claim; Piranesi might have raised an eyebrow. However, as Stephen Cairns and Jane M. Jacobs argue in their provocative literary work *Buildings Must Die*, the bricks and mortar of architecture itself has always typically manifested a false allusion towards being something infallible.[4] While observing the cracked and dishevelled marble and concrete of cemetery tombstones, barely two generations old, we might be inclined to attribute their sorry state to the likes of dampness or ground movement. In actuality, it is our own expectation of how longevity should be aestheticised that confronts us the most.

Cemeteries and by association, death, have a far more intricate presence in our cities and lives than the traditional dualism divulges. There are myriad lenses by which this realisation can be interrogated. For example, Australia's First Nations peoples never made the same assumption that the land we walk on or even the dead themselves were insentient and unconscious.[5] There are complementary shades of this non-anthropocentric respect for the earth captured in, say, contemporary ecofeminist thought. A similar acknowledgement of urban complexity is digressed in Foucault's interpretation of the cemetery as a type of "heterotopia:" a quasi-world within a world situated in a contemporary epoch that is less concerned with hierarchies of public space and more so with "simultaneity" and "juxtaposition."[6]

The most descriptive yet concise analogy for complexity and multiplicity is captured by Italo Calvino's venerable work of literary fiction, *Invisible Cities* (1972). It is here that we find the allegorical *Eusapia*: a city possessing an identical copy of itself that is constructed underground, in which its inhabitants are said to be delighted by their unrivalled ability to "enjoy life and flee care."[7] Over time in this narrative, it is the living who replicate the innovations of the underground—until a mythology escalates in *Eusapia* whereby it becomes indistinguishable as to who is truly dead or alive, let alone who built the above ground city to begin with. This story may sound entirely whimsical.

However, the relationship of colonial Australia's garden suburb planning to its precursor, the 19th century 'garden cemetery'—which was developed as an Eden, distinct from the ill effects of the newly industrialising city centre—may be understood as a parallel to Eusapia's ambiguous, blended duality. This seemingly idyllic mode of suburban living that underpins the 'garden suburb' is effectively modelled on conditions that were initially created for the un-living.

Former cemeteries sequestered beneath the likes of Sydney and Melbourne came to be 'hidden' due to pervasive growth of colonial cemeteries, that was both driven by, and paralleled, the act of colonial expansion itself. The first ships to Australia from 1788 onwards were often rife with disease, and on-board deaths were not uncommon.[8] Poor medical facilities in the fledgling Sydney settlement as well as harsh working conditions took their toll.[9] Subsequently, makeshift burials took place in several areas now more readily identifiable as The Rocks and the city centre.[10] Moreover, Old Sydney Burial Ground (1793-1869), the city's first official cemetery, eventually became the site of the Town Hall (Est.1889). Seemingly, as the city expanded and cemeteries became full, then a new cemetery would be built on the equally 'new' outskirts. Hence the initial placement of Devonshire Street Cemetery (1820-1901), before it too was swept beneath the city rug of what is now Sydney's Central Station. What is also startling to note in all this, and particularly so for the Old Burial Ground, is that only a few decades had passed before the people that lay there largely become strangers to the rest of society.[11] To quote the eminent historian Grace Karskens:

> The key conclusion by 1867 was that the dead had no place in the modern city; they were part of an increasingly irrelevant past, a hindrance to development; they depressed property prices and should be moved out.[12]

Reflecting this attitude, site workers for the new Town Hall were reportedly afforded a mere day to relocate as many human remains as they possibly could to a new cemetery.[13] Human remains continue to be discovered whenever site works associated with maintenance are performed at this locus. It is a similar case with Melbourne's Queen Victoria Market (Est.1878), whereby the presence of thousands of human-remains left from its previous use as the city's first cemetery (1837-1853) continue to pose an ongoing challenge to the site's redevelopment. On one hand, contemporary apprehension about intervening into this site may be attributed to a tempering of early developmental fervour. On the other hand, this passivity could also simply be attributed to a particularly Australian brand of indifference. An astute writer for a Sydney-based newspaper at the turn of the 20th century has gone so far as to wittily suggest that even if there were any spirits upset by the 'desecration' of the Old Devonshire Street Cemetery graves, they were scarcely likely to do anything about it because, after all, they too lived in "a land whose secret motto is 'Can't Be Bothered!"[14] Bearing in mind that the rate of skeletal decomposition varies considerably depending on a variety of factors, such as soil composition, depth, moisture and climatic conditions it is therefore difficult to know with any certainty, how long remains are likely to remain identifiable, in any of these cases.[15]

While the development of centralised cemeteries ensured that society could literally and metaphorically compartmentalise death away from lived experience (something that very much persists today) it didn't allow the cemetery to escape the commodifying tendencies of the urban grid. This colonial urban planning mechanism—the grid—has relentlessly been at work subsuming thousands of years of Indigenous history attached to the landscape.[16] Not far away from Sydney's CBD for example, is the harbour-side suburb which we refer to presently as Rose Bay. Prior to colonisation, the area was a traditionally sacred burial ground and a place where tribal punishment took place using ritual combat by First Nations peoples.[17] Even colonial illustrations prior to urban development show this place as picturesque and seemingly well-maintained.[18] At least, this was until it was decided that the site would also make a pleasant location for an exclusive golf course. Disconcertingly, though unsurprisingly, repeated findings of pre-colonial Indigenous Australian remains and precious artefacts amongst the course's many sand traps continue to make mainstream media headlines today. Again, this is far from a Sydney-specific phenomenon. Neighbouring Melbourne's Tullamarine Airport (and another golf course) is the Keilor Archaeological Site—an Indigenous Australian burial precinct with human remains and artefacts dating to over 14,000 years ago.[19] This is an issue that finds common ground in all Australian cities, and which demands reconsideration by way of architecture and urbanism. An Australian academic concerned with 'sacredness,' Lyn McCreddin writes, "Aboriginal history simmers beneath the surface of the city: a scar is alive, the dead languages are remembered and can escape, even if momentarily."[20] Australian Aboriginal designer, Alison Page, echoes the sentiment of a *tabula rasa* of bitumen and concrete smothering precolonial history:

> Cities like Sydney are lacquered with so many impermeable layers of Western thinking that architects, designers and builders must decide how each layer can dig below the surface and reveal the original story of Country. How can we, as designers, pick the scabs and allow Country to breathe again?[21]

Neither of these authors were referring to cemeteries or burial grounds specifically. However, as evoked by the visceral, anthropomorphising metaphor of 'scars' and 'scabs' there is an evident compassion for being more aware of the vital *genius loci*: the spirit of a place.

The historic hierarchy between city spaces, whether they be sacred, profane or otherwise, has become increasingly obsolescent. For architects and urban planners, however, there is an uneasy feeling in Page's call to engage with Country that we may have missed something when it comes to these hidden burial spaces in Australia. Part of this problem is that evocations of 'sacredness' are typically reserved for the Australian landscape at large—the "wide brown land" as poet Dorothea Mackeller famously immortalised it—not the city, nor suburbia, where most of the population actually live.[22] In actuality, sacredness can manifest itself in all these realms. Yet, we tend not to see it that way. For example, although the Australian public were rightly outraged by the destruction of the sacred Aboriginal Australian caves of Juukan Gorge in 2020, cases of suburban development and soil quarrying having disturbed former burial grounds remain lesser known. Nevertheless, at a time when architecture and the construction industry are developing, moving earth and tunnelling at an unprecedented rate,[23] whether we remain open to it or not, the Australian city is still very much a place "in which sacred and secular jostle each other ambivalently, sometimes tooth and claw."[24] Rather than simply considering this dynamic across the horizontal plane of the "wide brown land," we must also remember that there is a vertical axis. As Australian academic Marilu Melu Zurita argues, we tend to assume the ground below us is some sort of "sub *terra nullius*," exempt from the post(colonial) critical dialogue that is performed on the Earth's surface.[25] Fundamentally, in the context of burial grounds, postcolonial history, or even the geology of a place, urban designers and planners in Australia have much to gain by picking into that which is deeply-temporal.[26]

Tongue in cheek, cultural historian Luke Stegeman recently wrote, "How useful the dead can be, ferried back across the Styx and up into the world of the living where there are clear political roles for them."[27] It is a wise phrase of caution for anyone regarding the geopolitical implications of this discussion, let alone designers or planners in the urban environment. For the latter, the point here then, is not that the remodelling of sites such as Old Melbourne Cemetery constitutes an irreconcilable ethical dilemma of posthumous harm, nor whether such sites can still remain sacrosanct, nor even whether they even were so in the first place. Instead, akin to an old home that over the years has had its floorboards covered in beige carpet or handmade brick walls plastered over, somewhere along the way we have been left architecturally and culturally poorer for opting not to engage with subterranean history at all. Whether it be through ignorance or conflicting values, historical richness has given way to an urban uniformity to the point whereby we reside with this oddly anomalous, if not grossly untenable position which sees the likes of golf balls being whacked out of sand traps bearing the sacred remains and artefacts of our First Nations people. Ironically, it is media images such as those showing the destruction of Juukan Gorge, which generate a sense of moral obligation to act. However, in talking about train stations and market places, we are also talking about places that we traverse every day. As a reaction, we could simply despair that our cities are already 'built' and there is little we can do to reverse the process. Or, like the analogous old house being 'rediscovered,' or even a piece of Japanese kintsugi pottery, we could understand that architectural thinking will, at times, need to happen in reverse: finding breaks, scars and fissures like our old cemeteries and mending them with seams of gold.

Frontispiece: 'Laudomia,' image courtesy of Serena Fanelli.

01 Jason, W. Moore, "The Capitalocene, Part 1: On the nature and origins of our ecological crisis," *The Journal of Peasant Studies* 44, no. 3, (2017): 594.

02 Alexis L. Boylan, *Visual Culture* (Cambridge: MIT Press, 2020) 15.

03 Étienne-Louis Boullée, "A Treatise on Architecture," in *The Emergence of Modern Architecture: A Documentary History, from 1000 to 1810* by Liane Lefaivre and Alexander Tzonis (London: Routledge, 2004), 471.

04 Stephen Cairns and Jane M. Jacobs, *Buildings Must Die: A Perverse View of Architecture* (Cambridge: MIT Press, 2014), 15.

05 Deborah Bird Rose, *Country of the Heart: An Indigenous Australian Homeland* (Canberra: Aboriginal Studies Press, 2002), 14.

06 Michel Foucault, "Of Other Spaces," *Diacritics* 16, no. 1, 1986, 22.

07 Italo Calvino, *Invisible Cities*, translated from the Italian by William Weaver (London: Vintage Books, 1997), 98.

08 Katherine Reynolds and Carol Liston, "Surgeon-superintendents and Penal Discipline: The Transportation of Female Convicts 1818-1835," *Health and History* 22, no. 1, 2020, 30-31.

09 Fiona Starr, "The 'Sidney Slaughter House': Convict Experience of Medical Care at the General 'Rum' Hospital, Sydney, 1816-1848," *Health and History* 19, no. 2, 2017, 60-89.

10 Keith A. Johnson and Malcolm R. Sainty, *Sydney burial ground 1819-1901: (Elizabeth and Devonshire Streets) and history of Sydney's early cemeteries from 1788* (Sydney: Library of Australian History, 2001).

11 Grace Karskens, "Raising the dead: attitudes to European human remains in the Sydney region c1840-2000," *Historic Environment* 17, no. 1, 2003, 42.

12 Ibid., 43.

13 Ibid., 42.

14 "A Visit to the Devonshire Street Cemetery," *Clarence and Richmond Examiner*, October 1, 1901.

15 Franklin E. Damann and David O. Carter, 'Human Decomposition Ecology and Postmortem Microbiology,' in *Manual of Forensic Taphonomy*, eds. James Pokines, Steven A. Symes and Carl Roper (Boca Raton: Taylor and Francis, 2013), 44.

16 Domenic Trimboli, "Interpretive Urban Cemeteries: Urban Cemeteries Reinterpreted," Paper presented at the 37th Annual SAHANZ Conference: *What if? What Next? Speculations on History's Futures*, The University of Western Australia, 2020.

17 Paul Irish, *Hidden in Plain View: The Aboriginal People of Coastal Sydney* (Sydney: NewSouth Publishing, 2017) 69-70.

18 G. H. Hammersley, *View of Sidney* [Sic] *in New South Wales (taken from Bell mount)*, ca. 1814, in *Australia Illustrated*, ca. 1777-1855 (London: James Whittle & Richard Holmes Laurie, 1814). Copy held by Mitchell Library, State Library of New South Wales.

19 Shaun Canning et al. "Recent archaeological excavations of Pleistocene deposits at Brimbank Park, Keilor Victoria," *Archaeological Heritage* 2, no. 1, 2010, 27.

20 Lyn McCredden, "Contemporary poetry and the sacred: Vincent Buckley, Les Murray and Samuel Wagan Watson," *Australian Literary Studies* 23 (2007) 164.

21 Alison Page and Paul Memmott, 'Objects and Spirituality: Building on Country' in *Design: Building on Country*, ed. Margo Neale (Port Melbourne: Thames and Hudson, 2021) 17.

22 Lachlan Brown, "The Way of Our Streets': Exploring the Urban sacred in Three Australian Poems," *Religions* 7, no. 12, (2016), 138.

23 M. van Iersel, "Heavy World," in *Rewriting Architecture-10+1 Actions: Tabula Scripta*, eds. Floris Alkemade et al. (Amsterdam: Amsterdam Academy of Architecture/Valiz, 2020), 29.

24 McCredden op. cit. 153-67.

25 Maria de Lourdes (Marilu) Melu Zurita, "Challenging sub terra nullius: a critical underground urbanism project," *Australian Geographer* 51, no. 3, 2020.

26 Maria de Lourdes (Marilu) Melu Zurita, Paul George Munro and Donna Houston "Un-earthing the Subterranean Anthropocene," *Area* 50, no. 3, 2017.

27 Luke Stegeman, *Amnesia Road: Landscape, Violence and Memory* (Sydney: NewSouth Publishing, 2021) 25.

ZOOM AND THE SEGMENTED SUBJECT

Alexis Kalagas text, Ciro Miguel images

Zoom was never intended to foster intimacy. Launched in 2011 as an enterprise tool to monitor and optimise the productivity of a distributed workforce, it has transcended the narrow scope of its original design in a way that parallels the accelerated pandemic era collapse of divisions between labour and leisure, digital and physical, public and private, in which it has played a key role. Between December 2019 and March 2020, when global lockdowns and social distancing became an instant new feature of everyday life, Zoom's daily users exploded from 10 million to 200 million. Even early in the pandemic—a crisis "tailor-made for Zoom"—commentators opined that "we live in Zoom now."[1] Today, the company is actively building towards a pervasive platform future "where you live and work and spend your day" in Zoom; where its proprietary interface and architecture controls time, perspective and participation.[2]

Hybridised lifestyles predated the pandemic, driven by the non-stop connectivity of the smartphone as digital beacon and bodily appendage. But Zoom is hastening this migration to a cloud-first world. Lydia Kallipoliti has described the city today as "a vast array of disconnected bedrooms, microcosms that come together in an abstract digital space."[3] It is Zoom that constructs the architecture of this space, an architecture that places us in "multiple different rooms at once."[4] Remoteness is recast as a simulacrum of face-to-face proximity, until the grid multiplies and we are reminded that IRL interaction rarely involves a collective constant gaze. That is, if we even see beyond our room at all. Research suggests that people spend most time on a video call distracted by their own face. Or—to maintain the illusion of eye contact—staring at the small, glowing green light above their computer screen, "completely alone."[5]

The primacy of the distorted and disembodied face in a world of virtual meetings is shaping a new sense of self. Physicians have reported a surge in individuals with 'Zoom dysmorphia' seeking plastic surgery to alter their minutely examined appearance.[6] Three years ago, French cosmetics giant L'Oréal acquired an augmented reality (AR) filter company called Modiface, ostensibly to develop a 'try on' tool for future purchases. Last November, L'Oréal launched *Signature Faces*, its first line of virtual makeup. The software offers ten products compatible with a range of videoconferencing platforms (including Zoom), allowing customers to "sign [their] digital look with confidence and audacity." While the advent of AR-enhanced face filters on platforms like Snapchat had already led to the phenomena of users wanting to edit their physical appearance to match their augmented image, their application in this context constitutes a more habitual blurring of physical and digital identity.

If the face is the currency of Zoom, the background is where the framing of the everyday veers from reality to representation. The unprecedented incursion by Zoom into our private sphere is emblematic of a domesticity in flux. As technology and the demands of 24/7 availability undermine the idea of the home as a space of autonomy and disconnection, Zoom has erased the last pretence that domestic life exists as a world apart.[7] Amidst performative 'credibility bookshelves' and how-to guides to curating your 'Zoom corner,' the radical visibility at the edges of a video call reveals the vast economic and social disparities in the capacity for individuals and households to seamlessly adjust to the new normal of working from home.[8] These disparities are often expressed spatially; in the gloom of a light-starved bedroom, a housemate wandering through the frame, a living room strewn with toys.

Zoom's answer to the disorder of the home interior is the virtual background. First launched five years ago—though requiring a standalone green screen setup until early 2019—this now ubiquitous feature allows users to resist a forced intimacy by blurring their background, or replacing it with an image or video integrated in real time. An advance on simplified edge detection algorithms pioneered in the 1980s, the technology relies on AI-based neural networks trained to isolate a person in an image from the surrounding background through a computer vision technique called semantic segmentation. Each video frame must be extracted, segmented and added to the virtual background. To ensure a relatively high degree of accuracy in identifying the subject and maintaining frame-to-frame continuity, deep learning models are fed with large datasets of thousands of annotated images containing pixel-accurate locations of human bodies.

The role of AI in enacting our shared realities extends to the stock photography supplying the generic scaffolding for countless calls. Zoom offers three default virtual background options: the Golden Gate Bridge, dewy grass, and the earth seen from space. Designed for universal appeal, constantly updated 'microstock' databases are the source of much of the nondescript imagery that saturates contemporary online culture. As their scale grows exponentially, these databases rely on machine learning to remain searchable, using pixel patterns to identify visually or thematically similar photos. Such spatially aware visual search tools sort images based on abstract composition, and increasingly predictive pre-screening for 'high performing' content, determined by aesthetic and technical parameters. The mass outsourcing of image curation to AI represents a surrender to computer vision over human ways of seeing, in the face of inconceivably vast streams of visual media.

Last November, Nvidia introduced a new platform, Maxine, built on a machine learning technique called generative adversarial networks (GAN), which can produce real-time video content (for instance rotating a person's face to correct for off-centre camera angles in video calls). In January, OpenAI announced DALL-E, a text-to-image engine capable of generating plausible images from simple text prompts. Each represents a more fundamental shift towards computational photography—a form of photography both "speculative and relational."[9] Trevor Paglen has suggested that at this moment in history "most of the images made in the world are made by machines for other machines," the learning fodder of so many AI datasets.[10] As systems improve, unreal images will inevitably be made by machines for humans. These photorealistic renderings of digital dreams will become the backdrop to video calls where participants willingly untether themselves from spatial reality.

Despite the sophistication of its underlying technology, the Zoom virtual background embodies a narrowing but persistent lack of contiguity in how we experience the intersection of the digital and physical. Smartphones and other devices increasingly challenge this distinction, through a layering effect enabled by pervasive networked communications infrastructures, which results in an urbanism shaped by "augmented cognition."[11] In contrast, within the static frame of the Zoom window, the frayed edge of the segmented subject produces a kind of cognitive dissonance—clumsy cut-outs and warped glitches that betray presence, experienced as a tear in the virtual fabric. As gaps open and resolve themselves, exposing otherwise invisible algorithmic fingerprints, we are afforded fleeting glimpses of a closed-off world. These glimpses heighten the sense of interacting in a liminal territory, not fully rooted in the physical, and not yet entirely floating in cyberspace.

The economist Edward Glaeser defined cities as an absence of space between people that produces "proximity, density, and closeness."[12] But architect Andrés Jaque has highlighted how contemporary social settings are not defined by physical space, rather by technological networks of exchange and interaction.[13] On March 29th, 2020, Tinder users swiped 3 billion times—the most the dating app has ever recorded in a single day—at the exact moment when cities across the world were imposing open-ended lockdowns and strict social distancing measures. Jaque has argued that platforms like Tinder and Grindr have "become the city," a form of architecture operating at multiple scales that has "redefined what being in a room means, the notions of proximity we live by, what density is about."[14] Unlike the atomised cells of Zoom, these dating apps construct proximity between strangers, collapsing perceptions of intimacy and distance.[15]

Evidence of widespread 'Zoom fatigue' is mounting.[16] The next generation of online meeting platforms are focused on breaking free from the grid to recreate experiences of serendipity and immersive spatiality closer to real life. Gather, which recently announced a $35 million investment from Sequioa Capital—the same firm that backed Zoom and Slack—allows users to pilot a personalised digital avatar around a scrolling 2D environment, designed to evoke nostalgia for the pixelated aesthetics of early video games. As you walk towards another avatar, a live video chat window appears within the screen, simulating a more 'fluid' form of conversation. The integration of spatial audio technology means that a person's voice seems to emanate from a defined location in space (including during more complex group interactions), growing louder and softer as your avatar approaches, shifts orientation or retreats.

In 2018, Space Popular's Lara Lesmes and Fredrik Hellberg declared *10 Propositions for Virtual Architecture* as part of the exhibition *Value in the Virtual* at ArkDes in Stockholm. Contending that as the virtual world gains a third dimension it becomes a matter of architectural concern, these propositions included that "Virtual worlds will intensify our interest and appreciation of physical environments" and "Planetary scale virtual worlds will coexist with their physical counterparts." Lesmes and Hellberg have suggested that when interacting in social virtual spaces, it is not our image that is the priority, but rather a combination of the natural speech patterns supported by spatial audio and formal and gestural body language facilitated by inhabiting non-realistic avatars.[17] In this reading, the removal of the body from the gathering experience can create a more equitable space, while building empathy and understanding.

The use of the word 'avatar' to describe onscreen virtual bodies was coined in 1986 in the massively multiplayer online role-playing game *Habitat*, a first attempt at a large-scale commercial virtual community. The term was famously popularised by Neal Stephenson in *Snow Crash*—his 1992 science-fiction novel that also introduced the concept of the 'metaverse.' A Silicon Valley obsession, the metaverse represents a collective, interactive and immersive virtual space—an always-on virtual reality that subsumes the mobile internet of 2D web pages and apps. In April, Epic Games, creator of the online game and cultural phenomenon *Fortnite*, developer of the Unreal Engine (one of two dominant platforms for building virtual worlds) and owner of the pandemic hit *Houseparty*, announced it had raised $1 billion towards constructing its version of the metaverse. Epic is already integrating features into *Fortnite* to bolster its use as a social platform, including *Party Royale*, a gathering space designed explicitly for shared experiences outside gaming.

While *Fortnite* recently hosted a live in-world concert by rapper Travis Scott 'attended' by 12 million people, players could only see and interact with a group of 50 people at one time. Current network technology is incapable of hosting an entire synchronous metaverse, separating users into 'shards'—siloed sections that limit the population of a server-defined area. Truly planetary scale virtual worlds will require a programming model that does not yet exist.[18] This type of decentralised and collaborative approach, which reflects the open standards and protocols crucial to the development of the internet itself, is antithetical to the proprietary 'walled gardens' that have been produced via the monopolising tendencies of platform capitalism.[19] Even as Zoom aspires to become the singular digital setting for our embryonic hybrid lives, the race to control the emergent architecture of the metaverse reflects a more all-encompassing idea of captive markets.

In the field of immersive technology, 'presence' refers to the experience of believing you occupy a virtual world. This is connected to individual agency: a sense of control and ability to influence that world. Presence does not explicitly require agency, but agency enables higher levels of presence. For many, Zoom will be an involuntary first step towards a more immersive convergence of the digital and physical, where new forms of digital labour, the creeping influence of AI, and the personal and societal implications of platform logic driving entire world building will continue to raise countless issues, including of individual and collective agency. If tech platforms have become the city, operating simultaneously at multiple scales (from the bedroom to the planetary), then we must be alert to how they are restructuring what it means to inhabit that city, and the role of 'architecture' in the future spaces of everyday life.

01 Taylor Lorenz et al, "We Live in Zoom Now," *New York Times* (17 March 2020).

02 Eric J Savitz, "Zoom is Adding New Features to Prepare for a Return to Offices," *Barron's* (3 February 2021); Jeremy Neideck et al, "The Iconography of Digital Windows-Perspectives on the Pervasive Impact of the Zoom Digital Window on Embodied Creative Practice in 2020," *Body, Space & Technology 20*, no.1 (2021).

03 Lydia Kallipoliti, "Zoom In, Zoom Out," *e-flux Architecture* (April 2020).

04 T. Nikki Cesare Schotzko, "A Year (in Five Months) of Living Dangerously: Hidden Intimacies in Zoom Exigencies," *International Journal of Performance Arts and Digital Media* 16, no.3 (2020), 277.

05 Sherry Turkle quoted in Victoria Turk, "Zoom Took Over the World. This is What Will Happen Next," *Wired* (August 2020).

06 Shauna M Rice et al, "Zooming Into Cosmetic Procedures During the COVID-19 Pandemic: The Provider's Perspective," *International Journal of Women's Dermatology* 7, no.2 (2021).

07 See Jonathan Crary, *24/7: Late Capitalism and the Ends of Sleep* (2013).

08 Amanda Hess, "The Credibility Bookcase is Quarantine's Hottest Accessory," *New York Times* (1 May 2020).

09 See Hito Steyerl, "Proxy Politics: Signal and Noise," *e-flux* (December 2014).

10 Quoted in "The Autonomy of Images, Or We Always Knew Images Can Kill, But Now Their Fingers Are on the Triggers," *Hito Steyerl: I Will Survive* (2021), 240.

11 Benjamin Bratton, *The Stack: On Software and Sovereignty* (2016), 148.

12 Edward Glaeser, *The Triumph of the City: How Our Greatest Invention Makes Us Richer, Smarter, Greener, Healthier and Happier* (2011), 6.

13 Andrés Jaque, "The Agency of Networks," *Volume 53: Civic Space* (2018), 64.

14 Andrés Jaque, "Grindr Archiurbanism," *Log 41* (2017), 84.

15 See Alexis Kalagas, "Satellites of Love," *trans 26* (2015).

16 See Jeremy N Bailenson, "Nonverbal Overload: A Theoretical Argument for the Causes of Zoom Fatigue," *Technology, Mind, and Behaviour* 2, no.1 (2021).

17 Lara Lesmes & Fredrik Hellberg, "From Scrolls to Strolls" in Guillermo Fernandez-Abascal & Urtzi Grau eds. *Learning to Live Together: Humans, Cars, and Kerbs in Solidarity* (2021), 134-135.

18 Dean Takahashi, "Tim Sweeney: The Open Metaverse Requires Companies to Have Enlightened Self Interest," *VentureBeat* (27 January 2021).

19 See Nick Srnicek, *Platform Capitalism* (2016).

SUPPORTERS OF THE MELBOURNE SCHOOL OF DESIGN

Lord Mayor's Charitable Foundation
Grant F Marani
Faith Bake & Brian Baker
Late William C W Chen & Betty V W Chen
Vera Moore Foundation
Regalia Group
Beulah International
SGS Economics & Planning
Hansen Yuncken Pty Ltd
& The Peter Hansen Family Fund
Hans Varney & Carolyn Varney
Bates Smart
Warren and Mahoney Architects
SJB Planning
SJB Architects
Peter Williams AM & Trish Williams
Mandy Yencken & Ted Yencken
John Wardle Architects
Richard Falkinger AO
Dato'Peter C H Tan & Phillip C Tan
Tony Isaacson

Gwenda Thomas
Julie Willis
Andrew Lee King Fun
Ron Billard
Kang Family
Raghav Goel
Yi Siang Ooi
Alexandra T Chu
Rebecca L Bond
Justin A Bokor
George A Michell AM
The Teng Family
George Hatzisavas & Jennifer Warburton
Kelvin J Steel
Robert McGauran
Douglas K Y Lee & Joaquina Lee
Steven L Pell
ABP Commencing Class of 1964
Architects Registration Board of Victoria
Haripriya Rangan

Christopher A Heywood
Andrew Middleton & Clare Harper
Dominique Hes
Phillip Goad & Anna Johnston
Tom Eames
Chris Harvey
AnnMarie Brennan
Patricia Morton & Bruce Morton
Robyn Dalziel
James M Macneil
Fred Coates & Faye Coates
Danial W Haskell
Charles R Freedman
Dario Nordio
Craig C Wilson
Thomas Y Lui
Jeffrey J Turnbull
Chris Smith
Maureen X Wu
Alan L Nance & Rhyll M Nance
David Beauchamp & Lynette Howden
Alasdair N Fraser & Jenny Fraser
Andrea Macdonald
Jacqui Remond
Matthew Bell & Melinda Wong
The Tibbits Family
Karl Brown
Elisabeth F Grove
Peter Epaminondas Tsitas
John Hasker AM & Jennifer F Hasker
Barry J Matthews
J H Holdsworth
Late Robin M Edmond & Elvira S Edmond
David N Moore
Roger B Beeston
Mary Traitsis
Elizabeth Ridge
Jeff Robinson

The Faculty of Architecture, Building and Planning is grateful for the generous individuals, families and companies who have donated to provide better opportunities for our students and staff.

To purchase this and other copies of *Inflection*,
please go to Melbourne Books at
https://www.melbournebooks.com.au/